Complete Guide
to Instrumental Jazz
Instruction:

Techniques for Developing
a Successful
School Jazz Program

Complete Guide to Instrumental Jazz Instruction:

Techniques for Developing a Successful School Jazz Program

John Kuzmich, Jr.
Lee Bash

Parker Publishing Company, Inc.
West Nyack, New York

Library of Congress Cataloging in Publication Data

Kuzmich, John
  Complete guide to instrumental jazz instruction.

  Includes index and bibliography.
  1. Jazz music—Instruction and study—Teacher
training. 2. School music—Teacher training. I. Bash,
Lee. II. Title.
MT86.K9 1984   375'.78542   83-21141
ISBN 0-13-160565-8

About the Authors

John Kuzmich, Jr. is the Coordinator of Music for the Kirkwood, Missouri, Public Schools in the St. Louis suburbs. He has been teaching instrumental music, grades 4-12, for over fifteen years. His marching and concert bands have won five gold medals at international and state band contests and his jazz groups have been featured at a Music Educators national convention. A prominent music and jazz educator, Dr. Kuzmich's education includes a Ph.D. degree in music education with an emphasis in comprehensive musicianship from Brigham Young University, plus post-doctorate studies in curriculum development, electronic music, wind ensemble literature, music computers, human relations, administration, and jazz education from such institutions as the Eastman School of Music, University of Illinois, Syracuse University, and Indiana University. He is active throughout the United States as a clinician, adjudicator, and researcher at national conventions, universities, and music festivals.

Dr. Kuzmich is a nationally recognized author/researcher with over eighty articles published in national music journals, including *The Instrumentalist, downbeat, Music Educators Journal, Jazz Educators Journal, Selmer Bandwagon, Accent,* and others. His appointments include: contributing editor for the jazz column in *The Instrumentalist* for five years, editor of the *Jazz Educators Journal* since 1978 and national improvisation materials chairman for the National Association of Jazz Educators, and former national chairman for NAJE's Research, Combo Materials, and Curriculum, K-12. His photo credits include cover photographs for *Accent, Jazz Educators Journal,* and "Discover Jazz" record album, plus published photos in *downbeat, International Musician, Radio Free Jazz* and *Woody Shaw,* volume 9 by Jamey Aebersold. He was also selected as a recipient of *downbeat's* 18th "Annual Year" award for special contributions to jazz, and received a grant from the National Endowment for the Arts to study jazz with Dr. Ramon Ricker at the Eastman School of Music in Rochester, New York.

Lee Bash received his Ph.D. in Music Education from the State University of New York at Buffalo with an emphasis on jazz improvisation. He has directed award-winning ensembles in virtually every setting within the educational community, from a private boys' high school to a major university jazz ensemble. His programs are award winning regardless of the setting.

Dr. Bash has had articles and research printed in NAJE's *Jazz Educators Journal, The School Musician, The International Musician, Proceedings from NAJE Conventions 8 and 9,* and *The New Grove Dictionary of Music in the United States.* In addition, he has done extensive research in the areas of jazz, improvisation, and futurism.

He has worked for the National Association of Jazz Educators since its inception, and is a past president of the Connecticut unit of NAJE, was the chairman of Festivals and Contests for many years, the advisory chairman for the NAJE Commemorative Stamp Committee, the organization's executive secretary, and is currently their director of development. He has also worked extensively as an adjudicator and clinician for many jazz events.

Dr. Bash received a grant from the Julian Park Endowment Fund at the State University of New York at Buffalo for his work on and completion of this book.

Together, the authors share a combined experience of over 30 years in public school and college jazz education. Both have participated in extensive national presentations, adjudications, clinics, and workshops. This background has contributed to a systematic, comprehensive handbook that addresses the instrumental jazz program at virtually all levels.

About This Book

The *Complete Guide to Instrumental Jazz Instruction* will help every band director to be better prepared for the first day of rehearsal, whether he or she has years of experience or is a novice. In this book, John Kuzmich and Lee Bash have meticulously covered all the vital areas of jazz instruction.

Today's colleges and universities unfortunately have no standard, across-the-board jazz education requirements for graduating Music Education majors. Very few institutions of higher learning have required courses in jazz ensemble rehearsal techniques, jazz history, improvisation, jazz combo techniques or jazz theory. As a result, there has been a great deal of confusion about how to teach jazz in public school music programs.

However, this book will help solve the problem, for both the new director approaching the job for the first time and the established jazz band director looking for ways to improve students' learning processes.

Jazz Education is here to stay. It emphasizes an important ingredient that all people possess to some degree: creativity. This book will simplify the teaching of creative skills, and make it more meaningful for both teachers and students.

The *Complete Guide to Instrumental Jazz Instruction* will help raise the level of musicianship and the performance of student jazz bands everywhere.

Jamey Aebersold

Introduction

This book is designed as a reference handbook for the jazz educator, and as a detailed guide for the director who finds him- or herself developing a jazz program with no prior experience. Since the establishment of the jazz degree in the mid 1940s at North Texas State University and Los Angeles City College, jazz education has seen exciting growth and changes. In the early 1960s, only about 5,000 high school jazz bands existed. A decade later, there were an estimated 16,000 high school and 10,000 junior high school bands across the country. In the past 15 years, jazz education techniques have become very sophisticated; as a result, instrumental teachers in the 1980s need "state of the art" knowledge to produce a solid jazz program. This book fills that need.

Today, jazz performance and instruction encompass virtually every aspect and level of music education. Jazz activities range from the use of strings, vocalists, and combos, to elementary music lessons and various ensembles at all levels of the school curriculum. The pervasive interest in jazz adds to the need for a guide to jazz instruction and has influenced us in making this book comprehensive and versatile, yet as practical as possible.

The handbook is divided into four distinctive sections that deal with the pragmatic, practical, technical, and philosophical elements of instrumental jazz education. It begins with the larger issues, including a philosophical rationale and historical perspective of the jazz education movement, progresses through jazz ensemble techniques to individual instrumental applications, and finally deals with extra-musical considerations. Whole chapters are devoted to a fresh, in-depth look at each individual instrument of the jazz ensemble. Organizing and pacing a jazz concert, selecting special equipment with a knowledge of desirable characteristics, and dozens of solutions to common problems are also among the many topics discussed.

Virtually every aspect of jazz performance is covered for the instrumental ensemble director, from how to develop the audition process to eliciting good public relations, from creating proper ensemble techniques to understanding the role of each individual in the group. The concluding chapter offers a self-evaluation format that will not only help you determine problems or weaknesses, but also direct you to the appropriate section where you'll find further remedial information. In addition, each chapter offers a bibliography with sources that will help you get a better perspective on any troublesome area.

In-service instrumental music educators will find this book easy to read and simple to understand; it's practical yet comprehensive enough to be useful every day.

John Kuzmich, Jr.
Lee Bash

Contents

Joining and Creating the Jazz Bandwagon

Why Join the Jazz Bandwagon?

This opening chapter presents the "what" and the "why" of the jazz education movement with a rationale for its existence in the public schools. *Perhaps one of the most difficult situations for the aspiring jazz educator is in dealing with school administrators. Justifying jazz as a fundamental part of the music program and expressing a solid philosophy of jazz education are essential first steps towards implementing a jazz program.* Subject areas covered in this chapter include what jazz is, why to teach it; and what developments and current trends are occurring in jazz education today. This chapter will help organize your thoughts when persuading school and music administrators, other music teachers, guidance counselors, parents, and students about the validity of jazz instruction in the public schools.

TOWARDS A DEFINITION OF JAZZ

Jazz is syncopation, improvisation, interpretation, elaboration, and interpolation, but why is it jazz? Jazz is literally a twentieth-century phenomenon that stands beyond any simple definition. When Paul Tanner, jazz historian/performer/arranger/educator, was asked to define jazz, he said, "I don't know, but I'll be perfectly willing to shoot full of holes any definition you get, if you would like."[1] The word *jazz* encompasses so many styles that it escapes a permanent definition.

Originally, jazz was a combination of two different musical cultures: African and European, which fused together in New Orleans around the turn of the century. The African characteristics included: (1) syncopation, (2) poly-rhythm, (3) call and response, (4) improvisation, (5) audience participation (singing, dancing and/or playing of rhythms), (6) the use of repeated figures and bass ostinatos, and (7) an emphasis on expression in the melody with free use of the voice by blending pitches, using growls or moans, wailing, and/or varying shades of vibrato. European traits included: (1) the playing of Western European instruments (winds, strings, and brass), (2) a system of notation, (3) a complicated harmony (with scales and chord progressions), and (4) a system of musical form. The result was the creation of an American native music called *jass* or *jazz* that developed a spontaneous evolution of rhythmic, melodic, and harmonic ideas through individual interpretation, improvisation, and tone color (emotion), with emphasis on rhythm and intricate syncopation built on chord progression.

Since the early 1900s, jazz has come to mean Blues, New Orleans Dixieland, Ragtime, Chicago Dixieland, Boogie Woogie, Swing, Bebop, Cool, Progressive, Funky, Third Stream, Gospel, Free Jazz, Fusion, Latin Jazz, and still a number of other styles. The history of jazz is a chronicle of all these styles as well as the constant mixture of ideas achieved with the ongoing process derived from diverse cultural, racial, and ethnic contributions. Today's jazz can truly be considered an international art form rather than simply a form of American folk art.

What makes the development of jazz so distinct from other kinds of music is its individual nature. Jazz requires not only an individual interpretation of melody, it demands spontaneous individual invention of new melodies, individual articulation of style and rhythm that exceeds notation, and individual interpretation of a total musical sound.

> Basically, a classical performer strives to play the way he thinks the conductor understands what the composer intended. On the other hand, in a jazz performance, if the performer does not include something of himself, his personality, and his background, the audience rightfully feels cheated. In classical music, it is considered that how a work is performed is never as important as the work itself. In jazz, the work itself is never really as important as the way in which it is played. Jazz, then, is not a composer's art; rather, jazz is the art of the performer, the performing ensemble, and the arranger. The quality of the art is dependent upon their creative ideas.[2]

So, what is jazz? For the purpose of general agreement, let's call it emotional music comprised of syncopation, improvisation, elaboration, interpolation, and individual expression.

CONFRONTING THE ISSUES:
A RATIONALE FOR TEACHING JAZZ

Jazz is a valid musical art form. Jazz requires emotional (without precluding intellectual) awareness on the part of the listener in order to be appreciated and understood. Jazz may have evolved from humble roots, but the development and wealth of material mark it as an art form. Dixieland, ragtime, and early classic jazz styles are still being performed throughout the country. Jazz became an art form after the second World War, with the development of a sophisticated written approach and acceptance by the masses. Since then, jazz has evolved and developed its scope through absorbing and being influenced by other styles.

Jazz is America's only original art form. Jazz music is American. It is essentially the only indigenous folk music our culture has produced that has risen to the level of formal artistic expression, and has received international recognition in the process. Jazz's influence on contemporary classical (or formal) composers from the 1920s onward (including Dvorak, Debussy, Ravel, Stravinsky, Milhaud, Hindemith, Krenek, and Gershwin) is in itself a recognition of the creative energy and vitality of jazz. The acceptance of jazz musicians by musicologists as contemporary serious music composers (Duke Ellington, Dave Brubeck, Eubie Blake, et al.), is an indication that jazz is being accepted as an equal to the artistic production of the European culture.

Theodore Tellstrom, former Music Educators National Conference (MENC) Executive Director, disapproves of those music educators who still fear or demean jazz:

> Refusal to accept seriously a distinct expression of American music only serves to strengthen the argument that the function of Art in America is badly misunderstood . . . it would be unfortunate if students are continually obliged to seek musical training outside the school when it is the responsibility of the music teachers to provide a sound, comprehensive program of music education.[3]

Jazz is a product of twentieth-century sociological and technological acceleration and change. Given its dramatic impact on the masses, no other lasting musical style has been so intricately tied up with and totally reflective of the sweeping social and technological changes that have taken place in the United States in the last hundred years. Jazz has become a viable art form only because of the technological and social changes that have taken place. Without the development of the phonograph and later, the radio, jazz might have remained a folk-art dance music. It would have been impossible to correctly notate jazz styles. The phonograph and phonograph record allowed white musicians to imitate and later practice what, up to that time, had been a black folk-art phenomenon.

The radio glamorized jazz and swing, making national celebrities out of dance band leaders and singers. Later, it was through film and radio that jazz became a part of the attraction and sophistication of urban life. Today, exotic sound-producing equipment, quadrophonic sound, color television, stereophonic FM radio, video and audio cassettes, synthesizers and rapid transportation allow us to enjoy the best that our modern technological society has to offer.

During this time, there were also tremendous sociological changes taking place. Shifts of population from the country to the cities, industrialization, mobility of Americans, and the struggle for civil rights and social justice were part of the changes and problems faced in America during the past hundred years. Jazz has matured with these changes. Indeed, jazz was born and developed in what has been the most accelerated period of change in the history of the world. Jazz, particularly the contribution made to world culture by the black musician, is part of man's struggle to understand and surmount his ever-increasing social problems in an ever-shrinking world. If music is an international language, then jazz eloquently speaks of the balance essential to the world for survival. Jazz is an axis between the intellect and the emotion of man: the world today needs that same sense of balance.

Jazz education is a valuable, integral part of music education and American culture. Jazz education in the public schools began in the early 1950s and has steadily continued to grow. Jazz education hasn't become "today's fad: tomorrow's throw-away," but rather, the curricular aspects of jazz education are both innovative and comprehensive in that students are involved in performance organizations (band, strings, vocal, large ensembles, and combos), listening (history, improvisation, and style study), applied comprehension (theory, arranging, composition, and performance), and creativity (improvisation).

Both students and teachers are seeking relevance in their music education as it applies to performance practices of the past, present, and future. Students are no longer satisfied to solely study the music and artistic styles of another culture. Today's students need roots as a means of helping to find their own identity. In addition, the student is looking at what he or she considers valid while the teacher is trying to create a fulfilling experience for the student. The inevitable—and proven—answer is jazz education.

No other aspect of music education can develop originality and creativity better than improvisation, which is the heart of jazz. Improvisation is the core of jazz instruction. It is the developmental techniques of improvisation that distinguish jazz from all others and that give jazz education validity. The spontaneous creative experience of the students using improvisation is, by itself, enough to justify the teaching of jazz.

> There's something about jazz music that ignites fantasies which have to do with creative thinking. That's what the whole world needs today: more creative thinking. Improvisation is the basis of creative thought: improvisation should be compulsory.[4]

The use of improvisation in jazz is typical of most of the ethnic music in the world today. Only Western Europe, under the influence of industrial technology and reading experience and learning, has departed from the inclusion of improvisation and spontaneity in its musical art. The balance between the preconceived in jazz and the spontaneous meets a real, aesthetic need in our world today.

Jazz avocations and vocations are prominent in today's society. Jazz is a cultural by-product of modern industrialization and urbanization. With popular music being an integral part of this technological and sociological change, jazz offers many lucrative avocations and vocations in your student's future.

When most instrumental music students finish high school or college, their active participation in music will probably end. This is usually due to the fact that: (1) not everybody has the time or desire to pursue the performance medium; and/or (2) professional employment, either as a vocation or avocation, is limited in traditional music. With a jazz background, however, there are additional opportunities that can make it lucrative to continue an association with jazz beyond a student's formal education experiences.

The following fields for jazz vocations and avocations are summarized:

Music education requires more and more that one have a background in jazz, including clinicians for workshops, artists-in-residence, and adjudicators for jazz festivals.

Live performance mediums (jazz, blues, rock, pop, etc.) offer a broad range of opportunities, from weddings/cocktail lounges/disco gigs to a full-time studio musician in a live performance/recording/movie situation.

Arranging/composing opportunities are closely aligned with the performance field, but can be applied to education as well.

Private teaching is available to anyone who wants to supplement his or her income while providing assistance to any students who want to receive specialized jazz instruction.

Broadcasting media include recording, film, and TV opportunities which involve production, A & R director, recording engineer, disc jockey, film music editor, graphic designer, and contractor.

Publishing and journalism careers that deal with editing, copying, publishing, writing (criticism, interviews, freelance, reviewer, etc.), and printing at the magazine, newspaper, and book levels are available.

Manufacturing and merchandising represent billion dollar (minimum) business operations covering instrument design, instrument sales, retailing, and instrument or accessory manufacturer positions.

Highlights in the Public School Jazz Education Movement

- Prior to the second World War, most high school jazz ensembles were student-directed with little or no encouragement from the school band director.

- The educational objectives of many school-sponsored dance bands were to improve the sight reading and rhythmic skills of the students participating.

- Early jazz education influences were mostly found outside of the schools and colleges before the late 1940s.
  a. local clubs and dance halls
  b. private teachers
  c. listening to records and the radio or watching films

- Post World War II brought a trend of big bands, directed by band directors, to the public schools.
  a. new band directors with dance band experience or jazz background from service bands during the war
  b. jazz became accepted and fostered as an American Art by the State Department through sponsored tours
  c. "name" bands disappeared which left a vacuum to be filled
  d. there was a rapid expansion of schools
  e. curriculum was liberalized

- The first high school jazz festival took place in Brownsville, Texas in 1953.

- By 1955, there were still a serious lack of charts published for jazz band, but jazz clinics and festivals started to appear in the public schools with professionals and educators (Don Jacoby, Buddy DeFranco, Marshall Brown, Matt Betton, Stan Kenton, M. E. Hall, Father George Wiskirchen, and others) becoming increasingly involved.

- With few notable exceptions, the jazz ensemble developed in secondary schools at a faster rate than in higher education during this time.

- Secondary education jazz ensembles played primarily for dancing until the 1960s when ensembles such as Marshall Brown's at Farmingdale, New York proved that a high school ensemble could play representative jazz.

- In the late 1950s, the music industry began to hire professionals as clinicians and composer/arrangers for special arrangements designed specifically for the schools. Graded jazz charts began to be published.

- The 1960s showed the first evidence of real expansion for jazz education. It is estimated that in 1960, there were only 5,000 school ensembles, and by 1970, the number had increased to 15,000.

- The first Stan Kenton Summer Camp took place in 1961.

- Jazz instruction gradually shifted to the public schools during the 1950s and to the colleges in the 1960s.

- Jazz education materials and methods began to emerge in the 1960s.

- An increased availability of more specialized arrangements and methods became evident in the mid-1960s.

- The Tanglewood Symposium took place in 1967. Here, educators indicated the value of jazz as a subject of study and a performing medium. MENC (the sponsor) emphasized "youth music."

- The National Association of Jazz Educators (NAJE) was organized in 1968.

- By the late 1960s, there was such a great demand for professional clinicians that musicians like Clark Terry and Rich Matteson spent most of their time working in schools.

- The late 1960s saw the production of a large quantity of charts with a jazz/rock concept.

- In the early 1970s, the libraries of the "name" bands (Stan Kenton, Thad Jones, Woody Herman, Count Basie, Maynard Ferguson, Don Ellis) became widely published.

- The 1970s heralded annual awards, provided by the National Endowment of the Arts, totaling almost $500,000 each year in grants for jazz/folk/ethnic music.

- Many colleges emphasized jazz education techniques as a part of their degree program in the 1970s.

- In the 1970s, the concept of the all-state stage band and jazz choir became a common practice as part of the public school scene.
- The 1970s became the decade where tremendous increases in the publication of jazz education materials took place with:
  a. improvisation materials
  b. big band, jazz choir, and combo charts
  c. transcribed solos from earlier recordings
  d. clinics/workshops materials
- During the 1970s, the use of the term "stage band" was slowly replaced with the term "jazz ensemble."
- The use of jazz elements were incorporated into Kodaly and Orff methods as jazz instruction spread to the elementary school level during the 1970s.
- Many more jazz periodicals and journals emerged during the 1970s.
- Jazz choirs and combos became an established part of the 1970s public school curriculum.
- The first nationally publicized summer combo camp took place in 1972 through Summer Jazz Clinics.
- The first NAJE National Convention took place in Chicago in December, 1973 (with an annual convention thereafter).
- In 1976, NAJE established a K–12 Curriculum Committee to survey trends of jazz education in the public schools. The concept of a comprehensive music program (that is, one which gives the student an opportunity to experience and study all types of music including jazz) was stressed. The formation of a national curriculum was designed by this committee in the early 1980s.
- In the early 1980s, NAJE has a total membership of well over 5,000 and is the second largest Associated Organization within MENC.

Making Jazz Education a National Project

Since its inception in 1968, the National Association of Jazz Educators (NAJE) has provided leadership to the jazz education movement. Gradually, jazz clinicians, jazz festivals, jazz publishers and even other music periodicals became more in-tune to the leadership that NAJE was providing. NAJE's periodical, the *Jazz Educators Journal*, is the only full-time jazz education magazine produced today. The NAJE objectives, as outlined in its charter, are exemplary for jazz education movement:

1. To foster and promote the understanding and appreciation of jazz and popular music, and its artistic performance.

2. To lend assistance and guidance in the organization and development of jazz and popular music curricula in schools and colleges to include stage bands and instrumental ensembles of all types, as well as choral organizations and vocal ensembles.

3. To foster the application of jazz principles to music materials and methods at all levels, to include elementary and secondary schools, junior colleges, colleges, and universities, both private and public.

4. To foster and encourage the development and adoption of curricula that will explore contemporary composition, arranging, and improvisation.

5. To disseminate educational and professional news of interest to music educators.

6. To assist in the organization of clinics, festivals, and symposiums at local, state, regional, and national levels.

7. To cooperate with all organizations dedicated to the development of musical culture in America.

A Checklist for Your Jazz Curriculum

The following list is provided for general information to assist you in understanding the benefits and desirability of having your own jazz program.

- The jazz program provides an outlet for creative music ability through improvisation. A keen interest in chord formation and the structure of music may develop, serving as the basis for a desire to study music theory and composition.

- Students develop a keener sense of intonation, balance and blend because of greater responsibilities which they must assume as individual players (one player on each part). Individual responsibility to the group is a strong incentive for students to listen and learn. Peers may provide the most effective criticism and praise.

- The student is involved in music which he or she can relate with as being relevant. Interest is sustained and learning the mechanics is made less tedious.

- Students participating in jazz often develop leadership qualities as a part of their responsibilities as section leader, lead player, soloist, etc.

- Jazz study provides a form of "advanced placement" for the young group when professional group arrangements are performed.

- Jazz ensemble participation offers a unique opportunity to the student: unusual rhythm patterns, more frequent sight reading experience, exposure to more diverse key signatures and modes are all components not frequently encountered in other music ensemble experiences.

• The jazz ensemble student often develops a high level of musician-ship. The technical proficiency demanded by the music, allowing the student to advance beyond the standard ensemble levels, creates a better all-purpose musician. Students have a tendency to achieve beyond their aptitude when they perform music they enjoy and want to play.

It is even more important to understand the potential problems associated with the school jazz program. Given this information, you can anticipate difficulties and be prepared for any objections raised about your jazz program. BEWARE of the school system where:

1. the jazz ensemble performance is overemphasized to the exclusion of other ensembles.
2. there is little (or no) emphasis on jazz combo training.
3. the creative aspects of jazz instruction are minimized:
   a. improvisation
   b. student arrangers/composers
4. listening skills are not stressed to the students.
5. the students lack a historical and biographical jazz perspective.
6. too few students are actually involved with the jazz curriculum. The program doesn't "reach out" to involve students either not formally involved with traditional ensembles or are younger and less experienced.
7. negative values are incurred by an overemphasis on festival competitions.
8. a teacher is overextended by excessive demands on every aspect of the music program.

NOTES

1. Wheaton, Jack W. "The Technological and Sociological Influences on Jazz as an Art Form in America," (unpublished Doctoral dissertation, University of Northern Colorado, 1976), 251.

2. Tanner, Paul, and Maurice Gerow. *A Study of Jazz*, Dubuque, Iowa: Wm. C. Brown, Co., 1973, 7.

3. Tellstrom, Theodore A. *Music in American Education: Past and Present*, New York: Holt, Rinehart and Winston, Inc., 1971, 278.

4. Kenton, Stan (in a panel discussion at the first annual NAJE national convention), Chicago, December 1973.

How to Organize the High School Jazz Program

Music educators are typically looking for "how to" recipes and short-cuts. They are usually not interested in long-term planning, especially if it involves searching hard for solutions. Consequently, curriculum planning among teachers is usually not a high-priority item. This chapter offers the "hows" of organizing a successful and creative jazz program. Step-by-step guidelines are suggested for developing the curricular aspects of a jazz program that will have far-reaching effects on students, administrators, teachers, and parents. Time and effort spent now on curriculum planning will save you painful moments later.

Teaching music through performance should provide students with the opportunities for critical evaluation and creative interpretation. The teacher's taste should not be absolute, nor should the purpose of teaching be to present a fixed concept of musical values for unquestioned student acceptance. The useful way to cultivate creativity through your teaching is to guide students to become conceptually acquainted with their musical environment.

Learning theorists seem to agree that the role of the educator is primarily as a facilitator of student learning. Many of these authorities have agreed that students learn more effectively if they are intrinsically involved in discovering the structure of the discipline itself. In the classroom, the discovery method means that the pupil will learn through his or her own investigation rather than from the teacher's spoken words. When a student has sufficient first-hand experience with music through listening, performing, improvising, and analyzing, he is better able to conceptualize musical knowledge.

When the pupil thinks musically, he is applying his musical experiences while moving towards a lasting behavior, in contrast to accumulating transient knowledge (which is discarded as soon as a course of study is completed). To the neophyte jazz educator, this emphasis on individuality might sound too idealistic, too democratic, or unworkable; rather, it is practical for today's educational environment.

Consider that the over-emphasis on teaching performance techniques has indeed limited the quality of music performed in all areas of high school instruction, including jazz. During the past decade, considerable emphasis has been placed on re-evaluation of the music curriculum. In the appraisals of the music program, the role of performance groups has been particularly scrutinized.[1] The concern centers primarily around these questions: Are students in band, orchestra, and choir actually gaining an understanding of the music they perform? Are they developing concepts of style and form? Or are they, in fact, only reading notes mechanically?

Music students at the secondary level, though in many cases proficient in their performance techniques, are usually weak in integrating knowledge of music history, literature, and theory with their applied skills. "Many of these students become music teachers and carry with them this basic deficiency. These findings are in evidence at annual solo, ensemble, band, and orchestra festivals."[2]

You need to deal with the core problems that jazz programs face, so read on and let's get started with thoughts and decisions about how jazz instruction can best be offered through your particular teaching situation.

STEP ONE: INCORPORATING A PHILOSOPHY FOR MUSIC INSTRUCTION

Organization is the key to beginning, maintaining, or revitalizing a jazz program. Without organization, it would be difficult to deal with any of the following questions you might encounter: What are teachers trying to do through the jazz medium? How can teachers best accomplish goals stated for the above question? What kinds of innovations in jazz education are possible? How can these innovative concepts be implemented? How can students be more comprehensively instructed in jazz within the confines of a single course offering? Can a teacher identify what the differences are for ALL the parts in the ensemble? One of the fundamental reasons jazz is flourishing so well in the public schools is that many music teachers are successfully matching the challenges of the above questions to their students' needs.

It is essential that all music instruction be based on a philosophy so that an effective curriculum can be designed and implemented. Jazz is often perceived by administrators as a frill to a music program, particularly in this era of decreasing enrollment, rollbacks of tax proposals, budget cuts, and inflation. The following rationale is offered as a broad base from which one may stress the nature and values of jazz instruction. This rationale is intended to encompass all avenues of the public school curriculum: general music, vocal, instrumental, and theoretical, and not just the jazz ensemble. It is not intended to imply that jazz should replace existing instruction, but it should be included as an integral part of a music program because of its relevant qualities as discussed in Chapter 1.

Music Rationale

1. To expand ability, based upon the pupil's natural love for music; to respond to the music with greater and deeper understanding through a knowledge of its melodic, rhythmic and harmonic properties. To develop an understanding of the organizational concepts of music.

2. To emphasize the intellectual and emotive qualities of music by helping the student recognize the means of expression most suitable to him and to offer him the opportunity to explore and develop his talents in music.

3. To involve each student to the degree of optimum capacity in order to make the student a more sensitive, discriminating, and creatively aware person.

4. To acquaint the student with his musical heritage. A total curriculum should include the great folk music and classics of the non-Western as well as the Western world in order that appropriate recognition can be given to all artistic expression which has contributed to present-day culture.

5. To provide an effective medium through which students can learn to relate to one another as well as to society and the world.

6. To motivate the student to explore a variety of musical literature in order that he may discover the value of music as a desirable mode of expression. An appropriate musical setting should be established through a repertory to include not only music of the past but of the present as well.

7. To help students find values through aesthetic expression.[3]

STEP TWO: CONSIDERING CURRICULAR GUIDELINES

The educational obligation and responsibility of a music curriculum can be summarized as follows:

1. To develop the talents of those who are gifted musically.
2. To develop the aesthetic sensitivity to music of all students regardless of their individual levels of musical talent.

In order to meet these standards, it is important that you take note of the various ways in which the basic musicianship concept can be taught.

Listener	–	those skills related to the perception of sound through the awareness of musical structure (melody, harmony, form, rhythm, tone color, texture) and their relationships.
Analyzer	–	those skills related to the understanding of musical concepts through musical terminology, verbal descriptions, or transcribing.
Creator	–	those skills related to the creation of music through improvisation, arranging, or composing.
Performer	–	those skills related to the production of musical sound via singing or playing an instrument.

In terms of jazz instruction, there are three areas of development where these behaviors can be taught. They are identified as: (1) skill development, (2) musical knowledge, and (3) attitude. Outlined below is a breakdown of the types of courses/class activities that are presently being offered in high schools across the country. The activity indicated in each behavior heading coincides with that heading's main emphasis; this does not exclude a relationship with any other category.

Skill Development

a. Jazz ensemble/jazz-rock ensemble/jazz lab band
b. Jazz choir/swing choir/show choir/gospel choir
c. Combo
d. Studio orchestra
e. Electrified string ensemble
f. Rock group

Musical Knowledge

a. Music theory/harmony
b. Music composition/arranging
c. History and literature of jazz
d. Improvisation

Attitude Development

a. General music/music appreciation
b. Music laboratory
c. Class guitar
d. Electronic music
e. History of rock and jazz
f. Folk music lab
g. African music lab
h. Piano lab
i. Folk guitar
j. Rock guitar
k. Banjo

STEP THREE: STARTING AT THE BEGINNING

There must be a balance in a music curriculum between jazz and non-jazz course offerings. An inadequate music program refers to a one-sided emphasis of instruction. Outlined in Tables 2-1, 2-2 and 2-3 are three quality comprehensive music programs for small, medium, and large school districts respectively. The point of these illustrations is not only to show what can be done in terms of curriculum design, but to emphasize that these programs were not established overnight. With adequate planning music programs can grow in predictable patterns. The establishment of such programs represents a multiple-emphasis approach for music achievement, public relations, feeder systems, curriculum development, and so on.

The big problem, though, is how to get a jazz program off the ground when there is no program! Initially, most jazz programs will need to begin with a single course offering, typically meeting before or after school hours, to be added later into the academic schedule as its worth and student participation increase. Most administrators will go along with such a program if there is real desire shown by you and your students and if the rest of the music program will not suffer. You must be prepared, however, to make sacrifices if you want a jazz program. Most jazz programs have started with a director who typically rehearses twice a week before or after school for no extra compensation. Once the validity of the program is self-evident, the director is in a position to negotiate: (1) a more satisfactory schedule, (2) additional course offerings, and (3) appropriate compensation.

TABLE 2-1

Pattern of Offerings – Music Department – McMinnville (Oregon) Public Schools

KINDERGARTEN (Music by Kindergarten Teacher)

ELEMENTARY CLASSROOM MUSIC (by Music Specialist)

Grade		
1	Basic Text 1-6	Orff Instruments (Diatonic)
2	*Exploring Music* (1971 ed.) Holt, Rinehart, Winston	
3		
4	*Threshold of Music* Mary Helen Richards Harper & Row	Recorders
5		
6	Grace Nash Materials (Kodaly approach)	Guitar

ELECTIVE INSTRUMENTAL MUSIC (by Specialists)

Beginning Strings
Second Year Strings
Beginning Band
Second Year Band

JUNIOR HIGH SCHOOL MUSIC (No Required Music Classes)

Grade	7th Grade Mixed Chorus 2 Sections	Treble Choir	Swing Choir	Concert Choir	General Music	Guitar	String Orchestra	Beginning Band	Adv. Band	Stage Band
7	7th Grade Mixed Chorus 2 Sections				7, 8 & 9 Given each sem.		7, 8, & 9	7, 8 & 9	7 & 8	
8	8th & 9th Mixed Chorus	8 & 9	8 & 9	8 & 9		8 & 9			Concert Band 8	8 & 9 Must take Concert Band
9									Band 9	

HIGH SCHOOL MUSIC (No Required Music Classes)

Grade	Exploring Electronic Music	Concert Choir	Swing Choir	Music of Today	Music Fundamentals	String & Full Orchestra	Concert Band	Stage Band
10	Exploring Electronic Music 10,11, & 12	Concert Choir 10,11, & 12	Swing Choir 10 & 11	Music of Today 10,11,12	Music Fundamentals 11 & 12	String & Full Orchestra 10,11,12	Concert Band 10,11, & 12	Stage Band 10,11, & 12
11	Electronic Lab 10,11, & 12		Twilighters 11 & 12	Guitar Lab 10,11,12			Pep Band	Must be taking Concert Band or Orchestra
12							Ensembles	

18

TABLE 2-2

Sequence of Music Offerings – Kirkwood (Missouri) R-7 School District

ELEMENTARY CLASSROOM MUSIC
(by Music Specialist)

K	Silver Burdette Series
1	Kodaly approach
2	Eurhythmics
3	Threshold of Music
4	Orff Instruments
5	Recorder

ELECTIVE INSTRUMENTAL MUSIC
(taught by Instrumental Specialists)

Beginning Strings	Beginning Band
2nd Year Strings	2nd Year Band

MIDDLE SCHOOL MUSIC

6	Living Arts Team Teaching (1 Music, 1 Drama, 2 Art teachers) Required Course	6th Grade Beginning Strings Strings	6th Grade Band	Beginning 6th Grade Band
7	7th Grade Team Teaching (1 Music, 1 Home Ec, 1 Art and 1 Speech/Drama teacher) Required Course	7th/8th Grade Strings	Cadet Band (7th/8th grades)	
8	8th Grade Chorus / Music Lab Required Course / *Swing Choir Extracurricular		Concert Band (7th/8th grades)	Stage Band Co-curricular (must take band)

HIGH SCHOOL MUSIC (No Required Classes)

9	9th Grade Chorus	Music Theory I & II 9-12	*Symphonic Orchestra 9-12	String Orchestra 9-12 (not presently offered)	*Symphonic Band I & II 9-12 Supporting Activities: Ensembles Marching Band Pep Band Orchestra Winds	Concert Band 9-12 (not presently offered)	*Stage Band I & II 9-12 Extra-curricular (must take band)
	*A cappella Choir 10-12	Mixed Chorus 10-12 (Four sections)	Vocal Solo & Ensemble 11-12	*Swing Choir 10-12			Jazz Combo I & II 9-12 Extra-curricular (must take band)

*Advance Performing Group – Entrance by audition

TABLE 2-3

Music Curriculum—Seattle (Washington) Public Schools

Course	6	7	8	9	10	11	12
Chorus	6	7	8	9			
Vocal Ensembles		7	8	9			
Concert Choir					10	11	12
Intermediate Choir					10	11	12
Madrigal Singers					10	11	12
Swing Choir						11	12
Chamber Singers						11	12
Class Piano	6	7	8	9	10	11	12
Piano I	6	7	8	9	10	11	12
Piano II	6	7	8	9	10	11	12
Piano III			8	9	10	11	
Piano IV							12
Introductory Piano					10	11	12
Folk Guitar I	6	7	8	9	10	11	12
Folk Guitar II					10	11	12
Guitar I			8	9	10	11	12
Rock Guitar					10	11	12
Classic Guitar					10	11	12
Beginning Band		7	8		10		
Senior Band				9	10		
Cadet Band					10	11	12
Concert Band					10	11	12
Marching Band					10	11	12
Jazz Ensemble					10	11	12
Brass/Percussion Band					10	11	12
Woodwind Band					10	11	12
Junior Orchestra		7	8				
Senior Orchestra			8	9			
Orchestra				9	10	11	
Concert Orchestra					10	11	12
Intermediate Orchestra					10	11	12
Chamber Orchestra						11	12
Miscellaneous Instrumental		7	8	9			
Beginning Instrumental					10	11	12
Instrumental Ensemble						11	12
Handbells	6	7	8	9	10	11	12
Senior Handbell Choir					10	11	12
Recorder	6	7	8	9			
General Music	6	7	8	9			
African Music Lab	6	7	8	9	10	11	12
Beginning Banjo					10	11	12
Folk Music Lab					10	11	12
Theory					10		
Harmony						11	12
Evolution of Music						11	12
History of Music						11	12

SCHEDULING JAZZ IN THE CURRICULUM

Once a jazz offering has proven successful as an extracurricular activity in terms of enrollment, achievement, and public relations, the next step is to pursue academic scheduling during the school day. There are numerous advantages to scheduling jazz ensemble during the day, as shown in the following list:

1. Improvisation can be more thoroughly dealt with as the core of jazz instruction. Jazz ensembles that meet beyond school hours usually require more time to be spent with ensemble technique with little time left to devote to improvisation or ear training techniques.

2. Ear training, which is the most fundamental skill used in jazz education, requires adequate time if jazz improvisation is to be seriously presented in class. Daily instruction lends itself to this type of format.

3. There are more opportunities to develop listening sessions for the purpose of style, concept, and historical awareness during daily classes. Listen to historical records for ensemble style (phrasing, articulation, rhythm section feel, and arranging style) and for solo style and approach (structure, use of space, vertical vs. horizontal approach, use of leading tones, paraphrase solo, tonal modification, dynamics, etc.). Be able to distinguish verbally and aurally the major periods and artists of jazz.[4]

4. Several combos can be organized on a regular basis since there are fewer scheduling conflicts. The time before or after school is now free and the students can organize their own combos if they want.

5. More jazz ensemble time per week is available for both rehearsals and sight reading. This gives the group more flexibility and opportunities to stress whatever needs most attention.

6. Attendance problems are minimized since the class is part of the regular schedule. There are no conflicts for jazz ensemble students who want to participate in other extracurricular activities.

7. Increased opportunities to expand the budget for jazz exist since it is a regular course that meets during the school day.

AN IDEAL MODEL:
TEXAS STATE CURRICULUM GUIDELINES

Band directors at Texas junior and senior high schools do not have to hassle with their administration as to whether it is proper to offer jazz ensemble daily for academic credit. In 1976, the Texas Education Agency sanctioned jazz ensemble as an approved course for grades 7–12, which can be taught by any certified teacher. The course includes prerequisites, time, credit, and course description. Hopefully, other states will follow Texas' initiative. (The guidelines are provided by the Texas Education Agency, 201 E. 11th Street, Austin, Texas 78701.) The guidelines state:

Jazz Ensemble – State of Texas

Grade Placement: 7–12

Prerequisite: Concurrent membership in band or orchestra; exceptions permitted for piano or organ, guitar, bass, and/or vocalist(s). Student assignment determined by the director.

Time: Semester plan – 130 clock hours minimum
Quarter plan – 135 clock hours minimum

Credit: Semester plan – ½ to 4 units
Quarter plan – 1,2,3 quarters per year, up to 12 quarters

Description: The jazz ensemble is a musical organization serving as a laboratory for students of instrumental music. Instrumentation is flexible, but organizations maintain sufficient size and balance of instrumentation to perform literature authentically and artistically. The jazz ensemble provides students with an opportunity to explore alternative styles of instrumental techniques utilized in American jazz and jazz-driven musical idioms; fosters creativity through improvisation; and serves as a basis for music vocations and avocations. The jazz ensemble may serve as a vehicle for performance of student compositions as well as commissioned and published materials. The jazz ensemble is under the direction of a certified music teacher.

FINALLY: PUTTING IT ALL TOGETHER

Even if jazz ensemble is given academic status during the school day, there's no assurance that any of the musical advantages previously outlined will be achieved. Again, organization is the key to running a successful jazz program. Since most high school isntrumental music teachers cover a variety of courses (including marching band, concert band(s), music lessons, jazz, and sometimes strings or chorus), that teacher needs a systematic, efficient approach to jazz instruction.

In order to deal with those common weaknesses inherent in jazz instruction (see Chapter 1), several curricular guidelines are provided in sequence below that can vastly expand the development of jazz ensemble students within the confines of a 55-minute daily rehearsal. Programs that meet less than daily can alter these plans appropriately.

Plan A: Multi-Curricular Approach

While it is natural to expect any rehearsal situation to be designed to emphasize preparation of music for an upcoming concert, theory, improvisation, history, style, listening, and/or sight reading are too frequently ignored activities appropriate for this time. Plan A makes two separate class offerings out of jazz ensemble with separate title, content, and evaluation taking place during the same class period. For example, the jazz ensemble meets Monday, Wednesday, and Friday, while Tuesday and Thursday are devoted to improvisation and theory. During these classes, listening and history may also be presented. With each section (jazz ensemble and improvisation) having its own course content, you are offered greater flexibility so that the ensemble can rehearse during an "improvisation session" if needed. The students benefit from a more comprehensive approach that allows immediate transference from one aspect of the program to another.

Plan B: Single, Comprehensive Approach

Plan B is a more comprehensive approach than Plan A since it includes specific sections for history, improvisation, and jazz ensemble. You may implement this program on a regular schedule or a rotating schedule. You are still afforded an "emergency" rehearsal if you need to work on preparation for a concert during an improvisation or history section, but the students are offered the opportunity to encounter jazz instruction at a level that is much more than the normal one-dimensional rehearsal. A rotating schedule that utilizes rehearsal, improvisation, and history is indicated in Table 2-4.

TABLE 2-4

| | WEEK | | | |
	1	2	3	4
MONDAY	Jazz Ensemble	Improvisation	Jazz Ensemble	Jazz History
TUESDAY	Improvisation	Jazz Ensemble	Jazz History	Jazz Ensemble
WEDNESDAY	Jazz Ensemble	Jazz History	Jazz Ensemble	Improvisation
THURSDAY	Jazz History	Jazz Ensemble	Improvisation	Jazz Ensemble
FRIDAY	Jazz Ensemble	Improvisation	Jazz Ensemble	Jazz History

The advantages of this type of scheduling include variety (where the students do not get into a "rut" with their schedule), flexibility, and generalization (where the class can study scores and records of a group in the history section; analyze solos and style in improvisation; and perform the music during rehearsal). This well-balanced approach will contribute greatly to your ensemble's ability to perform jazz in a correct, authentic fashion.

Plan C: The Extensive and Integrated Approach

A third plan offers still another opportunity to use each day for rehearsal, but with comprehensive instruction and incorporating all four basic musicianship behaviors into an integrated, decompartmentalized approach. The arrangement shown in Table 2-5 can expand the learning levels of jazz ensemble students within each 55-minute daily rehearsal. It should be pointed out that this type of format offers the ultimate flexibility, so the following might represent only one week out of a year where no two weeks are quite the same.

TABLE 2-5

MONDAY	10–15 minutes:	arranging, improvisation, or theory
	45–40 minutes:	jazz ensemble rehearsal
TUESDAY	20–25 minutes:	combos or improvisation
	35–30 minutes:	jazz ensemble rehearsal
WEDNESDAY	15–20 minutes:	history, style, or listening
	40–35 minutes:	jazz ensemble rehearsal
THURSDAY	20–25 minutes:	combos or improvisation
	35–30 minutes:	sectional rehearsal
FRIDAY	55 minutes:	jazz ensemble rehearsal

Now that you've been presented with three separate plans, you will need to analyze each to determine which plan will best meet your needs. Be realistic in your analysis of your program and objectives. If you find the plan you choose is unsatisfactory after a trial period, be prepared to choose another.

Individualizing Curriculum Design

Perhaps your school system has a scheduling situation that doesn't lend itself to any of the plans previously offered. With planning and cooperation from your administration, it is possible to design your own plan. Since any curriculum design takes extensive preparation, be sure you have a clear idea of how you want to implement your plan. Give yourself plenty of time in advance since each step along the curriculum design path takes longer than you might imagine. Finally, be quite certain you have the very best design for your immediate and foreseeable future needs; it is often easier to initiate a plan design than to change it.

NOTES

1. Papke, Richard E. "The New Breed of Band Director . . . Think Comprehensively," *Music Educators Journal*, November 1970, 40.

2. Disiderio, Anthony R. "Teaching the History of Western Music through Instrumental Performance in the Secondary School" (unpublished Doctoral dissertation, University of Southern California, 1966), 2.

3. *Music in the High School.* The State University of New York; The State Education Department; Bureau of Secondary Curriculum Development; Albany, New York, 1972, 2.

4. Wiskerchen, Rev. George. "The Roots of Excellence, or . . . 'Bird' Who?" *Selmer Bandwagon*, Volume 73, 28–31.

The Large Jazz Ensemble: The Backbone of Your Program

How to Organize a Jazz Ensemble Program

In Chapters 1 and 2, the curricular foundation, philosophy, and rationale for jazz instruction in the public schools were considered. This chapter covers the organizational aspects of the large jazz ensemble, which is the backbone of the entire jazz program. Obviously, there is considerably more to organizing a group of musicians than just passing out music and giving the downbeat! Every dimension of a jazz ensemble program is carefully considered in Chapter 3 and, for your organization, is presented in chronological order.

ESTABLISHING THE PRELIMINARIES

Identifying Membership Prerequisites

Care needs to be exercised to insure that the jazz ensemble will function smoothly within the total music organization. A preliminary procedure that will help develop a well-rounded instrumental program and insure cooperation among all the music teachers is to require all members of the jazz ensemble to be members of some other performing group. While some jazz ensemble programs exempt guitar, piano, and bass players, others use these players in choral groups or any performing group where they can make a contribution. This plan provides jazz ensemble members a fuller musical experience and reassures the music faculty that the jazz ensemble is part of the program rather than outside it.

Conducting the Jazz Ensemble Audition

Well-run auditions are an important factor in a successful jazz ensemble program. During an audition, the applicant's musicianship is evaluated, but more importantly, a tacit statement about the ensemble is presented to the auditioner. A well-organized audition with clearly stated objectives implies the standards and aspirations of the jazz program.

In order to attract as many applicants as possible, the audition should be well publicized in advance of the audition date. It would be beneficial if guidelines can be made available so that interested students can prepare for the audition. Make use of your school newspaper, public address system, and bulletin boards to publicize the audition.

Ideally, an audition should be a learning experience, not a negative reminder of what the student doesn't know. The advantage of having an organized audition procedure is that students can improve their performance level and basic skills while preparing for the audition. Select audition material that reflects the difficulty and style of the charts you plan to perform. Select a variety of styles. Wherever possible, choose music that is recorded so that interested students can take the initiative to study their parts. If one of your criteria is improvisation, select blues changes in two or three keys. Make it clear in advance what you expect!

The audition sequence should include a rhythm section tryout first. You might select your rhythm section according to the same procedure that is indicated below, but it will be helpful later to have the rhythm section taken care of first. If your rhythm section doesn't have any major problems with keeping time, struggling over chord changes, and so on, it should provide the foundation for the remainder of your audition activities. Besides the rhythm section, you should have separate auditions for each section. For each piece of music, you may: (1) rehearse the section; (2) move people within the section; (3) ask individual players to perform the rehearsed section by themselves; and (4) replace players within the section in order to try all possible combinations. At any point, go back to any other level rather than merely following steps 1–4. One of the main advantages of this procedure is that the rhythm section can get valuable time together as it works behind the auditioners.

Once you have heard all the section combinations, you will want to hear soloists. Improvisation should be an objective of jazz education so that any student who can't improvise should not be made to feel inadequate. Encourage all auditioners to try to improvise, but do not insist if a student seems unwilling; a big portion of success in improvising is *confidence*. Don't make any student's contact with improvisation a threatening, negative, or traumatic experience.

FIGURE 3-1

AUDITION EVALUATION FORM

Instrument _____ Date _____

Name _____ Phone _____

Address _____

	1	2	3	4	5	6
Time						
Tone or blend						
Articulation						
Range						
Intonation						
Sight reading						
Improvisation						

1 = Very weak

6 = Excellent

Time	Rhythmic precision; tempo does not drag or rush; a good rhythmic "feel."
Tone or blend	Contributes to section concept; balanced dynamic level; quality of sound.
Articulation	Uses attacks, releases, and breathing to achieve proper jazz concept.
Range	Produces extreme notes without pressure or distortion.
Intonation	Quality of playing in tune within section and alone.
Sight reading	Technical accuracy; musical rather than just mechanical.
Improvisation	Appropriate style, changes, and creativity.

A typical audition evaluation form is shown in Figure 3-1. It's a good idea to have your evaluation form posted on a bulletin board in advance of auditions so that the students can see what you are looking for and how they can best prepare. Also have an evaluation form for yourself so that you have a reference in case any questions or problems arise in the future; you could then later discuss each student's performance.

A good evaluation form should be simple to use and easy to understand. It should be valid for future reference and should contain an explanation of grading.

Choosing the Right Musician for Each Part

The best all-around player in your sax section should be your lead alto. Be sure to select someone with a good feel for jazz as well as a superior ability to read and play strongly. Playing "lead" means being responsible for the entire section since the section must emulate the lead player's style. He or she should be one of the section's most extroverted players and possess power and tone quality to carry the section. If a timid player is selected, the sax section will probably be dominated by the tenor players.

The first tenor should be your second best all-around sax player. The majority of improvisation is usually given to the first tenor. In addition to top improvisational skills, feel, tone quality, power, and extroversion are important and desirable qualities.

The contribution of the baritone saxophone should not be underestimated. This player will generally have fewer technical demands, so select accordingly. This player needs to help the first alto in carrying the section with power. Never select the weakest player for this position. If you have two students who have about equal technique but not lead alto material, always select the one with the bigger sound to play baritone sax!

A good spot for the younger alto player is second alto. Encourage the second alto to emulate the lead alto.

The younger tenor player can observe and emulate the first tenor by playing second tenor.

Criteria for selecting a lead trumpet for the trumpet section should be based on a good upper register, endurance, good pitch concept, strong tone, a centered sound, and the ability to lead the entire band in the phrasing, articulation, and interpretation of ensemble passages. Obviously, a good lead trumpet player is important to the success of any jazz ensemble. It is imperative that this person have both "chops" and musicianship. Because the part is so demanding in range and power, it is sometimes advisable to select an assistant lead player to share the burden (though never doubling the part!), so that a strong, confident first part is consistently covered.

The responsibility for improvisation is usually given to the second trumpet part. In addition to soloing, the second should be supportive of and complementary to the lead trumpet with good range and rhythmic concept.

Balance and support of the lead trumpet is critical in choosing third and fourth trumpets. The parts demand sensitivity, ability and willingness to play up (in dynamics and intensity) to the lead player.

The fifth trumpet part is not written in every chart. You should use the same criteria as for the third and fourth trumpets except that the fifth part is often called upon to solo and sometimes double as the "screech" trumpet playing in the extreme upper range.

Use the same criteria for selecting your lead, second, and third trombones for your trombone section as is recommended for the trumpet section. With the trombone section, the lead part, rather than the second, usually has the solo responsibilities.

The fourth trombone and baritone saxophone are the bottom of the band and need players of above-average ability. Select a player with good power, especially in the low range. This player should be your second or third best trombonist.

In the rhythm section, the bass (acoustic or electric) is the most important rhythm section instrument, so finding a good bassist will often be a difficult task. A good feel for the rhythm and tempo is necessary, in addition to a knowledge of chords. It makes your rehearsals much easier if the bass player is able to read well.

The drummer must have a good rhythmic feel in addition to having an accurate sense of time, and an independence of hands and feet. The drummer should be able to read music and perform in a variety of styles (swing, rock, Latin, and so on).

Select your piano, guitar, and vibes players with a good sense and display of rhythm, tempo, chordal structure, and voicing. These players must have a good ear and be interested in playing both by notation and with creative freedom. Much of the music they will encounter may be written in chord symbols only.

If you have another good drummer and the appropriate instruments (conga, timbales, tambourine, vibra-slap, guiro, cowbell, etc.), it is possible to add another player on auxiliary percussion. The use of auxiliary percussion is extensively discussed in Chapter 9, but essentially, caution and control must be exercised.

SEATING AND SETUPS FOR REHEARSALS AND CONCERTS

The seating arrangement of a jazz ensemble can influence its performance, particularly in terms of balance and precision. Though different seating arrangements have a marked visual affect on both the performers and audience, the prime consideration should be on how well the group plays and is able to hear.

There are two fundamental seating arrangements used in concerts for the jazz ensemble: the block style or the spread formation. Each setup has numerous variations determined by the strength of the players and the number in the group.

A Comparison of Traditional and Spread Setups

Two versions of the traditional block are presented in Figures 3-2 and 3-3, along with a list of advantages and disadvantages.

Strong Points:
1. Gives the group the tightest, fattest sound of all setups.
2. Rhythm section is not spread out and can hear most of the band.
3. Uses the least space of all possible setups.
4. Can be used with or without risers.

Weak Points:
1. Saxes are not easily heard by brass players.
2. No eye contact between players.

Two versions of the spread formation with its advantages and disadvantages are diagrammed in Figures 3-4 and 3-5.

Strong Points:
1. Provides a very balanced sound.
2. Rhythm section is central to the group.
3. Visually attractive stage setting.
4. Good eye contact among players.

Weak Points:
1. Spreads ensemble out: very difficult on an inexperienced rhythm section and members of each section most removed from the center.
2. Brass section not solid.
3. Harder for some members to hear other sections.

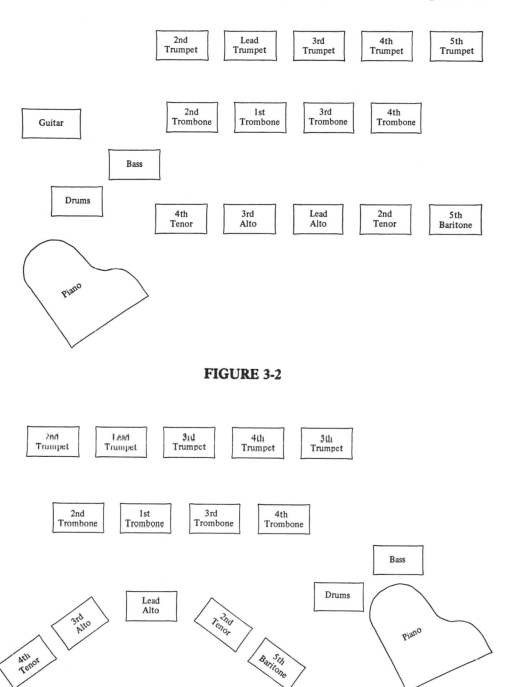

FIGURE 3-2

FIGURE 3-3

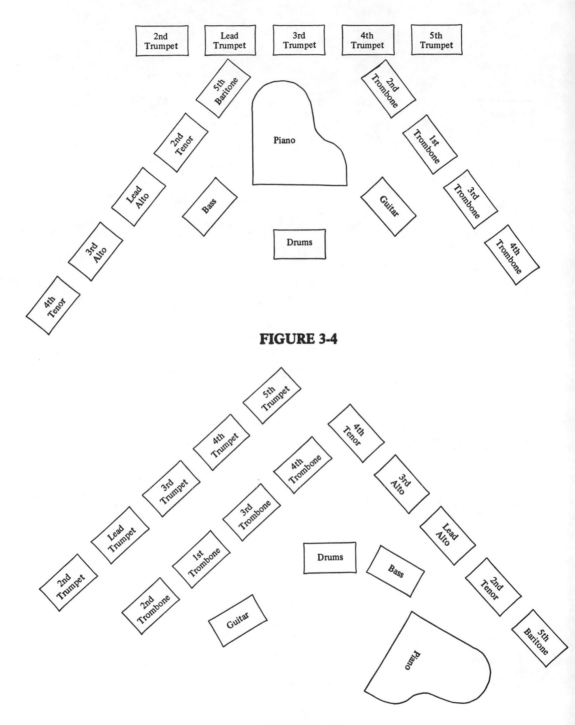

FIGURE 3-4

FIGURE 3-5

Setting Up for a Rehearsal

Take advantage of diverse rehearsal situations with the use of various setups. Primarily, of course, you want your group to set up the way they will perform on stage so that they are accustomed and comfortable to that format in advance. However, for variety or to solve a particular problem (getting the band to play a section "tight," hearing ALL the parts, developing uniform articulation and concepts, etc.), try the following setups (Figures 3-6 and 3-7) during your rehearsal.

Strong Points:
1. Brass can hear sax section easily.
2. Places the rhythm section in a new position where they are forced to listen more carefully.
3. This is especially helpful for groups that use the block setup. The similarities are obvious, yet it is new enough so that it can help the members of the group to hear things differently.

Strong Points:
1. The players can hear each other better.
2. The players can better understand how all parts fit together.
3. This is helpful for every group in a rehearsal where the director wants a new environment; it is well suited for the group that performs in a spread setup.

NOTE: The band that sits close together, plays together. Don't spread your group too much, since the distance will put a strain on the ensembles's intonation, balance, and precision.

The following pointers are a few additional guidelines to consider when seating a jazz ensemble:

- Lead players should sit in the center of each section.
- The rhythm section should be as close to the group as possible.
- Place the bass player behind the hi-hat of the drummer.
- The bass amp should be positioned so that the drummer and ensemble can easily hear it—the bass player should not stand directly in front of the amp.
- Place the tenor saxes on both sides of the altos in order to eliminate "tenor boom."
- The baritone sax and bass trombone should sit on the same side of their respective sections.

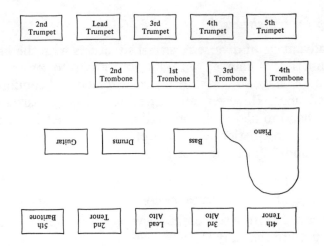

FIGURE 3-6

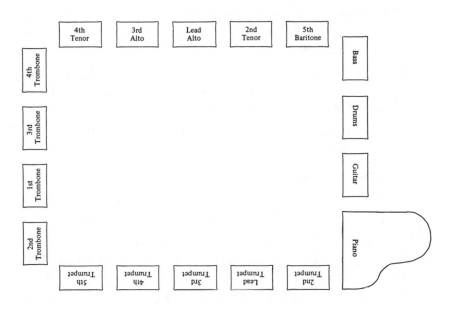

FIGURE 3-7

SCHEDULING REHEARSALS

Ideally, daily rehearsals are the preferred way to schedule a jazz ensemble. Too often, however, administrators, parents, and even students will not actively support such a schedule unless the ensemble has already proven its worth. In Chapter 2, several alternatives were provided in developing a comprehensive approach to jazz instruction. In this section, only the actual scheduling details will be examined.

The Sectional Rehearsal Concept

Regardless of the type of scheduling, sectional rehearsals are an important facet of the jazz ensemble program. The lead player should also be the section leader. Sectionals should be teacher-supervised until the section leaders prove their capability to direct the rehearsals alone. Sectionals are important in getting each section to play together in terms of blending, articulation, time, and phrasing. The section should strive to match the lead player. With this system, the director can deal directly with the section leader in terms of where the work should be done and the section leader can pass this on to the section, make musical decisions, and assume responsibility while gaining valuable leadership skills.

Generally, the most difficult section to manage is the rhythm section since each instrument is different and, usually, there is the problem that no student within the section is really qualified. The director should initially handle all rhythm sections, but there is still no reason why one member can't be identified and trained to handle the role of section leader. The rhythm section leader should be the student with the strongest musicianship and the most maturity. If there are some members of the rhythm section who are stronger in one area but not both, they will often not get the desired results if appointed section leader.

In addition to the sectional rehearsals, it is important that the lead trumpet, alto sax, and first trombone players have a "lead" sectional occasionally so that any tutti lick will be played exactly the same by each section within the band.

Since the lead trumpet is ultimately responsible for the style and phrasing of the entire ensemble, a "chain of command" becomes an important process to achieve group tightness and cohesiveness. Indicated in Figure 3-8 is a diagram to display each member's responsibility within the group. Ultimately, the director makes final musical decisions and should have a general sense of agreement and understanding with the lead trumpet player.

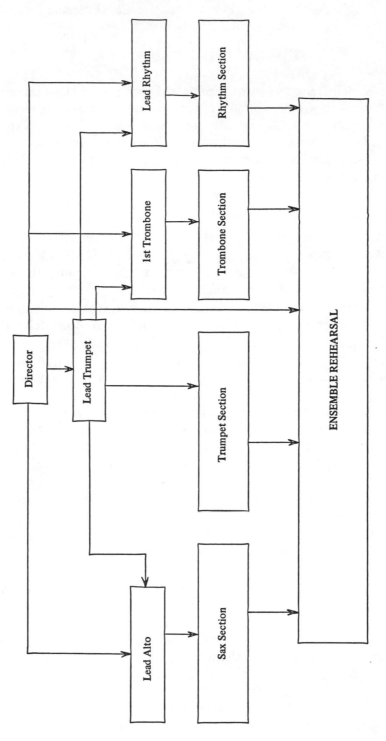

FIGURE 3-8

The Ensemble in the Extracurricular Schedule

Traditionally, one ensemble rehearsal per week is probably the most common approach to beginning a jazz ensemble, and there is no conflict with any classes if this is an extracurricular activity. In many systems it is possible for students to earn credit since they will receive eight hours of instruction per month for at least six or seven months. These rehearsals are usually at night between 6–8 p.m. or 7–9 p.m., since afternoon rehearsals would conflict with athletics and other extracurricular activities. It should be recognized that this plan represents a minimum of rehearsal time per week in order to operate a quality jazz ensemble program.

Another version features two after-school rehearsals per week. Here, two evenings a week are usually involved with two-hour blocks each. This can be a productive system, often more than doubling the single rehearsal plan. School credit for this class should be easy since the course meets approximately as much as any regularly scheduled class.

Before-school rehearsals work well for some school programs. If your school starts late enough and the students can get to school at least one hour before school actually begins, this form of rehearsal could work for you. Adequate time for brass warm-ups and rhythm section setup is an important consideration. There should also be a break between your extracurricular jazz ensemble rehearsal and the time when band is regularly scheduled so that brass players are not overly taxed.

Scheduling the Ensemble During the School Day

An alternating day schedule can be quite useful, especially if you follow a comprehensive approach as outlined in Chapter 2. In this situation, all jazz students would be getting more comprehensive instruction that would ultimately contribute to your ensemble's performance.

The epitome of in-school scheduling is represented by daily rehearsals, where continuity and efficiency are maximal. It is recommended that these rehearsals utilize a comprehensive approach.

If there are any problems with scheduling any members of the ensemble into a daily rehearsal, you may elect additional rehearsals to provide an opportunity for everybody to work together. Although this system can be physically demanding, it provides the group the opportunity to have complete instrumentation with the best possible players.

FINDING BASIC LITERATURE FOR JAZZ ENSEMBLES

One of the basic goals in developing a jazz ensemble should be to build a repertory of many jazz styles with an accurate historical perspective. A prerequisite to this is to teach the fundamentals of jazz musicianship: phrasing, articulation, and rhythm patterns. A working knowledge of the basics makes jazz charts easier to understand and perform. At the beginning and intermediate levels of public school jazz ensembles, the students don't know how to articulate jazz licks, how to swing, or understand jazz rhythms. A teacher might use a rote method where the parts are sung to the students with the proper inflections, but this process is time-consuming and not very efficient. Training books provide a faster and more thorough way to teach jazz basics. Many of these training books are designed for use in the heterogeneous setting with books in C, B^b, E^b, and bass clef. The following is a selected list of basic jazz ensemble materials, with information on still other types of materials listed in Chapter 4.

"Take One" Improvisation by Matt Betton and Charles Peters (Neil A. Kjos). This is a great book for elementary and junior high levels as a supplement to any standard Book II method. This series covers four areas of jazz instruction: (1) theory; (2) listening; (3) rhythm; and (4) creating.

Jazz-Rock & Harmony, Books I & II by James Ployhar, John Cacavas, and Fred Weber (Belwin/Mills). This is a sequential method book focusing on the student's development of rhythm and articulation skills as well as understanding improvisation basics.

The Elementary Stage Band Book by Gerald Sebesky (Belwin/ Mills). This book serves as a continuation of the series by Ployhar, Cacavas, and Weber.

The Sound of Rock by Sandy Feldstein and Joseph Sciani (Alfred Publishing Co.). Rock articulations and rhythms are covered in a very attractive, in-depth manner. The arrangements are catchy and appealing to younger groups.

The Sounds of Jazz by Carl Strommen and Sandy Feldstein (Alfred Publishing Co.). This work provides a musical treat for youngsters in learning jazz articulations and rhythms.

Developing the Stage Band by John LaPorta (Berklee Press). This has served as the standard training jazz band method book since the 1960s. It is solid, thorough, and provides abundant teaching applications. The book is still viable today.

ESTABLISHING A REPERTORY FOR A JAZZ PROGRAM

It is important that students be given opportunities to perform, listen, and study a wide variety of jazz literature. In establishing a music repertory, there is a tendency to build a lopsided library. Jazz has a rich history of development as well as diverse products. A balance of the following categories should be maintained in your music library for programming and study considerations.

Jazz written after the second World War would include the mainstream of most ensemble libraries. Charts of many of the top jazz bands commercially available include those of Buddy Rich, Count Basie, Thad Jones and Mel Lewis, Maynard Ferguson, Stan Kenton, Woody Herman, and many others.

This does not mean that the roots of jazz (that jazz written in pre-war times) can be neglected. The swing charts of Glenn Miller, Harry James, early Count Basie, Duke Ellington, Benny Goodman, and others are well worth the time to study and perform. Don't ignore the dixieland and ragtime pieces, either, because it is important that your students be aware of the evolution and development of jazz.

The fusion of jazz and rock in the 1970s gave jazz a broader and more diversified audience appeal. Charts by Blood, Sweat and Tears, Chicago, and Frank Zappa are available for the jazz ensemble. To fully understand and appreciate this music, listen to the recent jazz/rock sounds of Maynard Ferguson and Woody Herman to see how experienced big jazz groups are handling fusion.

Don't underestimate the importance of Latin-jazz charts. Latin-jazz (charts that feature a Latin flavor) can provide an exciting dimension to the jazz repertory. Latin percussion instruments (see Chapter 9) can be used for added interest to appropriate arrangements. Among writers who have used extensive Latin-jazz arrangements are Johnny Richards, Chico O'Farrill, Bill Holman, Don Menza, and Dizzy Gillespie.

Ballads are probably the most difficult form of jazz to play stylistically correct and the most demanding on the performers. The demands of a ballad should never be underestimated—sound support, section work, solid lead playing, intonation, and nuances like ghosting, falls, and flips, are just a few of the aspects that make ballads hard to play well. Have the ensemble listen to Stan Kenton, Thad Jones, and the Basie "Nestico" charts to get a good feel on how ballads should be performed.

TROUBLESHOOTING: HOW TO ANTICIPATE PROBLEMS

Sources of Jazz Charts

Today there's a wealth of excellent charts commercially available by arrangers who know the needs of public school educators at all levels of ability, from elementary school through college and professional. Many music publishers have records or tapes of their charts available upon request, which are helpful as a teaching aid. Many of the charts are from the libraries of famous jazz bands, such as Basie, Ferguson, Jones/Lewis, and Herman, and are commercially recorded.

It was once common for directors to duplicate and swap copies of unpublished charts with other directors. Now, most of the big-name artists and bands have many of their recorded charts published at a reasonable cost. Independent composers and arrangers, too, are making their charts available through their own publishing companies in increasing numbers.

With more than 300 publishers of jazz ensemble charts, it is not an easy matter to select music. The following list is compiled as a guide to help find good charts with a little less fuss. Write to each publisher directly for possible sound sheets, LPs, tapes, and/or study scores.

A. J. Productions
P.O. Box 1793
Beulah, MI 49617

William Allen Music, Inc.
P.O. Box 31334
Washington, D.C. 20031

C. L. Barnhouse
Music Publishers
Oskaloosa, IA 52577

Doug Beach Music
25 N. 5th Avenue
Maywood, IL 60153

Berklee Press
1140 Boylston Street
Boston, MA 02215

Blixt Publications
413 Rutland Avenue
San Jose, CA 95128

Alf Clausen
P.O. Box 3241
Hollywood, CA 91605

John Prince Cookbook
2050 Volk Avenue
Long Beach, CA 90815

Creative Jazz Composers
P.O. Box T
Bowie, MD 20715

Alfred Publishing Co.
15335 Morrison Street
Sherman Oaks, CA 91403

Artistries, Inc.
64-24 Grand Avenue
Maspeth, NY 11378

Mike Barone
P.O. Box 35216
Los Angeles, CA 90035

Belwin Mills
Publishing Corporation
Mehlville, NY 11747

Big 3 Music Corp.
729 Seventh Avenue
New York, NY 10019

Campus Music Service
P.O. Box A.A.
Hawthorne, CA 90250

Columbia Pictures Publications
P.O. Box 4340
Hialeah, FL 33014

Creative World
1012 S. Robertson Boulevard
Los Angeles, CA 90035

Dave Eshelman
10810 Minette Drive
Cupertino, CA 95014

David Diggs Publisher
P.O. Box 2601-L
Anaheim, CA 92804

Hansen Publications
1842 West Avenue
Miami Beach, FL 33139

Kendor Music
Music Publishers
Delevan, NY 14042

Laissez-Faire Music
810 N. Cumberland
Lebanon, TN 37087

Hal Leonard Publishing
8112 W. Bluemond Road
Milwaukee, WI 53213

Ladd McIntosh
7712 Alcove Avenue
North Hollywood, CA 91605

Outrageous Mothers, Inc.
P.O. Box 511
Lewisville, TX 75067

Pendulum Music
1944 Whitley Avenue #311
Hollywood, CA 90068

Don Rader Music
15859 Rose Street
Van Nuys, CA 91406

Southern Music Co.
1100 Broadway
San Antonio, TX 78292

Vegas Music
3105 Palora Avenue
Las Vegas, NV 89121

Steve Wright Music Endeavors
15631 Lexington Circle
Minnetonka, MN 55343

Young World Publications
10484 Glennon Drive
Lakewood, CO 80226

Forefront Publications
1945 Wilmette Avenue
Wilmette, IL 60091

Jenson Publications
2880 S. 171st Street
New Berlin, WI 53151

Neil A. Kjos Music
4383 Jutland Drive
San Diego, CA 92217

Norman Lee Publishing
P.O. Box 2733
Wichita, KS 67207

Marina Music Publishing
P.O. Box 2452
San Leandro, CA 94577

Menza & Pestrup
4425 Clyborn Avenue
North Hollywood, CA 91602

Palisades Publications
P.O. Box 35216
Los Angeles, CA 90035

Theodore Presser Co.
Presser Place
Bryn Mawr, PA 19010

Script House
1609 Third Avenue
Los Angeles, CA 90019

Sierra Music Publisher
P.O. Box 5433
Pasadena, CA 99107

Studio P/R Inc.
c/o Columbia Pictures Pub.
P.O. Box 4340
Hialeah, FL 33014

Warner Bros. Publications
75 Rockefeller Plaza
New York, NY 10019

Wynn Music
P.O. Box 739
Orinda, CA 94563

Solutions to Incomplete Instrumentation

If your jazz ensemble doesn't have a full complement of students for all the parts needed to be covered, consider the following recommendations:

- Try to have a minimum of three sax parts covered: lead alto, 1st tenor, and baritone.
- When you have only three trombones and a chart that calls for four, have the 1st, 2nd, and 4th parts covered. If a tuba player is available, use the tuba to cover the 4th part.
- If you have no bass player, consider these options:
  a. Have the piano player play the bass part on an electric piano. Better yet, have a second pianist play the bass part on a Fendor Electric Keyboard Bass, which comes close to sounding like an electric bass.
  b. Find a guitarist to learn electric bass since the concept is easy to transfer.
  c. Find an instrumentalist who plays in the lower register (tuba, bass clarinet, baritone sax, trombone, etc.) to learn bass.
  d. Check the orchestra to see if one of the acoustic basses or cellists would like to play bass in the jazz ensemble.
  e. Have a pianist play bass lines on a synthesizer.
- Never double parts! This only creates musical problems with intonation, blending, dynamics, and concept. What you end up with is a concert band that plays popular music in an inaccurate fashion.
- Use trumpets on lead, 2nd, and 3rd parts—in that order—when a full section is not available.
- If only two trombones are available, cover the 1st and 2nd parts.
- If no baritone sax player is available, cover the part with another instrument (bass clarinet, bassoon, even baritone horn) if that person is a good musician.
- Use French horns to cover trombone parts, especially 1st and 2nd.

Elementary/Junior High School: Where the Program Begins!

The high standards of some junior high jazz ensembles have come to rival some high school jazz groups as revealed at recent NAJE and MENC national conventions. The future of jazz education looms especially bright with the musical quality and success of these feeder systems. The purpose of a feeder system is to teach the basic skills of jazz through performance training. Developing rhythm sections, theory, improvisation skills, playing experience, sectional ensemble cohesiveness, and, above all, awareness and appreciation of jazz, are the reasons for having a jazz feeder program. Some suggestions for high school directors who want to improve their feeding programs (or the feeder/directors who want to improve their programs) include the following:

1. Keep a good working relationship among the elementary, junior high, and high school band directors. The feeder directors should be made to feel welcome at high school rehearsals and performances. If possible, have the feeder director take part in concerts and tours with the high school jazz ensemble. If possible, high school lead players should occasionally be able to sit in with the younger group.

2. Have the high school jazz ensemble perform at the junior high/elementary schools that feed your program on a regular basis. Exposure to these students encourages interest in your program from an early age.

3. Actively encourage younger players by personally visiting feeder schools and talking among the students whenever possible.

4. Invite the elementary and/or junior high jazz ensembles or concert bands to perform with your group at one of your concerts.

5. Develop a summer jazz camp designed to work specifically with younger music students.

6. Issue a specific invitation to the elementary/junior high school jazz ensemble students for each jazz activity (clinic, workshop, concert, etc.) at your school. Make it obvious what the high school program offers, and share guest clinicians and soloists with these students.

7. Pass on outstanding recordings or radio and TV programs for the younger students to hear.

8. Record your concerts and send the tapes to your feeder systems for listening.

9. Inform and encourage feeder teachers to attend jazz clinics, festivals, and workshops. Check with local music stores about getting clinicians through instrumental manufacturers and publishers for a clinic in your district.

10. Develop a master plan to maintain balanced instrumentation. Keep a running "inventory" of student participation by instrument for each year so that you can anticipate "holes" in your future instrumentation. Identify guitarists and pianists before they get to the high school level.

11. Send copies of the *Jazz Educators Journal* to feeder teachers and encourage them to join NAJE. If convenient, organize a NAJE student chapter at your school to include junior high school students.

12. Pass along pertinent articles and jazz ensemble chart reviews from the *Jazz Educators Journal* and *The Instrumentalist* to feeder teachers.

13. Encourage feeder teachers to introduce and teach jazz phrasing and improvisation concepts within the traditional concert band setting. Charts by Phil Hardymon published by Wynn Music are excellent for this purpose.

The three essential ingredients to building a fine jazz program at all grade levels include *broad involvement, good communication,* and *musically motivated* students. Each of these aspects is vital to a comprehensive program's success; without that success, the high school jazz ensemble director is forced to be at the disadvantage of training students for jazz when they get to him or her.

Selecting Jazz Equipment

The spectrum of equipment used in jazz today includes both the acoustical instruments of sax, brass, percussion, bass, and an array of electronic equipment like electronic guitars, amplifiers, P.A. systems, and more. Since music educators make budgetary decisions as well as performance judgments, it is important that they know what is available and how to select equipment that best meets their needs.

SELECTING SAXOPHONE NEEDS

How to Choose Saxophones

Saxophones can differ widely in both tonal and intonation characteristics. It is important to become familiar with the differences that can be found. Listed below are some guidelines that might be beneficial when considering the purchase of any saxophones.

- What is the intensity or projection rate? Have someone listen for comparison as various models are played from a distance.
- Does the horn respond at its lowest and highest dynamic levels throughout the instrumental range? Have the instrument played at ff and pp at the top, middle, and bottom of the register.
- What is the basic sound quality in terms of brightness or darkness? A silver finish produces a brighter sound than a gold finish, and a lacquer finish gives a darker sound. Generally, a newer model will produce a lighter sound.
- Are there any noticeable intonation problems? Check the most frequently out-of-tune notes (low B, C, C#, D, Middle D_2, E^b_2, and high C# up); test the intonation in fifths and octaves.

- Is there evidence that the instrument is irregularly out of tune at the top of the register? It is better to be *progressively* out of tune than *irregularly* out of tune.
- Are some key fingerings awkward to finger (especially low B, C, C#, G#, high D, and above)? Is the key mechanism sluggish? The height of the keys should be consistent and not too high. In order to cope with fast passages, the fingering action should be as light as possible.

Woodwind instruments frequently used in jazz are the soprano, alto, tenor, and baritone saxophones, flute, and clarinet. Other common doubling woodwinds are piccolo and bass clarinet. Most major manufacturers produce several grades of instruments from student to professional models. Listed below are prominent manufacturers.

Armstrong P.O. Box 963 Elkhart, IN 46515	C. G. Conn, Ltd. 2520 Industrial Parkway Elkhart, IN 46516	LeBlanc Corporation 7019 30th Avenue Kenosha, WI 53141
Buffet, Crampon & Cie 55 Marcus Drive Melville, NY 11746	King Musical Instruments 33999 Curtis Boulevard Eastlake, OH 44094	Selmer Co. P.O. Box 310 Elkhart, IN 46514
	Yamaha Musical Products P.O. Box 7271 Grand Rapids, MI 49510	

Considerations for the Sax Mouthpiece

There are several reasons why individual players will not sound the same when playing on one particular mouthpiece. Various characteristics that can affect sound are the differences in individual physical makeup, size and thinness of lips, jaw function, teeth, as well as concepts of sound and performance techniques. Certain brands of instruments can add to the variance with darker or brighter sounds, and even reeds and ligatures can have an impact on the tone.

Frequently, sax sections in a jazz group are unable to compete with brass sections in terms of sound production and blends. Consider the following questions when evaluating the status and effectiveness of the present mouthpieces of your sax section. You might want to consider using mouthpieces that could better enable your players to "cut" the total sound to be better heard.

- Does each player blend with the other saxes in the section in terms of warmth and edge? control the attacks consistently? maintain the sound quality when playing all degrees of dynamics?

- Can each player play the lowest and highest notes comfortably, and play softly and loudly consistently throughout the entire range of the instrument?
- Is the intonation consistent and controllable for each player?

Believe it or not, mouthpieces and various kinds of facings can actually affect the output of sax players in your section. Sound projection, articulation response, intonation, and blends are some basic areas of consideration. Materials used to manufacture mouthpieces have their own characteristics. These include:

Hard Rubber: more durable than plastic and very popular.

Plastic: slight differences exist between hard rubber and plastic; though it tends to warp, plastic is low in cost and has a high degree of performance strength.

Metal: there is generally brighter and faster response here than with hard rubber or plastic; metal mouthpieces are rugged and can be tooled to fine tolerance. The outside dimensions can be made smaller since metal is stronger, which is a distinct advantage to tenor and baritone players who prefer the feel of a smaller mouthpiece. These are very popular with professional jazz saxophonists.

Glass/crystal: the facing does not change for these mouthpieces. Although a very stable material, it can be broken easily.

Facings on mouthpieces can vary greatly from closed to open. When students are trying mouthpieces with different facings, be sure to use reeds that match the facing. Generally, the more open the mouthpiece, the softer the reed; and the more closed the mouthpiece, the harder the reed Listed below are some popular brands of jazz saxophone mouthpieces.

Berg Larsen Mouthpieces
c/o Charles Ponte Music
142 W. 46th Street
New York, NY 10036

Brilhardt Mouthpieces
c/o Selmer
P.O. Box 310
Elkhart, IN 46514

Bobby Dukoff Mouthpieces
P.O. Box 5612002
Kendall, FL 33156

Guy Hawkins Mouthpieces
Meyer Mouthpieces
Otto Link Mouthpieces
Wolfe Tayne Mouthpieces
c/o J.J. Babbitt Co.
1505 W. Beardsley Avenue
Elkhart, IN 46514

Gale Mouthpieces
c/o Charles Bay
P.O. Box 3955
Westlake Village, CA 91359

Lawton Mouthpieces
c/o Saxophone Shop, Ltd.
918 Noyes Street
Evanston, IL 60201

Santy Runyon Mouthpieces
P.O. Box 1018
Lewisburg Road
Opelousas, LA 70570

Selmer Mouthpieces
P.O. Box 310
Elkhart, IN 46514

Strathon Mouthpieces
Herb Couf Mouthpieces
c/o W.T. Armstrong
1000 Industrial Parkway Dr.
Elkhart, IN 46514

Since each manufacturer uses its own numbering system for mouthpieces, it is difficult for a person to equate one mouthpiece facing with one from another system. The comparison chart in Table 4-1 helps make it easier to compare various numbering systems.

While more open mouthpieces are used by those involved with jazz performance, concert band performance usually favors a more medium facing. Jazz requires a brighter and more forceful sound than that desired for use in an orchestral setting, which wants a darker and less edgy sound.

Remember, there are numerous influences on the tone quality of a saxophone. Careful analysis and experimentation with the instrument, mouthpiece (brand and facing), reeds, and even ligatures are necessary in order to achieve the preferred result. Here are some outstanding sources for saxophone and saxophone supplies.

Progressive Winds
c/o Bob Ackerman, President
5127 W. Amherst
Dallas, TX 75209

Ernie Northway
1946 East 4675 South
Salt Lake City, UT 84117

Claude Lakey
Box 2487
Sepulveda, CA 91343

ARB Inc.
c/o Elmer Beechler
Box 15
Encino, CA 91316

SELECTING BRASS NEEDS

What to Look for in Trombones and Trumpets

When selecting a trumpet, there are several factors to be considered before making a decision. It should be understood that there is no single instrument suitable for all types of playing. A trumpet specifically designed for lead playing in a jazz ensemble (using a smaller bore) is unlikely to meet the needs of an orchestral player. Conversely, a trumpet with a large bore for symphony (producing a darker, more full-bodied tone) will lack brilliance and prove too tiring for use in jazz playing. An all-purpose instrument requires a centered sound that is neither too large nor too brilliant, but projects well with consistent intonation. Thus, a difference of 0.10″ in

TABLE 4-1
MOUTHPIECE FACINGS COMPARISON CHART*

TIP OPENING | MANUFACTURER

	1	2	3	4	5	6	7	8	9	10
Close	2#	C	1, 1#, 2	2, 3	3, 3#	$\frac{70\text{-}75}{0}\ \frac{0}{0}$				
Medium Close	3#	C*	3, 3*	4	4, 4*	$\frac{80\text{-}85}{0}\ \frac{0}{0}$	4	4*3 4*4	4	4
Medium	4*	C**	4, 4*, 5, 5*	5	5, 5*, 6, 6*	$\frac{85\text{-}95}{0}\ \frac{0}{0}$	5	5*3	5	5
Medium Open	5*	D	6, 6*, 7, 7*	6, 7	7, 7*, 8, 8*	$\frac{95\text{-}105}{0}\ \frac{0}{0}$	6	6*3	6	6
Open	6*, 7*	E, F	8, 8*, 9, 9*	8, 9	9, 9*, 10, 10*	$\frac{105\text{-}130}{0}\ \frac{0}{0}$	7, 8 9, 10	7*3 9*3 8*3 10*3	7, 8 9, 10	7, 8 9, 10

Manufacturer Key:

1 = Herb Couf
2 = Selmer
3 = Brilhardt
4 = Meyer
5 = Guy Hawkins, Wolfe Tayne, Otto Link
6 = Berg Larsen
7 = Dukoff
8 = Lakey
9 = Lawton
10 = Beechler

Specially written
for this book by
Bob Ackerman, President
Progressive Winds
5127 W. Amherst
Dallas, Texas 75209

bore diameters of two otherwise identical trumpets can represent a world of difference in sound (stuffy to full) and feel (resistant to open). As a general rule, two characteristics should be looked for: an instrument with a medium to medium-large bore size, well in tune, and neither excessively dark nor bright in tone quality; and having a resistance level that is neither too easy nor too hard to blow.

A young player with poor air flow and support will likely find several top-line professional trumpets harder to play than many of the less expensive, less-resistant student model instruments. A young player should not reject a top-line trumpet simply because his playing has not yet progressed to the point at which he can achieve the energy level necessary to exploit the capabilities of a fine professional-level trumpet. Of course, any instrument that requires too much physical effort for the well-developed player is of questionable use. Be especially suspicious of fads or gimmicks, such as unique bell design, unusually large or small bores that have not been research tested and accepted by recognized professional performers and teachers, or anything else that has not been fully proven through time and research.

Here are a few questions that should be reviewed whenever you or one of your students intend to purchase a new horn:

- Is the instrument reasonably well in tune? Check both within the horn by chromatic scales and against another horn that is already proven from your ensemble to be accurately in tune.

- Does the horn have a uniform response throughout the various registers? Check especially in the bottom register and with high concert A, a note that usually tells a great deal about upper register response.

- Does the trumpet blow with an appropriate amount of resistance? Avoid extremes—too much resistance can produce a dull, stuffy tone, while too little resistance will lead to a brittle, overly diffused tone quality.

- Does the instrument project its sound well? Have someone else listen for comparison as various models are played from a distance.

- Does the instrument feel good and comfortable in the performer's hands? Check the placement of the valves, angle and position of the first and third slide rings, and response of the valves, hooks, and triggers. The trumpet should feel comfortable and fit like a glove. If it doesn't feel right in the hands, chances are that it will never feel the way it should—like the extension of the performer's body.

There are pros and cons concerning whether the instrument should be lacquered or plated. Though plating provides a somewhat longer-lasting finish, it also costs more. Generally, silver alloy will produce a brighter tone while a gold-brass alloy gives a darker, less brilliant sound.

A trombone section in a jazz band usually consists of three tenor trombones and one bass trombone. Because of the extra projection and edge needed to match the trumpet section, it is recommended that the tenor trombones be instruments with medium bores. Ideally, the lead player should have the smallest bore and each successive part should increase in bore size. This gradual increase in bore is not essential but it does point out the characteristics of the parts and requirements for the typical jazz ensemble.

Some concerns for the selection of a trombone might include the following:

- Is the slide action effortless? The slide should feel smooth and totally non-resistant.

- Is the instrument well balanced? When in the playing position, the instrument should not feel heavier at either end, but rest comfortably and feel perfectly balanced.

- Does the instrument have a uniform response throughout the various registers? (See the trumpet section.)

- Does the horn blow with an appropriate amount of resistance? (See the trumpet section.)

- Does the instrument feel good? Different manufacturers produce horns that may look essentially the same but are entirely different when held and played. The trombone should always feel comfortable. (See the trumpet section.)

Considerations for the Brass Mouthpiece

Mouthpieces need to be selected with as much care as when choosing one's instrument. Of all the variables found in brass playing (breath support, throat arch, embouchure, lip aperture, mouthpiece pressure, mouthpiece, and instrument), the mouthpiece is the easiest to manipulate and change. Though trial and error is one method for finding which mouthpiece is best for an individual, the following discussion on mouthpieces may provide some more efficient help. Since each student's teeth, jaw and lip formations differ, it is foolish to specify what type of mouthpiece would be most appropriate for the entire brass section. A mouthpiece should be perceived as a highly individual part of brass performance. A mouthpiece change should only be undertaken under the guidance and supervision of an experienced brass specialist. Casual or frequent mouthpiece changes should be avoided.

The following comparison charts are stated in the terms required to make broad, general evaluations about size and playing characteristics.

They are in no way presented to give a basis for the final selection of a mouthpiece derived from trial and performance. For our purposes, the following terms will be defined:

LARGE. Those mouthpieces that have wider and deeper cup dimensions than the mouthpieces found in the median range. As such, these mouthpieces allow a wider surface of lip area to vibrate and produce a generally darker, more resonant tone. These mouthpieces are typically found in orchestral-style performance.

MEDIAN. More than a "middle-of-the-road" classification numerically, these mouthpieces usually represent the sizes that are supplied with new instruments when they are sold to the initial consumer. The manufacturer of the instrument tries to identify the particular mouthpiece that will satisfy the performance requirements of the largest number of potential performers. In the case of mouthpieces used for original equipment by the instrument manufacturers, an asterisk (*) has been placed on the chart.

SMALL. These mouthpieces offer cup dimensions that are usually more narrow and more shallow than the median mouthpieces. Allowing a smaller lip surface to vibrate, these mouthpieces will slightly facilitate performance in the upper registers of the instrument. The sound tends to be more brilliant and is customarily found in commercial, jazz, and rock music.

The makers of mouthpieces included in Tables 4-2 and 4-3 present only a small fraction of the total number of mouthpieces that are manufactured by the various companies. Should you want further information, a list of most of the major and custom mouthpiece shops has been included. Most of the companies listed will be pleased to supply information about their products.

Vincent Bach Corporation
P.O. Box 310
Elkhart, IN 46514

Domenick Calicchio Co.
6409 Willoughby Avenue
Hollywood, CA 90038

Al Cass
Milford, MA 01757

Bob DeNicola
P.O. Box 386
Pennington, NJ 08534

Giardinelli Band
 Instrument Co.
151 W. 46th Street
New York, NY 10036

Bush Brass Mouthpieces
1859 Jadestone Drive
Sherman Oaks, CA 91403

Jerome Callet
756 7th Avenue at 50th Street
New York, NY 10019

C. G. Conn, Ltd.
2520 Industrial Parkway
Elkhart, IN 46515

Getzen, Inc.
211 W. Centralia Street
Elkhorn, WI 53121

Burt Herrick
c/o J. Marcinkiewicz
10320 Fairgrove Avenue
Tujunga, CA 91042

Frank Holton & Co.
Leblanc Corporation
7019 30th Avenue
Kenosha, WI 53141

King Musical Instruments
33999 Curtis Boulevard
Eastlake, OH 44094

John Parduba & Son
West 49th Street
New York, NY 10019

Bob Reeves
711 North Ridgeweed Place
Hollywood, CA 90038

William Tottle & Son
56 Botolph Street
Boston, MA 02116

Zottola Products, Inc.
40 Beach Street
Port Chester, NY 10573

Jet Tone
226 Kings Highway
Fairfield, CT 06430

Rudy Muck, Inc.
151 West 48th Street
New York, NY 10036

Peppy (John Pettinato)
1755 Broadway at 56th Street
New York, NY 10019

Schilke Music, Inc.
529 S. Wabash Avenue
Chicago, IL 60605

Tromba (Sarad Mouthpieces)
1859 York Street
Denver, CO 80206

L. Minnick Brass Mouthpiece
2484 S. Sepulveda Boulevard
Los Angeles, CA 90064

TABLE 4-2
TRUMPET MOUTHPIECE CHART*

MANUFACTURER	LARGE			MEDIAN	SMALL
Vincent Bach	1–C	3–C	5–C	7–C*	10½–C
Benge	1½–C	3–C	5–C	7–C*	10½–C
Benge-C.G. Series	C.G.	C.G.–3			C.G.–10
C.G. Conn, Ltd.	1½–C	3–C	5–C	7 C*	10½–C
Getzen		3–C	5–C*		10½–C
Giardinelli	3–C	6–C	7–C		10–C
Holton		3–C	5–C	7–C*	10–C
Jet Tone	T–2	D.S.	D.S.	2–D	6–B
King	1–M	3–M	5–M	7–M*	10–M
Purviance	5*3	7C3	4*3	4*04	4*7
Schilke	19	15	13C4	11	9C4
Yamaha	19	15		11*	

By its nature, this comparison must be considered in very rough terms. Each company was asked to make their own decisions about where in this spectrum their products belong.

Note that in the case of instrument manufacturers, the mouthpiece followed by * is the size that is supplied with their production instruments.

*Specially written for this book by Jan Nichols, 14156 Brandt Drive, Sunnymeade, CA 92388 (714/653-4802)

TABLE 4-3

TROMBONE MOUTHPIECE CHART*

MANUFACTURER	LARGE		MEDIAN	SMALL
Vincent Bach	6½ AL	7–C	12–C*	15
Benge	6½ AL	7–C	12–C*	----*
C.G. Conn, Ltd.	6½ AL	7–C	12–C*	15–C
Getzen	6½ AL*			
Giardinelli	3–D	4–M	5–M	6–M
Holton	6½ AL	7–C	12–C*	15–B
Jet Tone	JT–702	JT–701	JT–704	JT–705
Schilke	50	47	44	42
Yamaha	50	47*	44	42

*Specially written for this book by
Jan Nichols, 14156 Brandt Drive,
Sunnymeade, CA 92388
(714/653-4802)

By its nature, this comparison must be considered in very rough terms. Each company was asked to make their own decisions about where in this spectrum their products belong.

Note that in the case of instrument manufacturers, the mouthpiece that is followed by * is the size supplied with their production instruments.

Everything There Is to Know about Brass Mutes

There are many kinds of brass mutes available. Music educators need only be familiar with the basic mutes (straight, cup, and Harmon), as well as the special effect mutes. Various mutes are made from plastic, fiber, cardboard, aluminum, and rubber. If you are looking for a particular type of muted sound, check each manufacturer since a variety of different sounds can be produced on each type of mute.

The straight mute is the basic mute for many occasions. Like most mutes, it will restrict the lower register more than the upper register. The best straight mutes will have a brilliant, penetrating quality that maintains resonance through lyrical passages. Straight mutes have three or four strips of cork along the side to hold the mute in the bell of the instrument. The quality of the sound (as well as the response of the horn) will depend on the size of these corks. If the cork is too thick (making the sound too open), it may be carefully sanded down to produce the desired sound. Extreme caution should be exercised whenever changing something like the corks on a mute since a relatively expensive item can be easily ruined.

All mutes create some intonation problems. Usually, the player will sound slightly sharp when using a mute, so students should learn to automatically adjust the tuning to compensate.

The cup mute is simply a straight mute with a cupped resonator attached to the end. It provides a big, rich sound. The cup mute is versatile and, with a little experimentation, a number of different effects can be realized.

Stuffing cloth or other soft materials in the cup helps produce different sounds.

The Harmon mutes are also called "wah-wah" mutes. They offer the possibility of producing the most variety of effects and sounds and have been particularly popular with bebop and modern trumpet players. Harmon mutes feature a movable slide in the center of the mute allowing a maximum number of sound effects. These sounds can be dictated somewhat by the style of the music and the range of the performance. With the center stem in place, a bright, brassy sound is achieved. As the center stem is extended, the tone color is altered; when the center stem is removed, a much darker sound is produced. The bottom of the register is especially sensitive to the mute when the center stem is removed, which creates a heavy growl that is particularly effective. In addition, the Harmon mute can function as a wah-wah by covering and uncovering the bell of the stem with the left hand.

There are many types of mutes available, each with a specific design and purpose. The plunger mute is available in aluminum or may be purchased at the hardware store where it sells as a regular rubber plumber's plunger. It is especially effective for wah-wah effects. The Solotone mute is similar to the Harmon mute but is made of fiber rather than metal, and produces a softer, darker sound. The whisper mute is the softest of all mutes. It can be used very effectively for inaudible offstage warm-ups. The hat, or derby mute, gives a soft, far-away quality to the sound when placed directly in front of (while not touching) the bell. The velvet-tone mute takes off the hard edge of open brass.

Today's use of mutes is rather meager compared to that of musicians from the 1940s and 1950s. Mutes can provide an entire new dimension to soloing. With experimentation, a student can develop a wide range of effects and sounds that will give more variety to his or her expression.

Care and attention should accompany the application of any section that uses mutes. The director who would never think of having a section play out of tune or unbalanced will often ignore the subtleties when a section is muted.

For more information about mutes, write to any of the following manufacturers:

Humes & Berg Mfg. Co.
4801 Railroad Avenue
East Chicago, IN 46312

Jo Ral Mutes by Alessi
15 Anchorage Court
San Rafael, CA 94903

Tom Crown Mutes
c/o G. Leblanc Corporation
7019 30th Avenue
Kenosha, WI 53141

Selmer Co.
P.O. Box 310
Elkhart, IN 46514

For more information about brass instruments or equipment, you may contact any of the following:

Selmer/Bach
c/o Selmer Co.
P.O. Box 310
Elkhart, IN 46514

Getzen, Inc.
Box 459
211 W. Centralia Street
Elkhorn, WI 53121

Benge & King
King Musical Instruments
33999 Curtis Boulevard
Eastlake, OH 44094

Yamaha Musical Products
P.O. Box 7271
Grand Rapids, MI 49510

C. G. Conn, Ltd.
2520 Industrial Parkway
Elkhart, IN 46516

Frank Holton & Co.
Leblanc Corporation
7019 30th Avenue
Kenosha, WI 53141

Schilke Music Products
529 South Wabash Avenue
Chicago, IL 60605

E. K. Blessing Co.
1301 West Beardsley Avenue
Elkhart, IN 46514

SELECTING RHYTHM SECTION INSTRUMENTS

Building the Drum-Set

Music educators who are not drummers will typically purchase more drums than are needed for a drum-set. Essential to good drum-set playing (and thus, selection) is a creative use of the least possible drums and a comprehensive understanding of the use of cymbals. In jazz, the drums are used approximately 30 percent of the time, while the cymbals are used 70 percent. A standard drum-set should include a snare drum, one (or more) side tom-toms, one (or more) floor tom-toms, a bass drum, a hi-hat cymbal and stand, and one or more cymbals (ride, crash, etc.) with appropriate stands.

Durability is an important criterion for selecting good drum equipment. No matter how good a set looks or sounds, it *must* hold up to the rigors of extensive playing and moving! The trend today is toward larger-based, heavier hardware that lasts significantly longer than anything from the past.

The quality of sound you get from your drum equipment is also very important. You should examine the differences between fiberglass shells and wood shells to determine which you prefer because each produces a distinctive sound. When considering the purchase of a drum-set, the following guidelines can help in the final selection. It's a good idea to bring along an experienced drummer (or at least the student drummer from your group) to help in the selection process.

BASS DRUM. There should be no "ping" in the bass drum. This may require some muffling. Tension must be even all around the drum head. The 14″ × 22″ size is sometimes preferred for big band use, although 14″ × 20″ is usually considered standard size.

SNARE. This should have a nice crisp sound. The tension should be evenly spread around the head. Either 5″ or 5½″ × 14″ is considered an acceptable standard size.

TOM-TOM. Low, dark sounds are preferable. The standard size for a set of two tom-toms is usually 9″ × 13″ and 16″ × 16″. Tuning should be a perfect 4th between tom-toms and a perfect 5th between the large tom-tom and the bass drum.

This is the appropriate time to be considering the purchase of drum cases for each of these drums. Travel is perhaps harder on a drum-set than performance, so protection during travel is imperative. Look into purchasing the proper drum cases at the same time you select the drum-set. If the drum-set is stored in drum cases, it will be less tempting for other students to use the set and will assure minimum damage from general wear and tear.

For more information on drum-sets, contact the following manufacturers for literature:

Fibes Drums
c/o C. F. Martin
502 Sycamore
Nazareth, PA 18064

Ludwig Industries
c/o Selmer Co.
P.O. Box 310
Elkhart, IN 46514

Roger Drums
P.O. Box 4220
Fullerton, CA 92631

Slingerland Drum Co.
6633 N. Milwaukee
Niles, IL 60648

Tama Drums
c/o Elger Co.
P.O. Box 469
Cornwell Heights, PA 19020

Gretsch Drums
P.O. Box 1250
Gallatin, TN 37066

Pearl Drums
c/o Norlin Music
7373 N. Cicero
Lincolnwood, IL 60646

Remo, Inc.
12804 Raynor Street
N. Hollywood, CA 91605

Roto-Tom Drums
c/o Remo, Inc.
(see above)

Sonor Drums
c/o Alden Music
Southwest Industrial Park
Westwood, MA 02090

Selecting Cymbals

The selection of cymbals requires more time and sensitivity than choosing the drum-set. As already indicated, cymbals account for more than 70 percent of the sounds produced on a drum-set and, obviously, the right cymbal (the one that produces the exact sound you want) is most important to you.

Ride cymbals share a quality of dry sound without much ring or overtones. Listed below are various types of ride cymbals available and their characteristic sounds. The most popular sizes have been indicated to serve as a guide, although other sizes are available.

MEDIUM RIDE. Suitable for all styles of music, it is mid-range in pitch. The standard size is 20*"*.

FLAT TOP RIDE. This produces a high-pitched stick sound with no buildup of overtones. It is a popular recording and small-group cymbal. The standard size is 20*"*.

BEBOP. Similar to medium ride, it carries a lot of sound. Its standard size is 20*"*.

BOUNCE. This produces a lot of stick sound and a high pitch. The standard size is 18*"*.

PING RIDE. This is always medium-heavy in weight and produces a high-pitched "ping" sound with more definition than a medium ride cymbal. The standard size is 20*"*.

ROCK RIDE. This cymbal is heavy in weight and gives a strong bell sound with a dynamic ride beat. The standard size is 20*"*.

MINI-CUP RIDE. This is usually medium-heavy in weight. It is very high pitched and has very little buildup of overtones. The standard size is 20*"*.

Your initial purchase should be for a bebop or ping ride cymbal, 18*"* or 20*"* in diameter, with either medium or medium-heavy weight. A sturdy cymbal stand should be selected with a tilter, felt washer for the cymbal to rest on, and a sleeve to prevent metal-to-metal contacts.

When testing a ride cymbal, place it on a stand and tap it in various places from just below the bell to the edge. Next, play a rock rhythm or jazz rhythm fairly loud about ½ to ¾ of the way up the cymbal from its edge. Listen to make certain the stick rhythm can be heard easily and distinctly. Ask someone else to play the same rhythm while you step away to hear how well it projects. If the ring is overpowering the stick rhythm, it is an indication of a poor ride cymbal. Try several different kinds of ride cymbal to find a cymbal that projects the best while producing a ring without any stick sound.

The standard size for crash cymbals ranges from 15" to 18" with a medium-thin weight. When testing crash cymbals, strike the top edge of the cymbal with a stick. While holding the stick loosely in your hand, strike the cymbal with the middle of the stick rather than the tip: think of buttering a piece of bread by using a slicing motion. When a good crash cymbal is struck, it should give a splash or crash effect that produces a quick spread of both high and low overtones. The pitch will drop as the higher overtones tend to diminish quickly, allowing the lower sustaining partials to emerge and become more predominant. The ring should last at least 8 to 10 seconds. The longer the cymbal rings while maintaining the initial volume level, the better it is. For another test, strike the top edge of the cymbal and immediately strike it again near the center just below the bell or cup. Check for a primary pitch at each place. There should be a pitch difference of at least a major 2nd and preferably a minor or even major 3rd. If the cymbal's ringing makes the pitch differences hard to hear, examine the sound by choking the cymbal immediately after hitting it. Ultimately, your ear will be the final judge. If you are testing several cymbals of the same weight, the pitch of any two may be decidedly different. However, if several cymbals possess about the same sustaining and resonating properties, select the one with the high pitch as it will cut through the ensemble easier. If all cymbals have about the same pitch, choose the one that seems to sustain longest and resonate most.

Listed below are kinds of crash cymbals available with their sound characteristics. Again, the popular sizes have been indicated.

THIN. If only one crash cymbal is being purchased, this is the basic item. It produces a quick, bright high-end sound with good cutting power to help accent the beat. Sizes are 14", 16", or 18".

MEDIUM THIN. It is a good alternate cymbal to offer a variation of pitches for crash cymbals. This cymbal has slightly more weight than the thin crash, thus producing a slightly stronger high-end sound and longer sustaining characteristics. Sizes are 16" and 18".

MEDIUM. This produces a strong, high-pitched, full-bodied sound. This cymbal is best for large groups. The standard size is 18".

ROCK. This is a heavy cymbal producing the strongest, most powerful crash sound. It is especially good for cutting through amplified music. The standard size is 18".

A matched set of 14" or 15" cymbals is used for the high-hat cymbals. A penetrating "chick" sound is essential. A quick response when playing

16th notes on the top cymbal as you move the pedal up and down to the open and closed positions, or a good distinctive cutting sound with rock and jazz rhythms in a tight, closed position should be a good basis for your selection criteria.

The following examples provide a list of the different kinds of hi-hat cymbals available.

REGULAR. This set will provide a clean "chip" sound.

NEW BEAT. It provides extremely fast response, with powerful projection and pinpoint definition. It uses a mediumweight top and heavy bottom cymbal. The standard size is 14″.

FLANGE. This allows a drummer a full dynamic range with more body depth. This set uses a specially tapered medium-heavy top and a heavy bottom cymbal.

ROCK. This set provides a strong, solid beat for hard rock drummers with its high-pitched, heavyweight cymbals. The standard size is 15″.

MINI-CUP. This produces a high-pitched tonal quality and a "tight" stick sound. It is used in small groups and for recording; they have a medium mini-cup top cymbal and a heavy bottom cymbal.

When testing hi-hat cymbals, have them on a stand with the bottom cymbal properly tilted. Take enough time to learn a particular set's characteristics. Purchase only factory-mated or blended hi-hat cymbals. Choose the sturdiest and fastest operating hi-hat pedal with a tilter for the bottom and a height adjustment.

Listed below are the kinds of color cymbals available as auxiliary equipment for a drum-set. Most of these cymbals are medium-thin weight and 18″ or 20″ in diameter.

SIZZLE CYMBAL. Holes are drilled in the cymbal and six to eight rivets are installed near the edge to provide a "sizzling" or "buzzing" sound.

SPLASH CYMBAL. Small, thin cymbals are used for fast crash sounds that are then choked rather quickly. These are particularly popular for use in ragtime, dixieland, and Broadway show music, performances. The standard size is usually 10″.

CHINESE CYMBAL. Turned-up edges give Chinese cymbals a quick, dissipated "pie pan" sound. Sometimes six to eight rivets are installed for more sustaining power. Basically, a medium-thin cymbal can be used for both crashing and riding effects.

SWISH CYMBAL. This is also sometimes called a "knocker" cymbal and is used for funky sounds with a low-end spread.

PANG CYMBAL. This sounds more mellow than the swish cymbal, with a low "bottom" sound.

Remember, no matter what type of cymbal you are trying, listen for trueness, definition, and versatility. Any cymbal should produce three separate sounds—near the edge should be a distinctive crash sound; further in, a ride sound; and the center cup, clear bell-tones that are not distorted by overtones from the remainder of the cymbal. Try as many as possible the type of cymbals you want. Try different attacks and use the stick at various angles with different beats to produce a variety of effects.

For more information on cymbals, contact the following manufacturers:

Camber Cymbals
c/o Ambico
27 Wilbur Street
Lynbrook, NY 11563

Pasha Cymbals
c/o Grossman Music Corp.
1278 W. 9th Street
Cleveland, OH 44113

Avedis Zildjian Co.
P.O. Box 198
Accord, MA 02018

Paiste Cymbals
c/o Rogers Drum Co.
P.O. Box 4220
Fullerton, CA 92631

Tosco Cymbals
c/o Norlin Music
7373 N. Cicero
Lincolnwood, IL 60646

Developing Auxiliary Percussion Equipment

Since the 1970s, the use of auxiliary percussion equipment has gained popularity and prominence. Companies like Latin Percussion have done extensive promotion and research in order to preserve and improve original instruments from Brazil, Cuba, and Africa. Combined with the fusion of jazz/rock/Latin music, the use of auxiliary percussion in the school jazz ensemble has grown rapidly. There are virtually hundreds of auxiliary percussion instruments. A basic collection of auxiliary percussion should include the following:

CONGA DRUMS. There are usually two of these (11¾ ″ and 12½ ″) set on conga stands.

TIMBALES. These contain two drums (14″ and 15″) placed on a timbale tilter with a central cowbell post for one or two cowbells to be played with the timbales.

MISCELLANEOUS. This includes cabasa, cowbell, vibra-slap, guiro, maracas, wood block, claves, and tambourine.

While the above list indicates the common instruments usually encountered in a standard jazz ensemble, there are more exotic instruments, such as: tambora, bongo drums, bata drums, agogo bells, rhythm clackers, talking drums, castanets, native ankle beads, shekeres, African shakers, African tambourine, pod shere, raffia stick, Moroccan castanets, African log drums, cuica, samba whistle, spring guiros, surdo, saximi, pandiero, and many, many others.

For more information and details on auxiliary percussion instruments, contact the following manufacturers:

Cactus
c/o Camco Instruments
1716 Winchester Road
Cornwells Heights, PA 19020

Gon Bops
2302 E. 38
Los Angeles, CA 90058

Latin Percussion, Inc.
160 Belmont Avenue
Garfield, NJ 07026

Ludwig Industries
c/o Selmer Co.
P.O. Box 310
Elkhart, IN 46514

Carroll Sound Inc.
351-53 West 41st Street
New York, NY 10036

Hondo
c/o Internation Music Corp.
P.O. Box 2344
Fort Worth, TX 76101

Slingerland Drum Co.
6633 N. Milwaukee
Niles, IL 60648

Selecting Bass Amplifiers

There is a wide selection of amplifiers available, varying in quality of sound, durability, and the ability to remain distortion-free. A good amplifier should not just reproduce the signal that is run into it; rather, it should enhance the instrument being played by imparting its own special sound characteristics to the notes. The misconception that a bass amp must be big is another popular but false premise. Any amp that provides 50 to 100 watts RMS power output will be more than sufficient for most school-playing situations. A single 15-inch speaker is considered the standard bass speaker, but 12" or four 10" speakers are common alternatives. Although many musicians believe that a 15-inch speaker will give a truer bass sound, it ultimately becomes a matter of personal preference and taste.

The solid state amps have no tubes and are a lot more trouble-free because they are more suitable for moving around. Another advantage for the solid state amp is that it's usually smaller and lighter than a tube amp of the same power. For some reason, solid state amps seem to work better for electric bass than string bass. In general, transistorized amps have greater brightness, crispness, and clarity than tube amps, while tube amps have a warmer sound and can aid the acoustic bass in getting a more natural sound.

Before buying an amplifier, you should establish criteria based on how and where the amp will be most frequently used. There are essentially three categories of amp, each with its own particular function.

SMALL PRACTICE AMPS. These include anything under 20 watts RMS in power rating. They are excellent for home or practice rooms and, in many circumstances, they can be miked with good results for larger settings.

MID-SIZE AMPS. Generally, these amps are from 20 to 100 watts RMS in power and are a handy size for transportation. If necessary, these amps can also be miked with nice results.

FULL-SIZE AMPS. These amps usually start at 100 watts RMS and go up. Frequently, the amps have separate head/speaker cabinet assemblies. Though they are often quite large, they are also the most ruggedly constructed for rigorous playing demands.

Since many school-owned bass amps do double duty and are used simultaneously for guitar players, it is important that they have separate volume/tone control adjustments and input plugs, so that both guitar and bass sounds can be accurately reproduced through the amp. There are usually controls for tremolo and distortion/master volume, with some amps even featuring graphic equalizers.

Whenever possible, try out the bass amp in the location where it will be used most. With a little preparation and cooperation, a music store should be willing to bring several different kinds of amps to your school auditorium for a live "on the spot" audition. This is the best way to nail down the amp that most perfectly fits your needs based on sound quality, power, and the room.

If you have to check out the amplifier in the music store, be concerned about any amp that loses its sound quality at less than half of its volume capacity. If distortion occurs at 5 on an amp dial that ranges from 1 to 10, there will be very little or no difference in volume above the number "5"— the rest of the numbers are for show. Also while in the music store, try to move as far away from the amp as possible while it is being played to better gauge its full characteristics.

Most of today's jazz bassists agree that the main criterion for a bass amp used in jazz should be clarity. There are some amplifiers that are intentionally distorted (dirty) while others can be adjusted to produce a different sound for either jazz or rock.

For jazz bands that do not have a bass player, a keyboard bass provides a viable alternative, particularly if there is more than one piano player available. The keyboard bass is essentially an electric piano with only the bottom two octaves of the keyboard. Acoustically, it will cut through easily since it projects from a bass amplifier. At the present time, there are two companies that make the keyboard bass—Fendor and Hohner. The Fendor keyboard is a duplication of the Fendor Rhodes electric piano. The Hohner is a little more complicated since it has three stops: (1) guitar, (2) tuba, and (3) string bass. In both cases, the keyboard bass is simple to operate with tone and volume controls helping to provide the precise sound desired. Information can be supplied for each of these systems by contacting the manufacturer:

Fendor Rhodes
CBS Musical Instruments
100 Wilmot Road
Deerfield, IL 60015

Korg Instruments
c/o Unicord
89 Frost Street
Westbury, NY 11590

M. Hohner, Inc.
P.O. Box 15035
Richmond, VA 23227

Acoustic Bass Amplification: Getting an Electric Pickup

Electric string bass pickups can easily be attached to the bridge or the body of a string bass and offer a variety of types of sounds. Pickups are basically divided into (1) the electromagnetic type and (2) the transducer type.

The electromagnetic type is fitted on the end of the fingerboard under the strings. The strings must be metal in order for the pickup to magnetically attract the vibration of their movement. This is similar to the principle of an electric guitar or bass. The disadvantage to this type of system is that the natural sound of the string instrument does not get amplified; instead, the vibration of the strings is the only element that is amplified. The main asset of the electromagnetic type of pickup is the volume range. It is comparatively easy to use high volumes with no feedback problems. In addition, the sustaining power is enhanced when using this type of pickup.

The more popular type of pickup used today by most professional bassists is the transducer type. These transducers are stuck onto the bridge or body of the bass by means of a sticky paste. There are various brands of transducers, each with special features. Many professionals say that the transducer made by Don Underwood is the clearest, truest bass reproduction and provides a wider range of volume than encountered by most other transducer types. It is not available in stores since it is handmade, so it can only be ordered through the mail. Another model, the Polytone, resembles a bullet and attaches to the inside of the legs of the bridge. It produces a warm sound that perhaps most resembles the natural sound of the acoustic bass. The sound can be altered by moving the contact points to different angles. Each of the indicated models is distinctive and offers some advantages over the rest. For best results, try to see each demonstrated, or talk to various professional bassists to help decide what is best suited for your needs. For further information, write to the following:

Barcus Berry Sales Corp.
5461 Springfield Street
Huntington, CA 92649

Don Underwood
P.O. Box 303
Carmel Valley,CA 93924

Polytone
1261 N. Vine Street
Los Angeles, CA 90038

Choosing the Right Electric Bass

Since there are so many electric basses currently on the market, approach this area with caution. Let your ear be your guide. A pretty good rule-of-thumb when looking at new or used equipment is: flashy styles, tempting price tags, or special features are no substitutes for good quality sound. As suggested with the bass amp and bass pickup procedures, solicit the help of an experienced bassist when trying out a new bass.

When selecting an instrument, be careful to check for evenness in the scale by listening for noticeable changes in timbre, dead notes, and questionable intonation, particularly in the extreme upper register. The E string should sound true when you play an open E and then first-fret F. In the upper register, check for notes that don't "make it." A bass with a smaller neck will have more intonation problems in the upper register, but, at the same time, it will be easier to get around on. Unless a bassist has large hands, a smaller neck might be more comfortable and, in the long run, aid in the overall pitch accuracy. The standard full-scale length is somewhere between 32″ and 34½″. The short-scale length is 31″ or less.

With the advancement of electronic technology, basses are becoming quite versatile in the sounds they can create. Nevertheless, the standard for the industry is still considered to be the Fendor Precision Bass, which has one pickup that is split in half, one volume, and one tone knob. Fendor does make numerous other models which include:

JAZZ BASS. This utilizes two pickups, one volume, two tone controls, and a slimmer neck that is useful if the player has smaller hands.

TELECASTER. This model uses one pickup, and has a thinner neck than the Precision.

There are two smaller models that have smaller necks and bodies: the Musicmaster and the Mustang.

The Gibson company also has several popular models. The EB0 or EB3 have smaller necks than the Fendor Precision. The Grabber or Ripper models are comparable to the Precision. The Gibson basses produce a rounder sound than the Fendor "punch" type of sound.

There are many other excellent companies producing electric basses. The Rickenbacker basses generally have an especially trebly tone. Other companies include C. B. Rich, Carl Thompson, Alembic, and Travis Bean. Again, the important thing is to find a bass that suits your needs and produces the sound you want for your ensemble. Try as many different models as you can to make certain: (1) the frets are all in tune; (2) the frets are all the same height; (3) the neck is straight; and (4) all the electronics are working properly.

Strings can also be an important factor in the sound you get. There are three basic types of strings: (1) flat wound; (2) round wound; and (3) nylon tape.

Probably the most widely used all-purpose string is the flat wound string. This string produces a less brilliant, dead ring and has a harder fingerboard action. This string gives a "chick" sound effect when used with a pick and produces a clean definition of sound.

The round wound string has less tension, resulting in a more brilliant tone and a longer "ring" duration. These strings are often used by blues players. One consideration is that round wound strings do tend to wear down the fingerboard and frets. They also build calluses on the bass player's fingers.

Nylon tape strings give a duller, deeper tone. They have a loose, easy-playing action particularly well suited for fret-less bass playing. Since there is no exterior metal, there will be less string rattle when these strings are used.

There are three general categories of string thickness or gauge to consider: heavy, medium, and light. The gauge of a string alone won't determine how "big" the sound will be—that is the job of the pickup system and amplifier. Medium-gauge strings are used most frequently by jazz bassists, while light-gauge strings are very sensitive and should appeal to players who like to bend notes or who have a light pluck action. One manufacturer makes a flat wound "rock" gauge, which is between the light and medium gauges. The company claims this gauge produces a bright, ringing sound suitable for rock. Don't hesitate to try out different types of strings. Have your bassist determine which feels best and experiment with the variety of sounds available through the instrument and amp. A few of the major companies producing strings include Fendor, Rotosound, La Bella, D'Addario, and Dean Markley.

The upright, acoustic bass player may find the fret-less electric bass a comfortable transition. It captures the freedom to slide smoothly over the fingerboard, yet helps to create the funky sounds associated with electric bass. In addition, the adjustments for intonation found on upright are possible on fret-less. If you are interested in purchasing a fret-less bass, you should beware of rattle in the fingerboard and check for clean note definition.

Considerations for the Electric Piano

The electric piano is a very resourceful keyboard instrument for public school jazz programs. Since it is portable, it guarantees a consistent, quality keyboard instrument at all of your public performances. In some makes or models, you are also offered a variety of tonal colors so that the piano can blend with one musical passage and cut through the next. In addition, the dynamics can be adjusted via the volume controls on the piano or amplifier (or, on some models, by the finger action). Finally, tuning stability is excellent and, on some electric pianos, tuning can be accomplished without a piano tuner. The result is consistency and diversity for any performance setting.

Though there are many manufacturers of electric pianos, there are basically only three types of units made: (1) the electrified acoustic piano (Yamaha); (2) organ stops or electro-mechanical piano with reeds (Farfisa, Yamaha, Roland, Hohner); and (3) electrified tuning fork mechanism (Fendor/ Rhodes). Each type of unit offers distinctive advantages in terms of structural construction. For example, the electrified acoustic piano has separate tone controls for bass, middle, and treble ranges that provide a variety of sounds ranging from a traditional grand piano to mellow sounds for soft ballads and funky jazz/rock. The finger action of the Yamaha is almost identical with that of Yamaha's full-size grand pianos.

The organ stop types offer a multitude of sound color ranging from an organ, clavinet, harpsichord, or synthesizer, to a steel guitar, zither, Hawaiian guitar, electrified strings, harp, or spinet.

While the electrified vibes sound of the Fendor/Rhodes has become a standard "classic sound" for the jazz profession, there are other reasons for the immense success of the Rhodes piano. These include numerous structural advantages and characteristics of the Fendor/Rhodes that should be considered for public school use.

TONE SOURCE. Fendor/Rhodes pianos derive their tone from the principle of the tuning fork. This allows endless variety in tuning without the need of a piano technician for stretch tuning or equal temperament

(A440) situations. The lower, more resilient leg (tine of the tuning fork) responds visibly to the blow of a hammer by vibrating in a wide arc at a specific frequency. The upper leg (or tone bar of the tuning fork), which is not visible, vibrates at the same frequency. It is this patented tone source that structurally makes the Fendor/Rhodes piano outstanding for school use.

Replacement of the moving part of the tuning fork (the tine) is simple and can be done by the consumer without technical assistance, simply by following instructions given in a replacement kit. When strings or reeds break down in other types of electric pianos, the repair or replacement is usually more complex. Tuning and servicing for other types of electric pianos need competent technicians.

VOLUME ADJUSTMENT & DYNAMIC RESPONSE. While the Fendor/Rhodes, Yamaha, Roland, and Hohner models incorporate dynamic touch keyboard actions in contrast to the organ touch (or door bell) action of other units, the former is closer to that of an acoustic piano.

TIMBRE SETTING. Tone coloring or timbre, which is the presence or absence of fundamentals and overtones, is fully adjustable on the Fendor/Rhodes. The range of tone color can vary from the dark heavy sounds to biting brilliant timbres. Organ stop ranges have already been described.

KEYBOARD SIZE. Fendor/Rhodes and Yamaha offer full-size keyboards of 73, 76, or 88 keys. Hohner provides 49 keys (4 octaves) or 61 keys (5 octaves). Roland has 61- and 75-key models.

There are still other structural characteristics to keep in mind when purchasing an electric piano for your school. They include:

POWER OUTPUT. This should be about 50–100 RMS.

SPEAKERS. They should be able to cover both the treble and bass responses. Generally, 12″ speakers can do the job adequately.

SPECIAL EFFECT. These should include fuzz box, reverberation, wah-wah pedal, attack/decay controls, glide pedal, and sustained effects.

PORTABILITY/DURABILITY. Can the instrument be comfortably handled and moved by two students? The covers should be waterproof, durable, and tear and abrasive resistant. Carrying handles should be comfortable, have easy access, and be structurally strong enough to deal with the weight of the instrument.

CONVENIENCE. The sound controls should have easy accessibility during performance for easy adjustment.

In summary, there are many manufacturers of electric pianos with a variety of characteristics and price tags. Write to the following manufacturers for more details about their products.

Baldwin Piano & Organ Co.
1801 Gilbert Avenue
Cincinnati, OH 45202

Farfisa Musical Instruments
1330 Mark
Elk Grove Village, IL 60007

Nova Line, Inc.
P.O. Box 574
Norwood, MA 02062

RMI Rocky Mount Instruments
Macungie, PA 18062

Univox
c/o Unicord Inc.
75 Frost Street
Westbury, NY 11590

Yamaha Instrument Corp.
P.O. Box 6600
Buena Park, CA 90620

Elka Pianos
c/o Coast Wholesale Music of
  San Francisco
200 Industrial Way
San Carlos, CA 94070

M. Hohner, Inc.
P.O. Box 15035
Richmond, VA 23227

Rhodes Piano Co.
P.O. Box 4137
Fullerton, CA 92634

Roland Corp. U.S.
2410 Saybrook Avenue
Los Angeles, CA 90040

Wurlitzer Company
DeKalb, IL 60115

Selecting Guitars and Guitar Amps

There are three basic styles of 6-string electric guitars: (1) solid body, (2) hollow body, and (3) semi-hollow body. Body design affects the tone and sustaining qualities of a guitar. For example, the larger and more compact the area of mass in the guitar body, the better the tone and sustaining qualities.

The solid body electric is the most widely used style. Since it is a solid piece of wood, there is no appreciable resonance added by the body. Consequently, the sound is very electric, with treble tones accentuated, sustained tones lengthened, and volume pumped way up.

The hollow body electric guitar is a much quieter guitar, more closely resembling the acoustic guitar. Like the acoustic, it features a top, back, and sides to the body with the top frequently featuring "F" holes to further enhance the instrument's acoustic qualities. By using an electromagnetic transducer pickup, the guitar produces a warm tone full of the rich overtones generated by the soundboard and string vibrations.

The semi-hollow body is the most versatile of the electric guitars. It features a separate top, back, and sides borrowed from the hollow body model, which contributes to the high level of warm, acoustic resonance available when amplified. In addition, the more compact design and solid back enables the instrument to take on some of the more desirable characteristics of a solid body guitar.

The choice of materials used to construct the electric guitar is an important consideration. Wood for the body of the instrument generally includes the more dense and solid types such as maple or mahogany, since they produce the best tone and sustaining quality. The choice of wood used for the fingerboard is also important. Woods like rosewood, maple, and especially ebony wear well under the constant wear and tear of performance. Hardware needs to be from high-quality chrome, particularly in the tuning heads, bridge, and tailpiece, so that tuning can be more accurate and consistent. Electric pickups can vary immensely between guitars. There are numerous types of pickups to consider that present a wide range in sensitivity and power. Again, it is best to try out as many versions as possible to determine which is best suited to your specific needs. In addition, volume and tone controls have no specific standards so that each model has to be considered by virtue of its own merit.

A full-scale fingerboard length is somewhere between 24″ and 26″. The short-scale fingerboard will be easier to play since the frets are closer together, but will offer more intonation problems in the upper register. Short-scale fingerboards are less than 24″ in length. The number of frets can vary between 20 to 24 according to the model of guitar. Pickups will also range from 1 to 4 in various models.

When selecting an instrument, be sure to check for evenness in the scale by listening for noticeable changes in timbre. Also be on the lookout for dead notes and questionable intonation, particularly in the extreme registers. Check the construction, materials, options, and size to determine which model will best suit your needs. If possible, take the three or four models you most prefer to the place your ensemble will be performing most frequently. Using your regular guitar amp, see which instrument you like best in that room.

And Then There Are Sound Modifiers

If there's any single area in the field of jazz/pop/rock that shows rapid growth and interest, it is the area that features the use of special effects. Sound modifiers are being used by a huge spectrum of contemporary musicians: guitarists accentuate the beat with their wah-wah pedals; keyboard players use phasers to add depth to their sound; bass players employ equalizers to give new meaning to the word "bottom"; and wind players play duets with themselves or distort the tonal qualities until the listener can't recognize the instrument. In jazz, this electronic experimentation is mainly taking place with combos, which can provide opportunities for more freedom. There is still frequent application in the large jazz ensemble, however. The sound modifiers to be examined in this section include:

DISTORTION PEDAL. This is often referred to as a "fuzz box" and has an easily recognizable effect of distorting the original sound. The distortion pedal is electronically connected between the instrument and the amplifier. Essentially, it distorts the incoming signal to a pre-set degree, creating various effects ranging from warm subtle distortion of an overdrive tube amp to the raucous, feedback-laden wail of a stack of 100-watters with everything on volume setting "10." Good distortion pedals should be solidly constructed with rugged components. Better units will feature both output gain control (to match the level of distorted-to-clean signals) and variable distortion control (which enables the performer to decide how much distortion to use).

WAH-WAH PEDAL. This is named for the distinctive sound it produces. The wah-wah pedal is a single potentiameter controlled by a seesawing motion with the foot. A connection is made between the instrument and amplifier so that when the foot pedal is activated, a range of high and low "wah" effects is performed. This effect is especially useful for solos and certain fills. Compare the tonal range offered by different models. The durability consideration for the wah-wah pedal is similar to the distortion pedal indicated above. Some pedals combine the wah-wah function with some other effect. If a model you are interested in has multiple features, make sure the different effects can be operated both together and separately. The main criterion for a wah-way pedal should be the distance between the highs and the lows. The more distance, the more distinctive the sound.

PHASE SHIFTERS. These devices take an input signal from an instrument, split it in two parts, pass one half through a series of filters, recombine the two signals (which are now "out-of-phase" with each other), and produce the resultant sound effect. This effect produces an illusion that more than one instrument is playing in unison.

FLANGERS. A flanger takes phasing one step further by involving actual time delay of a divided signal in terms of width and speed. This gives the impression of "thickening" the tone or adding depth to the signal. This extension of the phase shifter concept alters the original signal with even more intensity to produce an effect of even more instruments playing a unison line.

ECHO/DELAY. There are two categories of these types of units. First, there are tape units which employ an endless loop of recording tape going through two or more heads to produce repeated signals. There is also a non-tape unit which features a time-delay circuitry not very far removed from that of the flanger. These units are more compact, quieter, and more durable than the tape machines. Don Ellis made especially good use of the tape echo/delay unit by playing duets and improvising against himself in a big band setting. The better units feature variable time delay with reverb effects, doubling, chorusing, and vibrato.

ENVELOPE FILTERS. These modifiers employ two filters to electronically alter the aural shape (envelope) of each note as it is performed, to create a wah-wah effect without the hassle of constantly having to use the foot pedal. The variation of effects can vary from a quick, duck-like quack to a longer, more distinct vowel-type voicing.

EQUALIZERS. This unit adds versatility to amplifiers in shaping tone by emphasizing certain overtones (high, mid, and low range), thus offering more opportunity to attain both a unique sound and improve the instrument's sound in a room that is acoustically weak or undesirable. Playing music inevitably means playing places with less than optimum environment for good performance. Equalizers can allow total sound control. Whether it is a response change in the acoustic characteristics in a room or the elimination of annoying problems such as a buzz or hum in the speakers caused by light dimmers or fluorescent lights, an equalizer can do the job.

ELECTRONIC PICKUPS FOR ACOUSTIC INSTRUMENTS. There are many circumstances, especially in a combo setting, where a pickup is more convenient for a wind player than playing directly into a microphone. The pickup for a wind instrument is small, button-like in appearance, and convenient. For brass players, the pickup is usually incorporated directly into the mouthpiece by cutting a small hole and fitting it precisely into place. Although this equipment does not distort the sound in the same fashion as many of the other items indicated above, the electronic pickup for wind instruments is (in some settings) an important sound modifier. Make certain you see and hear one in action before making any final decisions.

For more information or details about sound modifier equipment, contact the following manufacturers.

Advanced Audio Designs
1164 W. Third Street
Eugene, OR 97402

Frogg
4121 Redwood Avenue
Los Angeles, CA 90066

Mutron
c/o Musitronics Corp.
Rosemont, NJ 08556

Randall Instruments
1132 Duryea
Irvine, CA 92705

DOD Electronics
495 E. 27th South
Salt Lake City, UT 84115

Morley
1811 W. Magnolia Boulevard
Burbank, CA 91506

MXR Innovations
P.O. Box 772
Rochester, NY 14603

Rex Bogue Guitars
P.O. Box 751
San Gabriel, CA 91778

Needless to say, modern technology is improving at a steady and rapid rate. Music educators of today and tomorrow need to know more about sound modification if they expect to remain up to date with the contemporary scene. All you have to do is listen to the radio to understand what a big role sound modifiers play in the record industry. Since these are the sounds the students are hearing, it is the wise music educator who has a working knowledge about this material when the student comes to ask questions.

Listed here is a selected discography of records featuring sound modifiers:

Maynard Ferguson: *Primal Scream* (Columbia PC-33953)

Brecker Brothers: *Don't Stop the Music* (Arista 4122)

Brecker Brothers: *Watch the Time* (Polydor I-6092)

Eddie Harris: *Bad Luck Is All I Have* (Atlantic 1675)

Eddie Harris: *How Can You Live Like This* (Atlantic 1698)

Don Ellis: *Tears of Joy* (Columbia G 30927)

Don Ellis: *Live at the Fillmore* (Columbia CG 30243)

SELECTING PUBLIC ADDRESS SYSTEM EQUIPMENT

The primary concern for this section is to provide a step-by-step guide on what to look for when purchasing jazz sound equipment (public address systems, amps, microphones, etc.) for your school. Initially, there are two essential questions:

1. What characteristics in equipment design are desirable for your use?

2. What are some testing procedures you can use to evaluate the equipment?

Many music dealers are willing to do a sound test in your school auditorium to help assess your specific needs. Basic criteria for public address systems and amps are discussed below.

For sound quality, the goal is to produce a clear, natural sound free of artificial coloration. A test for natural sound is simply a matter of application with objective listeners determining the quality under normal-use conditions. Put a drum-set through the system. If a speaker can produce the sudden peaks of sound instantly, with its cone moving from a dead stop to a full motion without delay, it has good transient response. This is the quality in live music that gives drums and other percussion instruments their crisp, sharp sound; a miked trumpet, its bright, breathy tone; or a solo violin, a slight raspiness when the bow first contacts the string. In a recording, it's the quality that makes it sound "live" rather than dull, mushy, and canned. Most amplifiers and P.A. systems today are capable of reproducing a sound exactly as it is introduced into the amplifier. The result is a flat response throughout the unit, usually requiring an adjustment of the unit to compensate for deficiencies in the acoustics, microphones, and/or speakers. This adjustment is usually accomplished by the use of various tone controls and equalizers.

Good sound quality from a P.A. system requires good microphones, speakers that have a flat frequency response, high efficiency, uniform dispersion, and a powerful enough amp to drive it.

SPEAKER FREQUENCY RESPONSE. This is the way a speaker responds in decibels to a constant input signal swept over the audible frequency range: low bass to the highest treble. Speakers with a flat frequency response over the intended range will sound more natural than those that favor certain frequencies. Given a musical passage where the bass is soft, the rhythm section medium-loud, and the vocalist most forward, it should sound exactly the same over a balanced speaker. The flat response has an additional advantage in that it reduces feedback potential. If a speaker has a large peak in response, the microphone may respond to that peak first and feedback will occur at the frequency where the peak is.

SPEAKER EFFICIENCY. A P.A. system characteristic checklist must include the power of the amplifier and the efficiency of the speakers. Both are of equal importance. Be sure the speaker system efficiency is the amount of sound a speaker system is able to put out for a certain amount of audio signal input. Efficiency is rated by a percentage—the higher the percentage, the better the speakers in terms of power projection. For instance, 5% represents a high-efficiency direct-radiator speaker system. You should realize, however, that efficiency is not in any way related to quality. Of course, if in comparing two speakers, all other areas of performance are equal, the more efficient speaker is a greater value because you may use it with a less (and thus more economical) amplifier.

> *For example:* In order to perceive a doubling of P.A. system power, it is necessary to increase the power output by 10 db (decibels). Yet doubling the amplifier power or adding a second speaker system gives only an additional 3 db increase in output. The same results can be achieved by using a speaker with twice as much efficiency (2–5%). Instead of doubling the size of the amp (which becomes very bulky), the speaker size could be nearly the same.

DISPERSION COVERAGE. The dispersion coverage requirement will vary according to the room where the system will be predominantly used.

Higher frequencies tend to become narrower in their dispersion in comparison to lower frequencies. Check to see if the speaker dispersion coverage has a relatively uniform rate for most frequencies according to the needs of your auditorium. Some common dispersion coverage problems include:

1. Room reverberation swamps your voice (this is especially common in gyms). The further a listener is from the speaker in a reverberant room, the less chance of understanding what is being said.

2. High frequencies miss some of the audience (P.A. needs wider dispersion). To check for this, stand in front of the speaker and listen to the *hiss* for a few seconds. Then, move slowly all the way to each side of the room, always keeping your face toward the speaker as you move, so that both ears pick up the sound. If the sound remains fairly constant as you move around the speaker, it means good dispersion. If the sound becomes lower in pitch, or softer, or duller, you need wider dispersion.

Any multiple channel P.A. system affords the capability of mixing, where individual microphones are used for miking each sound source. This process is very subjective and usually winds up the way the operator chooses. Since the operator's taste in mixing does not necessarily match that of the audience, mixing can be a very big problem. Mixing vocal and instrumental sounds through a P.A. system to achieve balance can be very effective and, yet, simple. A drum-set with several microphones is a good means of assessing the mixing capabilities of your system. If the resultant sound can be made to remain true to the original, you have the right facilities. When using amplifiers, it is best when there is only one source per amp. A guitar and bass both plugged into a bass amp will work but the guitar will not get the good high frequencies that are available from a regular guitar amp with smaller speakers, nor will the bass/guitar separation be as good as when individual amps are used.

Six input channels, each with its own volume, tone, and reverberation controls, will probably be adequate for most public schools. For larger, more sophisticated use, 12 or 16 channels might be advisable since the current trend is to mike ALL the sound sources. While individual miking of sound sources can be productive, it requires a considerable amount of sophistication in the mixing process and lots of money for equipment.

Filters and anti-feedback controls are desirable since they offer a method for overcoming numerous deficiencies in microphones, speakers, and acoustics. Many microphones have a peak in their response curves at some particular frequency. This often causes feedback at that particular frequency even when the overall sound is at a relatively low level. Compensation for this weakness allows a much higher overall sound level to be achieved without materially changing the quality. The same is true of speaker or acoustic performance (either is a potential cause of feedback). Feedback can also result from improper placement of speakers—speakers should always be placed in front and on a different plane from the microphone. Therefore, proper equipment (filters and anti-feedback controls) and proper placement will insure no annoying feedback.

High impedance units are generally much lower in price than low impedance units. High impedance inputs generally tend to be noisier and are subject to hum and extraneous noise pick-up. The microphone cable has to be limited in length to avoid attenuating the higher frequencies because the capability of the cable becomes a much more limiting factor at the higher impedances. Low impedance units, while costing considerably more, offer great flexibility and freedom from most of the problems experienced with high impedance units. Microphone cables of considerable length can be used with very little attenuation of the higher frequencies and almost complete freedom from extraneous pick-up. Where you can afford to, choose low impedance units.

There are additional considerations to help in your selection of a P.A. system.

PORTABILITY. There are many systems available with multiple channels which include a built-in power amplifier. Portable units are available with output power from 60 to at least 300 RMS. They are generally quite ruggedly constructed and, when used with the portable enclosures for which they are designed, make a very effective combination. Most portable equipment is built to withstand a considerable amount of abuse, which is of importance for the school setting. Often, the equipment is operated by a number of different individuals who are in the process of learning how to manage the equipment and do not handle the controls well. Ruggedness is a primary consideration for choosing equipment.

REVERBERATION. Most of the P.A. systems designed today have a fairly good reverberation unit built into them. There is also usually a provision for external echo for when the internal reverberation is disconnected. Any adequate system should include reverberation.

POWER OUTPUT. The power rating of a P.A. amplifier is the measure of its ability to do work. A low power amplifier may be able to provide enough driving power for a single speaker, but to drive several speakers may require a substantial increase. There are several types of power ratings for amplifiers: RMS, peak, EIA, IHF. The true measure of an amplifier's ability is in its RMS rating (which must also include its distortion factor). Power output is a factor that is decided by the size of the area in which the system is to be operated and whether it is indoors or outdoors. Again, the system will only be effective in its particular environment if you make certain that the speakers selected are capable of handling the power and covering the area properly. Generally, 100 watts RMS is considered sufficient for most school uses.

MODULAR CONCEPT. Modular construction offers several advantages when dealing with a large sound system. First, parts of the system can effectively be used for a performance in a smaller room. Also, additional speaker cabinets can be stacked together to produce a "column effect" which provides long throw for auditorium and outdoor concert work. In addition, you can continue to build into your modular system, starting with the bare necessities and adding something each year until you feel it is complete. Finally, a large unit system that is modular is much more portable and, thus, easier to handle.

MONITOR SYSTEM CAPABILITIES. A monitor system can be very helpful, especially to the rhythm section and soloists. When the rhythm section is set off to the side of the horn players as in a three-deep setup, a monitor can be invaluable. Though many P.A. systems provide a monitor output jack, it is wise to see if you will need an additional power amplifier to drive the monitor speaker(s). In a P.A. system that does not require an additional power amp, check to see if the monitor volume is independent of the main output level. Unless the monitor system has a separate volume level, the monitor will match the house speaker system, which is inappropriate.

For more information concerning P.A. systems, write to the following manufacturers.

Ace Tone
c/o Multivox/Sorkin Music
370 Motor Parkway
Hauppage, NY 11787

Altec Corp.
1515 S. Manchester
Anaheim, CA 92803

Barcus-Berry Sales Corp.
5461 Springfield Street
Huntington Beach, CA 92649

Cerwin-Vega
12250 Montague Street
Pacoima, CA 91331

Acoustic Control Corp.
7949 Woodley Avenue
Van Nuys, CA 90620

Ampeg
c/o Selmer Co.
P.O. Box 310
Elkhart, IN 46514

Bose Corp.
100 The Mountain Road
Framingham, MA 01701

Electro-Voice, Inc.
606 Cecil Street
Buchanan, MI 49107

Gibson
c/o Norlin Music
7373 N. Cicero
Lincolnwood, IL 60646

Kustom Electronics
P.O. Box 669
Chanute, KS 66720

Peavey Electronics
711 A Street
Meridian, MS 39301

Shure Brothers
222 Hartrey
Evanston, IL 60204

Yamaha Instrument Corp.
P.O. Box 6600
Buena Park, CA 90620

JBL Sound Co.
8500 Balboa Boulevard
Northrup, CA 91329

Marshall
c/o Unicord Inc.
Westbury, NY 11590

Randall Instruments
1132 Duryea
Irvine, CA 92705

Sunn Musical Equipment
P.O. Box 402
Tualatin, OR 97062

DISCOVERING RECORDING EQUIPMENT

Whether you need a master tape for your next record album, a chronological library of every performance your jazz ensemble has ever performed, or just an analysis of last week's rehearsal, you need to know about recording techniques and equipment.

Matching Microphones to Your Needs

Perhaps the most confusing equipment to purchase for recording is the microphone. Individual prices vary from a few dollars up into the hundreds. The variety of specifications can be confusing and vary as does the cost. Since recording situations will differ according to environments, one microphone will not best suit all of your needs. It is important, therefore, that you decide your needs in terms of microphone design, impedance, the pick-up pattern, and the frequency response before you go shopping.

There are three basic types of microphones that convert acoustic energy (sound waves) into electrical energy (impulses or signals).

RIBBON MICROPHONES. These are so-named because of a moving ribbon in a magnetic field. This type is considered among the best for professional use in recording music (especially on brass instruments where the tone is complimented), broadcasting, and P.A. systems. These mikes are fairly high priced. They are normally used indoors due to their fragile nature—they can even be sensitive to wind.

DYNAMIC MICROPHONES. These have a moving coil in a magnetic field. They are relatively easy to make; practically indestructive; and are the most popular for general use. The frequency is normally smooth up to 20,000 cycles. Prices, styles, and types are offered in an extremely wide range.

CONDENSER MICROPHONES. These mikes use a motion of a charge plate to change capacities. Since this type of mike is electrically complex with a built-in internal amplifier (thus needing a power supply), it usually has a self-contained battery. Good condenser mikes have a wide frequency response with few dips and peaks. Electric-type condenser mikes can offer ruggedness comparable to dynamic microphones while yielding super performance at frequency extremes (highs and lows) when compared to dynamic models. They are most versatile and can be used in any situation. Condenser mikes have the most accurate directional characteristics of any of the directional microphones.

Impedance categories are broken into "high" (10,000 ohms or more) and "low" (600 ohms or less). High or low impedance values do not solely determine which microphone is better than others. The advantage of low impedance microphones is the amount of cable that can be used. Cable lengths of high impedance microphones must be kept under 15 feet or there will be a loss of high frequency signals and output level. Low impedance microphones do not have restrictions on cable lengths, so they can run up to hundreds of feet without serious deterioration of the original signal.

Microphones "hear" selectively and are designed to pick up sound for some particular direction. There are three general classifications based upon the directional characteristics of each microphone.

UNIDIRECTIONAL. These microphones pick up sound primarily from the front (one direction), while suppressing sound and noise from the back. The most popular unidirectional mike is the cardoid, which picks up sounds in a heart-shaped pattern: from the front best, then equally but less well from the left and right sides. These are great for recording large music groups while suppressing audience noises (coughing, shuffling feet, etc.). They are also handy for problems dealing with feedback. Since the rear of the microphone rejects sound, the mike can be placed so that sound projecting from the monitor speaker on stage cannot re-enter the mike to generate feedback. Performers can work much further away from unidirectional microphones than omnidirectional mikes. Cardoid microphones have one disadvantage—the closer they are to the sound source, the more prominent the bass response is. This effect is called the proximity effect.

OMNIDIRECTIONAL. The omnidirectional microphone picks up sounds evenly from all directions (360°)—front, back, and sides. In a sense, these mikes are nondirectional. They are useful for close situations since there is no proximity problem. The omnidirectional mike provides a lot of warmth to the sound, since it receives the overall sound including the reverberant effects of the concert hall. This type of mike is good for general purposes where feedback or the audience is not a consideration, but avoid using an omnidirectional mike where there is a stage monitor or house speaker nearby. Price ranges and response characteristics are widest for this type of microphone.

BI-DIRECTIONAL. The bi-directional microphone picks up sounds in the shape of a figure "8." The sides are picked up while the top and bottom are suppressed. This mike is best suited for use when performers are on opposite sides of the microphone.

The microphone frequency response refers to the ability of a microphone to reproduce various tones that are measured against the human ear's audible range—20 Hz to 20,000 Hz. Generally, the more extended the range of the microphone, the more faithful the reproduction will be. Microphone flatness refers to the frequency response ration of a microphone. Most jazz sound (amps, records, P.A. systems, mixers, etc.) will require a flat frequency response whenever possible. Sometimes, the right kind of microphone can help alter or improve the original sound. For example, a brassy trumpet will sound better if it is recorded with microphones that have a high flatness response, which will emphasize the high frequencies and add brilliance and edge to the original sound. A thin alto sax sound can have an emphasis on the low frequencies and added richness and fullness to the original sound if recorded with a low flatness response microphone.

If you've never encountered any extensive information about microphones before, the above information might seem overwhelming. Listed below are some guidelines to help you when selecting microphones. Remember, you must first assess how the microphone will specifically be used so that your final selection is based on your needs.

1. Use low impedance, matched microphones. If you already have good high impedance mikes, purchase the relatively inexpensive transformers needed to convert them to low-impedance units.

2. Start with good dynamic or condenser omnidirectional mikes. These offer the most versatility with live recordings of a large group, close mike work with a P.A. system, and studio recording. Cardoid mikes would be an appropriate move upward for use in large-group recordings later in the future.

3. Use microphones with relatively flat frequency response (50 Hz – 15,000 Hz).

4. Avoid bi-directional microphones until you are certain they can be of use in a specific situation.

5. Condenser mikes can noticeably improve P.A. systems because of their greater intelligibility.

6. Expect to pay between $90 and $300 for a good quality mike.

You may want to write to the following companies for more information concerning their microphones.

AKG Acoustics
91 McKee Drive
Mahwah, NJ 07430

Shure Brothers
222 Hartrey
Evanston, IL 60204

Sony
c/o Superscope
20525 Nordhoff
Chadsworth, CA 91311

Electro-Voice
600 Cecil Street
Buchanan, MI 49107

Sennheiser
c/o Norlin Music
7373 N. Cicero
Lincolnwood, IL 60646

TEAC
7733 Telegraphy Road
Montebello, CA 90640

The Multi-Purpose Tape Recorder

There are essentially two approaches to tape recorders, each designed for specific purposes and having distinct advantages. Make certain your microphones are compatible with your recorder.

The main advantages to the cassette recorder are convenience and compactness. In addition, a good cassette recorder is less expensive than a good reel-to-reel model. Nevertheless, the sound is almost as good. There are the added bonuses that a portable cassette recorder can tape a performance "on location" and the tape is compatible with all other cassette recorders.

The most important quality factors for cassette recorders are frequency response and flutter and wow. For a medium-to-deluxe priced cassette deck, you can expect the following: *frequency response*—25 Hz to 15,000 Hz ± 3 db, and *flutter and wow (%)*—0.12% to 0.10% or less.

Most cassette tape decks should include these features:

1. Recording-level meters (to indicate volume of sound being recorded on each stereo channel).

2. Microphone inputs (used for live recordings).

3. Headphone jack (enables a person to plug in headphones for private listening or monitoring during recording).

4. Fast forward and rewind.

5. Tape counter (provides reference numbers to facilitate finding any specific spot on the tape).

6. Dolby® noise reduction system (reduces tape hiss).

The following are optional features for cassette decks:

7. Tape memory (finds a desired place on the tape by stopping at a preset number).

8. Automatic shutoff (when the end of the tape is reached, machine shuts off).

9. Tape selector (permits adjustment for different kinds of tape: iron oxide, Fe_2O_3; chromium dioxide, CrO_2; and ferrichrome, FeCr).

10. Limiter or automatic level control (automatically reduces recording level when incoming signal is too strong).

11. Overload-warning light (flashes when recording level is high enough to cause distortion).

12. Input mixing (permits blending of a live recording with inputs from records, radio, or tapes).

13. Pause control (allows tape to stop briefly without having "play" or "record" buttons reset).

Reel-to-reel recorders, also called open-reel recorders, are designed to produce a higher-quality tape, with less emphasis on portability and convenience. Although there are relatively inexpensive reel-to-reel models available, if you opt for open-reel over cassette models, you should try to purchase the top of the line.

The main features of open-reel models include faster taping speeds than cassettes (which produces better quality fidelity) and a system that is specifically designed to produce the finest recordings. Because these models are both outstanding and desirable, it is wise to rig them on a wheeled table so that they can be moved to a performance area and returned to a secure storage location with a minimum of wear and tear on the machine.

Nearly all quality tape decks have a built-in Dolby® noise reduction system that eliminates much of the hiss made by the tape itself, so that the music emerges against a silent background. The Dolby® equipment can also be used to reduce FM background hiss for stations broadcasting Dolby®-encoded material (perhaps one of your performances). In both cases, the quality of sound reproduction is significantly improved.

Rehearsal Techniques for the Jazz Ensemble

The quality of any music organization can be directly attributed to the mastery of music fundamentals. Jazz ensemble directors frequently receive comments from adjudicators and clinicians that address the basics of musicianship. Jazz ensembles never outgrow the need to improve their tone, intonation, dynamics, breath support, blend, balance, articulation, rhythm development, and/or vibrato. This chapter is directed towards improving these needs.

Good tone and intonation involves the development of sound quality, embouchure control, and the ability to listen to yourself and others.

A list of common problems includes:

- overblowing and going flat
- tone without a center of pitch
- sharp upper registers, particularly in saxophones and lead trumpets
- bad notes on the instrument
- open octaves in brasses (this is especially treacherous)
- unison high notes in both brasses and reeds (very dangerous)
- crescendos and decrescendos in both brasses and winds (will present pitch variations)
- pedal tones on the trombone (will usually be sharp)
- different registers of saxophones (will often suffer poor intonation)
- In pp and p passages, the brass tends to be flat (usually caused by a lack of breath support)

An effective tuning method for the horns has been devised by Conrad Johnson, now retired, and Buddy Smith, a high school director, both from Houston, Texas. A matching tone system is used where a general tuning begins the process and then proceeds to a fine tuning called the "Bah" system.

First, the brass and saxes tune to a fixed pitch source so that there are no irregular vibrations. When the tones match, the players proceed to the Bah system in which several like instruments may be checked for tuning by attacking and sustaining tones. The first player attacks and sustains any given pitch while the second, third, and fourth players enter on that pitch one after another. All players hold the pitch on a full and straight tone. Any horns that are not tuned and matched will stand out immediately. The player or players who are not tuned make the necessary adjustment and match the line of tones until there are no noticeable irregular vibrations. This system should be used daily to sensitize your students' ears to differences in pitch and sound quality, which contribute to both improved intonation and tone quality. An example of the Bah system would look something like Figure 5-1.

The Bah system will detect the slightest intonation problem in any section after tuning. The Bah system can also be applied as a quick tuning check in the middle of any rehearsal.

Bands have a tendency to play at the same dynamic level (usually too loud) most of the time. There must be good dynamic contrast for any group to hold the attention of the audience. Never allow the members of the ensemble to blow at their maximum volume. Not only will intonation be more controlled, but tone quality will also improve when a group maintains dynamic control. You will also notice that the sound actually penetrates bet-

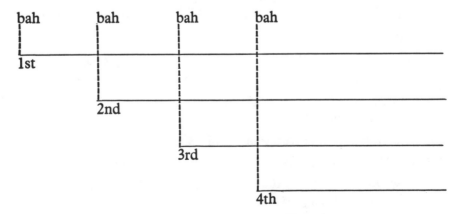

FIGURE 5-1. THE BAH TUNING SYSTEM

ter than just a loud sound. Overblowing or intonation ensembles produce a sound that cancels out the overtones, while a more controlled, in-tune ensemble reinforces and amplifies the overtones. Develop a true *p* and *pp* ensemble sound and your group will achieve more expressive and excitement —and ultimately, more appeal. Find and use charts that require dynamic changes. Be sure to add appropriate dynamic markings to the rhythm section parts since there are few markings usually provided. Be especially insistent about dynamics from the rhythm section during solo or soli sections where more sensitivity is required.

This problem can be especially difficult with an over-amplified guitarist and/or bassist. Even if the dynamic level is suitable, the tone quality can produce a biting treble sound for the guitar while the bass will often sound distorted. The guitar should have a round, warm, mid-range tone (listen to Wes Montgomery, Jim Hall, or George Benson), and the bass should have less bass and more treble emphasis to approximate the sound of the acoustic bass.

If the guitarist is playing a solid body guitar with two pickups and an amplifier, have him or her use the fingerboard pickup exclusively. The guitar tone control should be set about halfway for a rich, mellow, almost acoustic sound that is most desirable for jazz charts especially in the Basie tradition. The bridge pickup will produce an undesirably thin, nasal quality sound.

Many amps have two volume controls: master volume and channel volume. To obtain a clean, non-distorted sound, the master volume needs to be lower than the channel volume setting on the amp. If the master level is at a higher setting, overdrive distortion will result.

The balance of overtones can be controlled by the amplifier as identified by the three range bands: treble, mid-range, and bass. Start with each of these bands set at a flat frequency response near the midway point (usually 5). From here, you may make adjustments to suit your tastes. Bass players will need to set the treble higher while the guitarist will use less treble and more mid-range sound quality.

As much as breathing techniques are stressed by music educators, it still seems to be one of the major areas of concern as a basic fundamental for the band to master. Without good breath support, upper range, good pitch control, crescendos, decrescendos, in-tune dynamic extremes, balanced blends, and long phrases cannot be effectively developed. Whole notes are frequently short-changed with a diminuendo effect rather than the desired effect of sustained intensity. Breath support must also be utilized as a part of phrasing: a much smoother phrase is the result when the phrasing is not broken with too many breaths and when crescendos and decrescendos are more gradual and extended.

Everyone in the section should be made aware that they need to actively listen for the section leader and imitate that person in terms of dynamics and articulation (blend) when playing. All parts must support and enhance the section leader by "playing up" to him or her, especially in the harmony parts. It is a common error for some of the players to under-blow their parts and not play up to the dynamic level of the lead player. The unison parts require sensitivity to pitch, tone quality, and articulation. It is when playing harmonized passages that there will be discrepancies in balance between the section and lead players. Always have other players try to emulate the lead player's sound characteristics. Lower harmony (3rd and 4th parts) will generally need to be played stronger dynamically in order to establish balance with the 1st and 2nd parts.

For ensemble cohesiveness in the tutti passages, remind the band to use dynamic markings as an indicator of the volume only. The band must accurately and precisely follow the lead trumpet player without covering him or her, especially in the *ff* sections. The trick in tutti passages is for the section leaders to play up to the lead trumpet player's level of dynamics. Players in each section will then have dynamic guidelines to follow within their own sections as well as from the lead trumpet part.

> **Note:** High trombone players have a tendency to destroy the balance of the brass chords by overblowing the 4th or 5th trumpet players who are in the same tessitura.

Be sure to establish proper balance levels in rehearsal (this is a spot to work *without* the rhythm section). The rhythm sections should always be gradually worked into the piece and must *support* the ensemble balance rather than dominate it.

The easiest way to understand the concept of balance is to think in terms of a pyramid. The peak is the lead trumpet. On the next level down are the parts closest to the lead trumpet harmonically or in range. Those parts furthest from the lead trumpet provide the next level and the rhythm section provides the foundation or support base.

Jazz articulation is based on several practices and rules of interpretation and phrasing. Jazz attacks and releases require special attention and a willingness by all performers to match.

To begin, there are four basic articulations that focus on the attack of the note. Here is a brief description of each articulation.

LEGATO TONGUE. This holds full value. Use either a soft "doo" or a hard "d" sound for the attack.

STACCATO TONGUE. This creates a short, crisp but not heavy sound. Let the tempo be the guide for the actual degree of shortness so that a slower tempo receives a longer note. Use a "dit" attack style, which will provide a definite start and a controlled release that can quickly become uniform within the section. The space between notes is what is important, not the degree of shortness.

HEAVY, STRESSED ACCENT. This holds full value with an accented "doo." This type of articulation should not be played too short, especially at medium or slow tempos. Frequently, this attack crescendos to another note within the phrase.

HOUSETOP OR VERY HEAVY ACCENT. This holds less than full value. Use the "dot" or "dit" sound which provides a definite attack and will cut the note off a little shorter for a more abrupt and well-defined release. One danger of the very heavy accent is that the attack will dominate the sound to the point where only the tongue is heard while the pitch and sound quality are lost. To avoid this problem, increase the air velocity to the housetop for it to ring with clear tone quality.

What ultimately makes the articulation process so difficult to deal with is that each composer, arranger, and publisher may choose to use any articulation markings since many are not standardized. Some charts will be well edited for articulations, while others may only provide a few hints. Several publishers offer condensed scores and sound sheets upon request. A sound sheet can be particularly helpful when you can analyze someone else's performance to infer about articulation.

Note release is another concern dealing with articulation. Most groups are careful about starting the sound but careless or inconsistent about releases. All releases should be marked to indicate exactly when the note ends. Longer notes become more indefinite and require even more attention. Every note must have a clean release as well as attack to ensure precision.

Vibrato should be thought of only as "warming up" the sound and should never detract from the tone. Usually, in soli parts the lead player may elect to use vibrato. *Never use vibrato in unison soli passages since it will cause intonation problems.* "Dead tone" or "n.v." means no vibrato.

The interpretation of jazz rhythms is different from symphonic notation. To produce a jazz or swing feeling, rhythms must be interpreted in a relaxed manner since it is not easy to precisely notate them. The basis of rhythmic ambiguity lies in the eighth-note figures. The difficulty with eighth notes is how their character changes with different figures and tempos. Consider the rhythmic interpretation of the pattern of (♫). Although they may be written as (♫) or (♫), they are actually performed in a slightly uneven long-short triplet pulsation (♩♪). To add to the confusion, there is also a natural stress given to the off-beat note rather than to the downbeat note.

To vocalize this "swing" feeling may help to understand this concept. The spoken syllables "du ba, du ba" with the = 132 – 160 for a (♩♪) figure clearly indicates a compound meter relationship and approximates the jazz rhythm.

The use of phonetic syllables can help the student to feel the time and articulation concepts most difficult in jazz performance. It is often easier to vocalize the syllable and then play it rather than try to perform it first. The syllable "du" indicates a regular attack and the syllable "dot" indicates a distinct release. A "ba" release is more legato. Thus, a rhythm pattern written as (♫) would be verbalized as "du dot" and, if written accurately, would look like (♩♪).

Without a correct concept of style and articulation, a passage of eighth notes might be played too evenly or in a choppy manner. Consider using the phonetic syllables to alleviate this tendency with your students.

As a general rule, play eighth notes legato unless otherwise indicated. The legato technique of a smooth articulation is essential to jazz style, even when accents occur. The syllable "wah" is used for eighth-note off-beat accents (see Figure 5-2).

FIGURE 5-2. OFF-BEAT ACCENTS

A helpful aid in developing good interpretation of jazz swing figures is to include listening sessions for your students which cover a variety of jazz styles and an emphasis on all tempos.

Another method of teaching jazz rhythmic interpretations during the warm-up period is to initiate time drills. Use these time drills as a way of coordinating jazz articulations and those patterns you expect to rehearse that day. These drills should first be vocalized, then played instrumentally until everyone is playing them accurately and together. You may use these drills in any of the following ways: (1) in unison on any given pitch; (2) in a blues progression based on the progression's chord roots; (3) with harmonized chords previously worked out; and (4) using an arpegiated scale passage. Encourage a student to demonstrate how each figure should be played on an instrument. The rhythm section should always perform in a simple yet solid time feel in the background.

Figures 5-3, 5-4, 5-5 and 5-6 are examples of swing patterns with reference to traditional notation and how they should actually be performed.

Quarter notes are played shorter than a full beat, in a detached manner, unless notated otherwise, such as in tenuto passages.

written

played

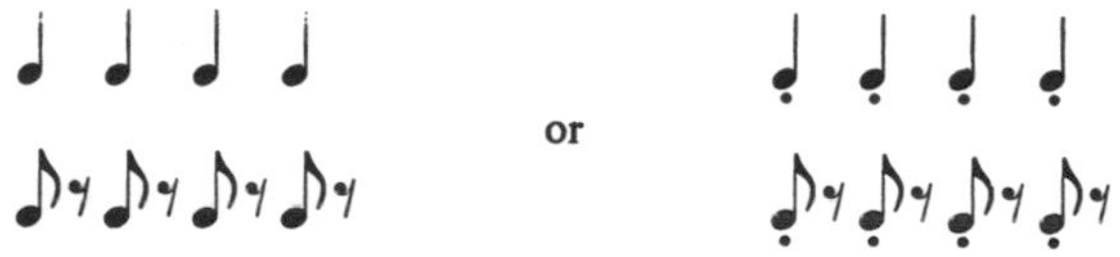

or

Notes longer than a quarter note are given full time value.

written

played

Single individual eighth notes written on the up-beat are played short as an anticipation of the next beat and accented.

written

played

FIGURE 5-3. RHYTHM PATTERNS

Patterns of two or more eighth notes are played with a lift and slight breath accent in a long-short manner similar to compound meter. All eighth notes are played legato unless otherwise indicated.

written

played

Patterns of two or more eighth notes slurred into a quarter note are usually followed by a tonguing articulation if the rhythm pattern continues.

written

played

Downbeat eighth notes are played longer (approximately ⅔ of a beat). Upbeat eighth notes are played shorter and later.

written

played

FIGURE 5-4. RHYTHM PATTERNS

Consecutive syncopated quarter notes are played like compound meter quarter notes with an eighth rest in-between unless otherwise notated. The faster the tempo, the shorter the syncopated eighth notes. In a laid-back tune, the space between the syncopated quarters is not as abrupt, with longer sounding quarters and shorter rests.

written

played

Upbeat entrances of eighths or quarters are played as an accented anticipated entrance of the next down beat.

written

played

FIGURE 5-5. RHYTHM PATTERNS

The goal of rhythm time drills is to develop consistency in dealing with jazz rhythms and articulations in the rehearsal. The following exercises are provided to be used as a part of the warm-up in a medium tempo.

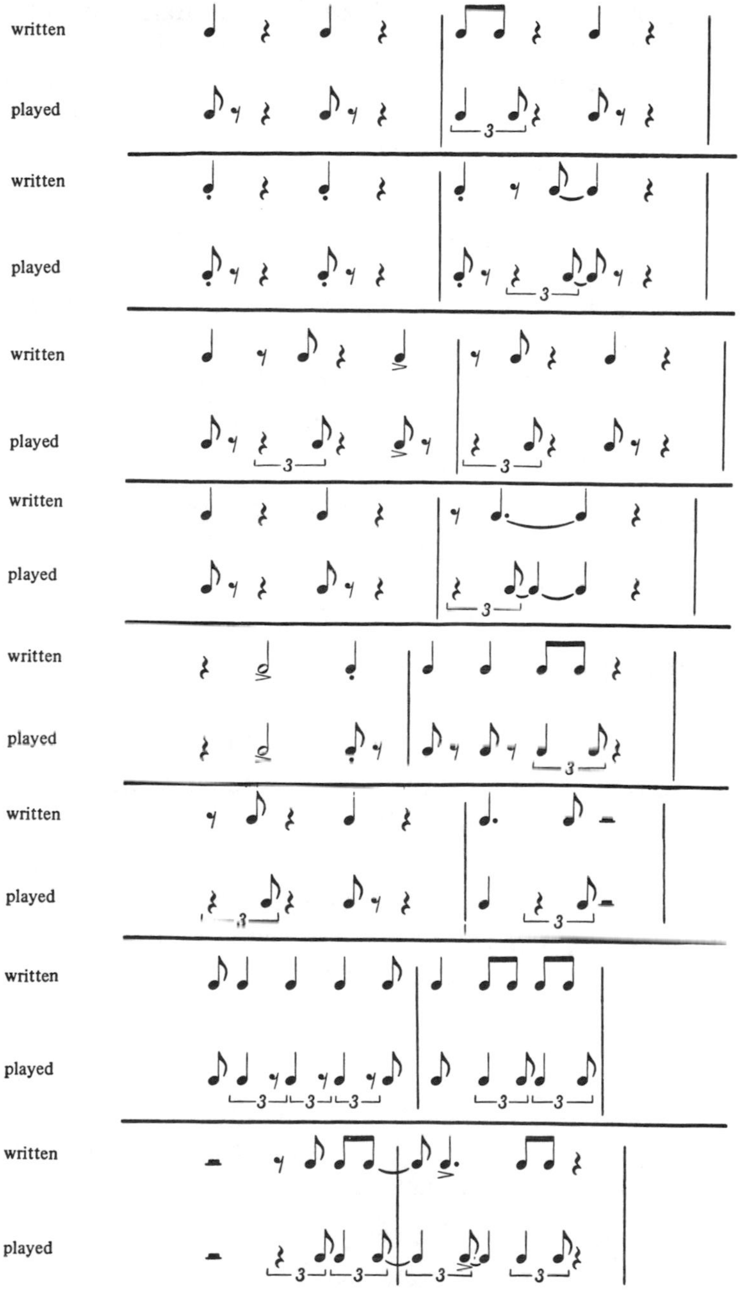

FIGURE 5-6. RHYTHM PATTERNS

PLANNING/ORGANIZING TIPS FOR EFFICIENT REHEARSALS

A successful jazz ensemble rehearsal requires preparation and planning to make it a valid music education experience. A rehearsal can be more productive if there is a disciplined procedure followed with some specific objectives clearly identified for the group to accomplish. The following ideas provide organization and planning strategies to help improve the quality of your jazz ensemble rehearsals.

1. Consider your seating arrangement. Don't spread members too far apart. Seat the rhythm section together. Different seating arrangements can influence the ensemble's balance and precision. Specific suggestions include:

- All lead players should be in the middle of their section.
- Saxophones should sit or stand in a semi-circle.
- First tenor should be nearest the rhythm section.
- Keep the two tenors apart to avoid a bottom-heavy sound in the sax section.
- Have the 4th trombone and baritone sax sit on the same side of the band when using the traditional setup.
- Brass players should point their bells slightly in towards the lead player and always above the top of the music stand.
- The bass player should be next to the drummer's hi-hat.
- The guitarist should be on the left side of the drummer.
- The pianist should be in front of the drummer and facing towards the band.
- All amps should be placed so that the rest of the band can hear them. Don't let the amps dominate the band's sound. Use the amps to support the band as a part of the rhythm section, not the other way around.

2. Develop a marking system for parts and insist that your students bring a pencil to all rehearsals. Don't allow your students to rely on memory! An abbreviation system such as the following can be helpful in making the students more efficient in marking their parts.

- Circle dynamics to stress changes.
- Attacks should be appropriately marked.
- Ensemble releases and breath marks need to be clearly indicated. Use a slash or number to indicate when a note will be released. (A number

can refer to a release on that beat and a slash can indicate a release on the upbeat.) Use a comma for breath marks.

- Ghosted notes should be indicated by a set of parentheses ( ).
- Crescendos and decrescendos should be made specific by indicating length and breadth.
- Added solos and/or repeated sections should be clearly marked.
- Downbeats can be indicated by the use of arrows during syncopated passages where there is any confusion (↓ ↑).
- Articulations that are not being played correctly should be circled.
- A copy of the score or of the lead trumpet part with all the appropriate markings should be posted on a bulletin board in the band room *before* the rehearsal so that members can mark their parts correctly in advance.

The director should study passages and decide how the music is to be played in terms of articulation, dynamics, tempos, phrasing, special effects, attacks, and releases. The music should be rehearsed in an organized fashion. Begin by focusing on the problem spots. Use a deliberately slower tempo until all the technical parts are mastered. Occasionally challenge the group by making them read through a chart at the proper tempo. Identify trouble spots and concentrate on procedures designed to eliminate the problem. Use patience and positive reinforcement to encourage the members of the group.

Develop good warm-up procedures. Like calisthenics before a ball game, use a gradual process that will allow brass players to achieve the right embouchure. Once you get past your favorite warm-up routine with your favorite scale/etude/flexibility/breathing exercises, consider warming up the group on a blues-riff tune. The benefits of such a procedure include:

- It establishes time for the horn players as well as the rhythm section.
- It provides ample opportunity to balance a unison line among horn players as well as help the rhythm section players properly adjust their volume level.
- It offers more extensive improvisation opportunities for individual members as it familiarizes them with the form and changes.
- It helps establish a good swing feeling without being locked into reading a chart.
- You can deal with many different musical considerations without interference since the group is working through a head chart and there is no written music to distract them.

Regularly scheduled sectionals can turn a rehearsal into a highly productive activity. They also help develop esprit de corps within a section and contribute to the development of stronger, more effective lead players. It is important for the members of the section to understand that the section leader is in charge and that he or she, in turn, is directly responsible to the director. Given regularly scheduled sectional rehearsals, the regular ensemble rehearsals can become more oriented toward ensemble concerns rather than sectional concerns. You should communicate your wants and needs directly to the section leader—develop a sense of responsibility in that person and the entire section.

Occasionally rehearse the full band without the rhythm section (let them have a sectional rehearsal or, if you feel it's important for them to be there, have them observe) like Count Basie during a recording. Not only will the band be more sensitive to dynamics, balance, intonation, articulation, phrasing, and time, it will also give the rhythm section (if they *listen*) a better idea of how to work with the band. Horn players need to be able to develop a rhythmic "feel" independent of the rhythm section: they make the band swing and the rhythm section *underlines* the swing!

Tune carefully. Try to get your students to establish a tuning regimen before the rehearsal begins. Get your bass and guitar players to tune by themselves in advance since their harmonics are not well suited for concert B^b tuning. Do not restrict tuning to one pitch. Tune to major chords (I, IV, V) or open fifths, and start your tuning with the lowest instruments and work up. The concept of good intonation is an ongoing process and should be stressed throughout the rehearsal. Members should constantly be examining how "in tune" they are with the rest of the section or band and making minor adjustments. If you don't see anybody making intonation adjustments during the rehearsal, it is a symptom that there is not enough attention being focused on good intonation. Be particularly concerned about unison lines where intonation is an especially difficult problem.

Use a tape recorder to illustrate weaknesses and problems. Record individuals, sections, or the entire band. Have whoever has been recorded listen with you so you can point out problems while describing solutions. The following suggestions include more uses of the tape recorder during rehearsal.

- Carry a microphone with a long cable and walk among the band while they are playing. Hold it near various instruments so they "stand out." Differences in intonation, articulation, phrasing, and entrances will become very obvious to the group when they hear this demonstration.

- Make your own "play-along" tapes with your rhythm section performing the chart being rehearsed. Have several copies for your soloists or any other members who would like to use them for practice.

- Use tapes to provide soloists with a means of analyzing themselves.

- Use tapes to gain "distance" for yourself. Pretend you're unfamiliar with the group on the tape to better determine whether the band is exciting, technically accurate, and/or playing the way you want in a total sense.

Change rehearsal seating arrangements periodically. It will allow members of the group to hear each other differently and usually proves most helpful to the rhythm section. Here are some other ideas you might consider.

- Have the soloist stand next to the rhythm section. Be sure that the soloist and rhythm section are conscious of one another and sensitive to what is happening in their interaction.

- Use a different rehearsal room to achieve a different acoustical feel and response to the music.

- Use an entirely new setup (see Chapter 3) than you use for concerts.

Utilizing rehearsal time efficiently is imperative! Good rehearsals don't just happen by chance. Practice the following "do's" and avoid the "don'ts" for maximum benefits for your rehearsals.

DON'T over-explain things to students. Keep your comments concise and accurate.

DON'T allow playing when you are giving instructions or directions. Insist on everyone paying attention even if what you're saying is of main concern to some other section within the group.

DON'T spend rehearsal time on what the band already does well. Rehearsal is an opportunity to improve and accomplish new skills.

DON'T stop the band unless you know what you want to say. Be specific and make it clear that you have a purpose in mind.

DO post what tunes you expect to rehearse in advance so that there is no wasted time hunting for music.

DO avoid interruptions: don't allow phone calls or messages to interfere or stop your rehearsals.

DO insist that individual parts be marked accurately and up to date.

DO avoid spending too much time on one small section or part in the music.

DO be positive! Make it a point to compliment and encourage individuals and the group when they produce what you're after. Be enthusiastic in your praise.

DO pace your rehearsal so that you avoid working the hardest music last. Begin and end the rehearsal with familiar material.

DO minimize your conducting. Conducting stiffens a rhythm section (especially when they are trying to swing). Basic conducting responsibilities should be restricted to:

- counting the proper tempo
- cut-offs
- dynamic changes
- solo cues
- rubato sections
- new tempos
- the ending

DO teach improvisation concepts regularly during rehearsals.

DO encourage soloists to memorize chord changes for their solos. This provides the double benefit of being more desirable for stage presentation and allows the soloist to get more into the music.

DO sight read on a regular basis. This is a skill that will actually contribute to your group improving in other areas.

DO pace your brass players. Use a split lead in both trumpet and trombone if you don't have strong enough players. Avoid charts that overextend players' range and endurance.

DO ask other band directors to help out by supervising a sectional rehearsal or chart for your band (make a trade by doing one for that person) in order to give your students a new perspective. DO invite college students and professional musicians to come and help out, too.

DO be concerned about the length of notes. Make it clear how long you want notes held. Remember, the slower the tempo, the longer the articulation, even if it is marked staccato or housetop accent.

DO check for blend and balance. Investigate if the inside parts of a section are playing up to the lead player in harmonized passages. All players must support the section.

SIGHT READING TO IMPROVE YOUR ENSEMBLE

Sight reading is one of those areas of music education that is too often ignored. The usual reason cited for sight-reading deficiencies is that there is not enough time during rehearsal. The purpose of this section is to convince you of the value of sight reading and outline some simple strategies so that you can fit the activity into your program on a regular basis.

All NAJE Approved Festivals now require sight reading as a determining factor to help choose the festival champion. Although your group may not plan to participate in an NAJE Approved Festival, the growth in number of these types of festivals is very evident and implies a growing emphasis on sight reading throughout the country.

The emphasis on sight reading should not be so much on duplicating rhythms and notes accurately (although this is *in part* important), but should concentrate on good phrasing, musical articulation, and a general effort to produce a sound that would be described as "complete" in the performance sense as possible. Select music that is initially within everybody's ability, continuously upgrade the material, and always stress "getting through" above allowing the band to stop for any reason. Spend at least five minutes of every rehearsal on sight reading and set your goal to hand out a chart to sight read on stage during one of your concerts. Keep a separate sight-reading folder so that you can go through the new music quickly and efficiently. The following suggestions are designed to help develop enthusiasm and attain success in your sight-reading endeavors.

- Spend a little time talking through the chart in advance of actually playing it.
- Indicate if the eighth notes are swing or rock style.
- Reveal any formal aspects of the music: repeats, D.S., D.C., Coda, endings, etc.
- Point out key signatures, time signatures, and ALL changes.
- Demonstrate the correct tempo.
- Have the band sing back any difficult rhythm patterns to you.
- Cover stylistic indications of articulation and dynamics.
- In syncopated passages, emphasize where the downbeats fall.
- Make certain there is no confusion as to assignment of solos.
- Point out tempo changes, cadenzas, rubatos, fermatas, etc.
- DO NOT STOP once you begin. Make the group understand that mistakes are acceptable in sight reading but that having to stop is not.
- Only deal with the bad spots if they are total disasters and, then, only with an eye towards improving future sight-reading sessions.

Sight reading is a stimulating and exciting part of music education and should be a regular feature of your rehearsal. Once past their initial hesitation, students can learn to love the feeling of discovery and accomplishment associated with sight reading. If you don't have a lot of charts in your library for sight reading: (1) swap sight-reading folders with a neighboring school (folders are collected after each rehearsal so there's no danger of losing borrowed music); or (2) purchase easier charts especially for sight reading when music is on sale at your local music dealer. Many fine older charts can actually have a list price of $5 or $10 and though the music might not be acceptable for concert purposes, it may be perfect for sight reading!

TRAINING METHODS TO HELP TEACH JAZZ ENSEMBLE CONCEPTS

There are some fine jazz band training methods and materials that are available and designed for the heterogeneous class. They provide valuable instruction on the fundamentals of jazz in a systematic and comprehensive manner without spending too much time on unnecessary details. These methods have conductor's manuals which provide additional guidelines for the director. General areas of instruction include interpretation, phrasing, dynamics, rhythm patterns, improvisation, arranging, sight reading, and typical concepts. Listed below are training band materials.

Elementary and Junior High School Levels

Take One Improvisation
Betton, M., & C. Peters
Kjos Music

Jazz, Rock & Harmony
Cacavas, J., J. Ployar,
  & F. Weber
Belwin/Mills

The Sound of Jazz
Feldsetin, S., & C. Strommen
Alfred Music

*The Elementary Stage Band Book
  I & II*
Sebesky, G.
Studio P/R

The Sound of Rock
Feldstein, S., & J. Scianni
Alfred Music

Junior and Senior High School Levels

For Swingers Only
Baker, D.
Pro Art

*A Guide to Jazz Phrasing &
  Interpretation*
LaPorta, J.
Berklee Press

The Time Revolution
Levy, H.
Creative World

Modern Stage Band Techniques
Hall, Dr. M. E.
Southern Music

Developing the School Jazz Ensemble
LaPorta, J.
Berklee Press

Contemporary Concepts for Stage Band
Eisenhower, W.
Bourne Publishers

6

How to Successfully Put Together a Concert

SELECTING APPROPRIATE JAZZ ENSEMBLE CHARTS

Selecting appropriate music for the band is one of the most essential areas of concern in the jazz band program. The music is "where it's at": the essence of the jazz program is based on the music itself. Therefore, informed and intelligent choice of music is a big key to the success of your program. Of further concern, of course, is the economic factor—no one can afford to purchase music that doesn't work for the group.

It is imperative that the strengths and weaknesses of the band be determined *before* examining music for the jazz ensemble. Consider the following questions in analyzing your band's capabilities:

- What is the practical range of each player in your band (particularly lead brass players)?
- What are the limitations of each section in terms of technique, rhythm, range, blend, intonation, articulation, etc.?
- Can the rhythm section play in different musical styles (shuffle, rock, swing, bebop, Latin, etc.) with the appropriate feel?
- Can all sections contribute to the proper balance in a tutti section and at all dynamic levels?
- Which instruments can the members of the sax section double and at what level of proficiency (beginning, intermediate, or advanced)?
- What is the endurance of the band (particularly brass players)?
- How well does the band hold tempos within different styles?

- Which players can handle improvised solos?
- Is the band solo- or ensemble-oriented (which feature is their "strong suit")?
- Are there extra players available to cover additional parts if they are called for?

Once you have a better understanding of the band's strengths and weaknesses, you will be able to analyze unfamiliar charts more thoroughly for the "best match." If a score only features a condensed version, take the time to examine the individual parts. Full scores are most useful but not always available. The best music is not only playable, it also shows off the best qualities of your group. Consider the following guidelines when examining charts for different levels of instruction and performance.

Beginning and Intermediate
(Elementary, Junior and Senior High Schools)

- No woodwind doublings
- Limited or modest range for all instruments (extreme ranges should be avoided, lead trumpet should top at concert F or G^b)
- Simple and recurring rhythm patterns through most of the chart
- Variable instrumentation: allows from a 10- or 11-piece jazz group up to a full jazz ensemble or concert band
- Inclusion of standardized jazz articulations
- Flexibility in the length and number of solos (optional sections may be opened up for solos)
- Scales and/or chords should be notated for all chord symbols in any improvised section
- Lots of ensemble work to keep everybody active and alert
- Written-out solos should be included whenever possible
- Stereo recordings should be available from the publisher
- Rehearsal instructions should be included with the chart
- Full score and a condensed score should be available
- Optional parts should include tuba, vibes, french horn, flute, percussion, and strings
- The quality of the manuscript should be clearly legible, not cramped, and easy for young students to interpret
- Transcribed solos (from recordings) should be provided

- Completely voiced piano, guitar, and bass parts should include chord symbols and a written part; the drum part should be written out rather than just slashes

Advanced (High School and Up)

- Should offer woodwind doubling opportunities
- Should include an expanded range for all instruments (lead trumpets move beyond high C) with noticeable range demands given to the inside trumpet and trombone parts
- There will be a much wider variety of rhythm patterns and time signatures encountered, with great emphasis on complexity
- Open improvisation sections are provided for maximum flexibility within the group
- Instrumentation is often much more exotic with string players, a solo vocalist and/or vocal jazz group featured

Advanced charts usually have everything offered in elementary and intermediate charts but with additional features. In some instances, advanced charts will eliminate those features that might be deemed as helpful but unnecessary for a professional-level chart (that is, written-out solos, drum parts, full voicings for rhythm section players, etc., are often not included).

Table 6-1 indicates the grading systems utilized by four main resources useful when selecting music. Since their criteria do not match, their gradings do not coincide; but with this chart, you can see how they compare.

ADJUSTING THE ARRANGEMENTS TO IMPROVE YOUR JAZZ ENSEMBLE

Often, you will encounter music that seems well suited to your group but upon closer examination, you find there are some minor problems. Rather than putting the chart aside, there are often remedial steps that you can exercise to repair the problem. The following suggestions may be used to adapt arrangements to your group.

Problem: Ranges of the trumpets and trombones are too high. The inner parts are also too demanding. The overall sound of the section is strained and forced.

Solution: Usually, the high school lead trumpet player can comfortably play to a high C or D. Since many of the arrangements take the lead player well above this point alternatives are:

TABLE 6-1. PROFESSIONAL GRADING SYSTEMS

NAJE	INSTRUMENTALIST	PHANTOM MUSIC	KENDOR MUSIC
I & II—Elementary or easy	I—Mainly for first year groups. II—For those who are definitely beyond beginning stage.	I—Easy: play at junior high level. II—Medium easy: better jr. high & inexperienced H.S.	I—Very Easy II—Easy
III & IV—Intermediate or Medium Difficult	III—For those who have acquired some technique. IV—For more advanced instrumentalists.	Intermediate III—Playable by average high schools & inexperienced colleges. IV—For the above-average group.	III—Medium Easy IV—Medium
V—Advanced or Difficult VI—Very Difficult	V—Mostly for college players.	V—Difficult For experienced college groups.	V—Medium Difficult
VII—Professional	VI—For the skilled professional.		VI—Difficult

• Rescore the entire section to unison (see Figure 6-1). Cut out lines of manuscript paper, recopy the lines and tape them over the existing part. Since the lead part in most cases is the main line, drop it one octave and assign all parts to this line. Do not simply drop all written parts one octave —this will create a muddy texture and may interfere with other parts in the ensemble. Also, the lead player may be able to rest during this unison section and save his or her chops for later demands.

• Most arrangements are scored for four trumpets. Check the voicing of the section. If the fourth part is an independent part, write a fifth part which is written as the first part only down one octave. This will help reinforce the lead part.

• If an electronic synthesizer is available, synthesize a brass-like sound and double it in the same octave as the trumpet. This should not be allowed to overpower the sound of the lead player.

• Add a piccolo (or flute) to essential lead lines. Assign two or three players on the part at the maximum. *Use this technique sparingly.*

FIGURE 6-1

Problem: The saxophone parts are too demanding. The passages contain too many notes and cannot be played with ease.

Solution: Examine the overall arrangement. Many times the arranger will add embellishments to the melody when scoring it for the saxes. If this is true, simplify the parts as they are found in other sections of the arrangement (see Figure 6-2). Be certain you retain the overall style of the section.

FIGURE 6-2

Problem: The bass player can't get the bass line out convincingly.

Solution: Give essential bass lines to the baritone sax and/or 4th or bass trombone. The baritone sax can read the bass part by changing the bass clef to treble clef (see Figure 6-3), raising the key signature up a major sixth (add 3#s), and altering any accidentals.

FIGURE 6-3

- Double the bass part in the piano or synthesizer.

- Add a tuba to the group and write the original bass part down one octave.

Problem: The chord changes are too difficult for the guitar player due to altered note chords or non-major, minor, and diminished triads and seventh chords.

Solution: Rename intricate chord symbols. As long as the bass part supplies the fundamental, the guitar player can concentrate on the upper extensions of the chord structure.

- Table 6-2 is designed to assist the young player in understanding and performing chord symbols. Encourage the player to learn all chords and their variations as soon as possible.

Problem: Guitar parts are frequently a duplicated piano part with many more chord changes per measure than actually makes sense for the guitar. The result is a very cluttered sound and often the guitarist struggles to keep up.

Solution: Streamline the complicated series of chords that change every beat to a more appropriate progression. Eliminate the passing chords to retain the original harmonic movement of the chord progression while at the same time reducing the awkward fingering patterns created by the original (see Figure 6-4).

FIGURE 6-4

TABLE 6-2. CHORD SYMBOLS

WRITTEN	PLAYED
E^b/B^b	This symbol stands for an E^b triad over a B^b bass. The guitar player can simply sound an E^b triad if the bass is supplying the B^b.
C MA 9 C Major 9 C MAJ 9	Since this chord is spelled C,E,G,B,D, a guitar player can sound an E minor 7th chord over the C in the bass.
C minor 9 C mi 9 C – 9	The chord is spelled C, E^b,G,B^b, D. The guitar player can play an E^b Major 7th chord over the C in the bass.
C mi 7^{b}5 C ½dim 7	This chord is spelled C,E^b,G^b,B^b. The guitar player can play an E^b minor triad over the C in the bass.
C 7#9	This chord is spelled C,E,G,B^b,D# (E^b). Depending on the scoring of the horn parts, the guitar could play a plain C7 or an E^b triad over the C in the bass.

Problem: Drum parts are exceptionally intricate. The drummer has trouble reading and playing the written part.

- There are three main types of drum parts. The first supplies time slashes and important brass and ensemble figures that are cued along the top of the staff (see Figure 6-5).

FIGURE 6-5

- The second, mostly found in older arrangements, has the part written in concert band format (see Figure 6-6).

FIGURE 6-6

- The third, and most common in today's school arrangements, has fills and figures written into the drum part (see Figure 6-7).

FIGURE 6-7

Solution: The young drummer should first become comfortable with keeping time throughout the arrangement. Supply him or her with the basic outline of the rhythm pattern (see Figure 6-8). Next, write in the main brass and ensemble figures. The first trumpet part can be helpful at this stage. Finally, refer to the original part for reference to solo fills, accents, etc. Remember, the function of the drum set is to: (1) keep time; (2) accent important figures and rhythm patterns; and (3) supply embellishments such as solo fills and kicks.

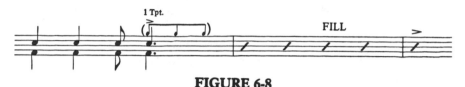

FIGURE 6-8

Problem: The pianist cannot understand the chord symbols written out in the part. The piano part only supplies time slashes and chord symbols.

Solution: Every young guitar and piano player should own a copy of *Standardized Chord Symbol Notation* by Clinton Roemer and Carl Brandt. This book contains many of the most common forms of chords and their spellings.

- Before rehearsing a chart, voice the chord changes at the beginning of each measure (see Figure 6-9). Do not merely voice the chords in block form—try to voice them in a keyboard-like manner. This technique should not be used as a crutch. Encourage the piano player to memorize these symbols and be able to voice them at sight.

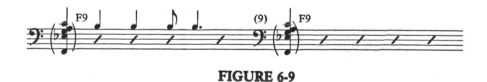

FIGURE 6-9

- Another helpful technique is to write in rhythmic patterns across the top of the staff. Use the basic drum pattern, with brass and ensemble figures for reference (see Figure 6-10).

FIGURE 6-10

By applying many of the above techniques, some of the charts that seem beyond your group can be modified to meet your ensemble's ability. This will not only help the sound of the arrangement but allow players to perform without danger of overextending themselves. Careful consideration of your students' abilities can greatly assist them to achieve steady and accurate progress.

> **NOTE:** Making arrangements of a piece of music is an exclusive right of the copyright owner, but under the Music Guidelines amplifying the *Fair Use* section of the law, the following is conceived to be a reasonable exception:
>
> "Printed copies which have been purchased may be edited or simplfied provided that the fundamental character of the work is not distorted . . ." From *The United States Copyright Law: A Guide for Music Educators.* National Publisher's Association, Inc., 110 E. 59th Street, New York, NY.

PUTTING TOGETHER THE CONCERT PROGRAM

Details! Details! Details! That's what preparing a successful concert is all about. If the musical responsibilities (selection, preparation, and problem solving) weren't enough, the organization and business aspects of the concert will tax the energy of the most experienced teacher. In addition to the musical considerations, a successful concert needs planning, responsibility and decision concerning publicity, ticket sales, programs, lighting, recording, sound amplification, physical setup, ushers, clean-up, etc. Presenting a successful concert will be dealt with in this chapter by focusing on: (1) musical considerations, (2) equipment management and considerations, and (3) master-calendar considerations.

Even before the school year begins, develop a preplanning strategy.

- Choose concert and dress rehearsal dates with ample rehearsal time provided. Make certain the concert site has no conflicts near the time!

- Let all participating members of the group and technicians know about the date AS EARLY AS POSSIBLE to make certain there are no conflicts. It is best to print the information at the beginning of the school year and hand it out to students and parents.

- Follow the musical, equipment, and calendar preparations outlined in this chapter.

Because the jazz ensemble often serves as a vehicle for school and community public relations, directors should carefully consider the musical tastes of each individual audience. Every concert should represent a balance between those pieces that are challenging to the group and perhaps not totally audience-oriented and those pieces that are pure pleasure and entertainment for the audience. Each concert has its own distinct personality—there is a great difference between a student assembly, a P.T.A. presentation, a performance for senior citizens, and a jazz festival presentation. There are four steps to programming that need your attention: (1) evaluating the audience, (2) concert format, (3) pacing, and (4) the lasting impression.

Assessing the Audience

In order to best evaluate your audience, you need to answer the classic journalist's questions concerning your anticipated performance: Who? When? Where? Why?

WHO will you perform for? How old will the members of the audience be? What do you think they already know about jazz? Are they paying to see your group or are you coming to them?

WHEN will you perform for your audience? Will it be in the morning? Will your performance be limited in duration? Will you perform during the weekend when there is a difference about time?

WHERE will you perform the concert? Will you be playing in a regular concert hall or will it be in a gymnasium? Will the place you are going to play be crowded or spacious? Will you be playing outdoors? Will the seats be soft or hard and uncomfortable? Will the acoustics be "alive" or will they be dull?

WHY will you perform? Are you performing for a group of youngsters who have had little or no exposure to jazz so that you will be providing an educational activity? Are you playing for a group of people while they are eating or walking past?

You must answer each of these questions and analyze your answers in order to be fully prepared for any specific performance. You should gear your presentation to the time, place, event, and people you will have for an audience. Above all, the image of your jazz ensemble should never be restricted to one type of program. It is important to be flexible and creative when choosing music for your concert. In addition to the charts that might have the most immediate appeal to the audience, occasionally slip in some chart that might be outside the audience's previous music experience, but remember: *add new music like a very strong spice and don't put in too much!*

Deciding the Concert Format and Length

Two factors that will contribute most to your success in concerts are: (1) the use of soloists, and (2) the length of the concert. Opening up solo sections will help break up the big-band "sheet of sound" as well as provide for visual and aural action around the band stand. Solos help promote and generate enthusiasm as well as provide for a variety of effects. Bill Watrous and his band is a good example of a roaring jazz ensemble that intermingles with many solo/combo performance effects. Watrous adds a whole new dimension to his group with the variety of soloists, which adds interest.

No matter how well a band plays, most people have a saturation point in terms of listening fatigue and patience. Audiences generally prefer concerts to last just under one hour without intermission or about 1½ hours if there is an intermission. In addition, keep your group's stamina in mind when deciding concert length.

A successful performance should have a sense of momentum all its own and a good measurement takes place whenever someone from the audience comments that, "Your concert should have lasted longer," or "You should have played more music." Be sure to invite these persons back to your next performance and keep the thought "Always leave 'em wanting more!" as a reminder that you have chosen the correct length.

An informal atmosphere is generally the rule for jazz ensemble concerts. Programs are often unnecessary and the director usually can announce the concert. Audience participation should be encouraged by a brief comment early in the performance regarding jazz performance etiquette (applauding for soloists during the piece immediately after the performance is considered appropriate). If you announce the concert, take a moment between each piece to indicate some tidbit about the composition, arrangement, composer, etc. This not only helps the audience gain a perspective on the music but allows time for the ensemble to rest embouchures and get up the next piece.

Pacing: How to Play to the Audience

Pacing a concert should be approached from two directions: (1) don't tax your brass players with too many demanding charts at any point of the concert, and (2) provide an order of performance for your audience that is appealing. Indicated below are a few considerations for helping you select the order of your concert.

- OPENER. You should choose a piece that is: (1) not too long, (2) not too difficult, (3) a solid ensemble-oriented piece, and (4) well rehearsed. If your opener doesn't catch the audience's attention or is shaky, you and your audience are off to a poor start.

- MAIN PRESENTATION. Consider a variety of selections using tempi, dynamics, and style to achieve contrasts. Use balance and try to choose music from different backgrounds and styles. Mix music from different time periods. Try to design the choice of your music so that the momentum starts high, eases off some, then drives towards a smashing finish. The contour of such a presentation might look like Figure 6-11:

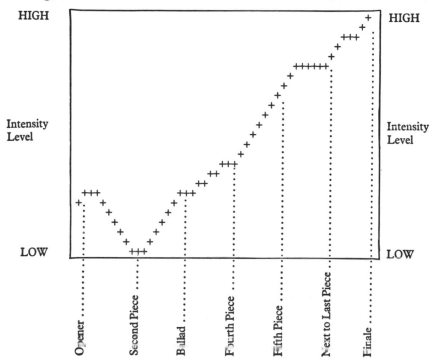

FIGURE 6-11. PERFORMANCE CONTOUR

- BALLADS. Don't put a ballad too far into the program since some ballads tax brass player's chops as much as a heavy chart! While a ballad has a strong appeal for the over-30 age group in your audience, there are many ballads that can work just as effectively for the younger members of your audience.

- ENDINGS. This is the piece of music you use to make a lasting impression. It should be exciting, well rehearsed, and end with a big ending. It should be the most dramatic piece of the concert.

Too many concerts begin loud and remain that way until the very end. *A successful concert will take advantage of contrast.* Also, avoid using more than two pieces by the same group (Basie, Kenton, Herman, Ferguson, etc.) on the same concert. Feature one section for each concert alone with just the rhythm section.

Finally, follow the old saying "When in doubt, leave it out!" concerning the length or number of pieces for a performance. If you design your concert well, you will pull your audience along with you to a glorious ending without overextending your players. If you choose to do an encore, make it brief and complementary to the rest of your program.

Creating a Lasting Impression

Just like it's silly to always reinvent the wheel, it is silly when you must always reinvent your audience. For any public performance, create a performance that has crowd appeal and interest and then be sure to invite your audience back for your next performance. In fact, ask them to invite someone new if they enjoyed themselves.

Considerations for Sound Reinforcement

Good sound reinforcement can add clarity, power, and enjoyment for the audience to a performance. Over-amplification can just as easily destroy an otherwise fine performance. Make certain that you have the opportunity to work with any sound system prior to any performance so that you are familiar with the room and equipment.

The goal of sound reinforcement should be to retain the acoustical properties of the group so that it sounds natural. Although the general guidelines for a sound system are indicated in Chapter 4, here are a few simple rules to help the audience enjoy the performance.

- Whenever possible, use omnidirectional microphones.
- If you mike the saxes, use three mikes.
- When miking the saxes, place the mike at the first open tone hole rather than at the bell.
- Don't mike the brass section.
- Mike the acoustic piano.
- Use one solo mike at the front of the band on the rhythm section side.
- If you use two solo mikes, the second should be on the rhythm section side near the trombones.
- Solo mikes should have an on-off switch.
- If you use a monitor system, it should only be loud enough for the band to hear soloists.
- Observe the three-to-one rule: Microphones must be separated three times the distance from each other as they are from each performer.

Don't Forget Music Stands!

Regardless of whether the band sits or stands with or without risers, the wind players are never to play directly into their music stand. When using the standard black music stands, have the saxes keep them as low as possible. Brass players should turn the top of the stand so it is almost horizontal to the ground. All brass players should play with their bells above the stand. Have the players put their folders aside and keep only the music that is to be played on the stand. Continue to remind your players to get their horns out of the stand and to play to the audience.

DEVELOPING THE MASTER CALENDAR

Even if all aspects of a concert are well thought out, there still needs to be a timetable established with all details organized and delegated. Listed in Figures 6-12A, B, C, and D is a detailed outline for organizing and promoting a concert. It can be adapted to a variety of public performances: an evening concert, a school assembly program, a clinic/concert with a guest artist, traveling to a concert, or any similar activity.

First, eliminate any items that are not appropriate for a specific activity. You'll probably be able to add or replace a few items of your own that will better suit your particular needs once you get the hang of the master calendar. The real benefit of such a calendar is that it allows you to delegate responsibility and anticipate difficulties in advance. Before using the calendar, meet with your band officers, jazz ensemble members, parents' booster club, etc. to communicate your needs and identify who will be performing which duties.

PREPARING FOR A JAZZ FESTIVAL

Preparing for a jazz festival is like preparing for a very intensive successful concert—usually the time of performance is much shorter and adjudicators are usually much more critical than your normal audience.

Since you have a time limitation for most festivals, you must distill the best from your normal concert setting. You will still need an effective opener. The opener should be everything an opener for any concert is but magnified. For a festival, all your music must be the very best and representative of its kind. Your middle piece (most festivals feature the use of three pieces) should be a distinctive contrast, so save your very best for last. Everything must be rehearsed until it is TIGHT and you are totally satisfied. Exercise the most discriminating selection process for the pieces you

CALENDAR CHECKLIST
SIX WEEKS BEFORE CONCERT

Activity	Done	Person in Charge

CONCERT

Select concert dress rehearsal date	☐	
Select numbers	☐	
Select special features	☐	
First rehearsal	☐	

TICKETS

Printer	☐	_____
Amount/cost	☐	
Color	☐	
Copy	☐	_____
Admission price	☐	
Delivery date	☐	
Numbered tickets	☐	

PROGRAMS

Printer	☐	_____
Number	☐	
Color, stock, ink	☐	
Copy	☐	_____
Cover design	☐	_____
Amount/cost	☐	
Acknowledgments	☐	_____
Ads	☐	_____
Delivery date	☐	

FIGURE 6-12A

MISCELLANEOUS

	Done	Person in Charge
Special transportation	☐	
Auditorium requested	☐	_____
Ushers	☐	_____
Sound crew	☐	_____
Lighting crew	☐	_____
Special rentals	☐	_____

CALENDAR CHECKLIST
FOUR WEEKS BEFORE CONCERT

Activity	Done	Person in Charge

PUBLICITY

	Done	Person in Charge
Posters	☐	_____
Background news releases to:		_____
TV	☐	
Radio	☐	
Newspapers	☐	
Pictures	☐	

CONCERT COMMITTEE

	Done	Person in Charge
Ticket takers	☐	_____
Ushers	☐	_____
Stage crew	☐	_____
Clean-up committee	☐	_____
Ticket sales	☐	_____

FIGURE 6-12B

CALENDAR CHECKLIST
TWO WEEKS BEFORE CONCERT

Activity	Done
Schedule piano tuning	☐
Mail complimentary tickets	☐
Distribute tickets	☐
Distribute posters	☐
Send publicity pictures	☐
Send news releases to:	
TV	☐
Radio	☐
Newspapers	☐

ARRANGE DETAILS

P.A. system	☐
Dressing rooms	☐
Warm-up rooms	☐
Room security	☐
Chair placement	☐
Lighting effects	☐
Backdrops	☐
Curtain cues	☐
Tape recording	☐
Video recording	☐

FIGURE 6-12C

CALENDAR CHECKLIST
JUST BEFORE CONCERT

Activity	Done
Send invitation letter to:	
Faculty	☐
District music teachers	☐
Administrators	☐
Pick up programs	☐
Check ticket sales	☐
Arrange dress rehearsal	☐
Time _____	
Place _____	
Send final news releases	☐
Use school intercom announcements for concert information	☐
Check with custodian	☐
Check assessory equipment:	
cords, mutes, stands	☐
Make certain everything is ready	☐

FIGURE 6-12D

will use in a festival since the choice of music is almost as important as the way the group performs it. Try to follow these simple guidelines:

- Try to avoid the use of "this year's most popular piece." No adjudicator enjoys encountering six versions of the same chart the same day at the same festival.

- Be judicious with your choice of soloists. Do not feature the same person for all solos, but be careful to select those soloists who will provide the most polished performances.

- Choose appropriate music according to the ability of your group. Nothing is more of a turn-off to adjudicators than hearing a group try to perform something that is obviously too difficult or too easy for the group.

- Familiarize yourself with the adjudication form in advance so that you will know what is expected and stressed about your group's performance.

Establish some goals and objectives for your group long before you go to the festival. These objectives are:

1. Communicate with the audience.
2. Generate enthusiasm during the performance.
3. Play as well as you know you can.
4. Feel good about the performance.

The objectives should NOT be to:

1. Win no matter what.
2. Get the first place trophy.

There are many types of "winning" and the wise director prepares the group for a festival to "win" by achieving the goals and objectives decided by the group. The band that leaves a festival feeling good about their performance and, more important, about themselves, is more a winner than the group that will only be happy by holding a trophy.

Applied Jazz Techniques: Developing Your Jazz Sections

The Sax Section

Each instrument of the jazz band has concepts and techniques unique to it. The understanding of these concepts and techniques will raise the level of musicianship for that particular section.

If players within the sax section don't have a concept of how they want to sound, that section as a unit will have an unsatisfactory sound. Having to contend with a battery of eight to ten brass players will only serve to exaggerate this problem.

THE BASICS OF JAZZ SAXOPHONE PLAYING

Tone Production Factors

Fundamentally, saxophone tone is produced by a column of air that vibrates the reed. The more reed that vibrates and the more air causing this vibration, the bigger and fuller the sax tone. A common misconception concerning sax tone is that a "big" sound is a loud sound. Rather, a big sound is one that has a direct, compact core (somewhat like a beam of light) rather than a spreading, conical dispersion. It also has a resonance with a slight edge in the color. The sound to be avoided would be either a weak, thin, or pinched type of sound, or the opposite, a loud, honking sound. Table 7-1 shows some of the common terms and definitions that can help in a diagnosis of the sax section's tonal quality.

Term	Description
CORE	This refers to a tonal center. Core is an ingredient of resonance that is necessary for stability of intonation and a center to the tone.
RESONANCE	Resonance is the generating or ringing quality of sound created by good breath support and correct embouchure control through the mouthpiece, the reed, and the instrument. It gives the tone its projection without the need for great volume.
INTENSITY	The energy of the sound produced is called intensity. It is closely related to resonance in that proper breath support and embouchure production are essential ingredients.
EDGE	Edge is the prominence of higher partials in the tone that enhances tone projection (there is often a slight hint of ''buzz'' to the sound). A certain amount of edge in a tone is desirable and can be influenced by mouthpiece/reed combinations.
COLOR	This describes the tone in terms of darkness or brightness (highlighting low or high overtones). A combination of both types is necessary in giving tone both body (low partials) and projection (high partials).

TABLE 7-1. COMPONENTS OF SAXOPHONE TONE

The saxophone is an instrument of great flexibility with its tone produced and influenced by external and internal factors. External factors include characteristics of each instrument: the type of finish, the thickness and quality of pads, the mouthpiece, and reed types. These factors were identified in Chapter 4. Internal factors can be identified as: embouchure, breathing and breath support, the oral cavity, the throat, and tonal concepts and tastes of the individual player.

If the mouthpiece/reed combination works right, a saxophonist should be able to play an octave scale with the mouthpiece and reed alone. In order to develop a full, vibrant sound, a student should start with a medium-faced mouthpiece (see Chapter 4). Projection requires a fairly stout reed (medium to hard) along with fast air velocity. The result is something the student has to blow against and can put more into the horn without closing down the reed. Resistance is particularly necessary in the upper register. As a student develops strong "chops," it will become obvious that harder reeds are not as strong as they once were. That would be the time for the student to look into getting a wider-opening mouthpiece. Often, musicians who use a wider facing can then select a lower-strength reed.

The inner chamber of the mouthpiece is another consideration. Medium-sized inner chambers are better than large, round, open chambers. Shallow chambers give a bright sound while large chambers produce a darker, symphonic sound. The medium chamber can give a good combination of high and low overtones, which is a good compromise. In summary, a combination of relatively stiff reed on a medium-faced mouthpiece that has a medium or smaller inner chamber should give a student the proper combination he or she needs to play with a good sound in the section.

The embouchure refers to all those physical elements and positions of the mouth and lips that cover the mouthpiece and reed so that no air escapes except through the mouthpiece when playing. The embouchure includes teeth, tongue, jaw, lips, and facial muscles. The setting for the sax embouchure is different from that of the clarinet. Clarinet players often transfer their embouchure to the sax as small and pinched due to the excessive pressure being applied and the small amount of reed that is capable of vibrating, since so little mouthpiece is actually in the mouth.

There are three basic areas where the reed is placed inside the mouth (see Figure 7-1): Area 2 is correct most of the time when 2/5th's of the playing surface of the mouthpiece and reed are actually in the mouth. Area 1 is for playing sub-tone effects, achieved by pulling part of the mouthpiece out and raising the lower jaw. Area 3 is for playing loud, funky sounds. Generally, students do not put enough mouthpiece in their mouths. Have your students experiment by putting more of the mouthpiece into their mouth to the point where the sound cracks and squeaks, that is, the point where the student has too much mouthpiece in the mouth, but only then.

To achieve the best tone quality, the saxophone uses the "fat lip" theory (as opposed to the "thin lip" used for clarinet). In the fat lip theory, the lower lip is turned out slightly, which results in several improvements in the tone quality. By rolling the lip outward instead of over the lower teeth (as in the thin lip method), (1) tension is reduced on throat muscles, (2) there is more maneuverability by being able to slide from Area 2 to 1 or 3 on the reed easily, (3) and there's less chance of cutting your lower lip since

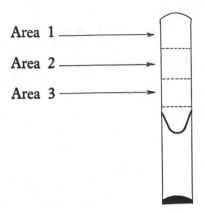

Area 1

Area 2

Area 3

FIGURE 7-1. REED AREAS FOR PLACEMENT

there's more cushion between the reed and teeth. This more relaxed position of the embouchure will allow more "lows" in the sound.

The oral cavity and throat are like a second mouthpiece. Producing a tone on the sax actually involves the use of two mouthpieces. "Mouthpiece" indicates the use of an opening and closing mechanism. In this case, the throat becomes the second mouthpiece, so equal emphasis should be placed on the throat, lips, and mouthpiece. Have your students sing some intervals of a perfect 4th or 5th and check the action of movement in the throat where the physical action of producing tones takes place. Both the throat and oral cavity need to be as open as possible. As indicated above, a fat lower lip will help to loosen the throat. This openness permits the air to travel freely from the lungs with sufficient pressure to make the reed vibrate and sustain the tone. A general rule for sax is: "The higher you play (especially on alto or soprano), the more critical it is to have a good open throat position." In addition, the oral cavity also acts as a resonating chamber.

Excessive shoulder movement, breathing through the nose, continual lack of air, and intonation that is drained by the phrase length, are all signs that the player is breathing improperly. Proper breathing involves the diaphragm (the large muscle that separates the lungs and organs), which pushes the air out and into the instrument. If your students are not breathing properly, establish breathing exercises as part of your regular warm-up program. One such exercise is described here.

1. Have your students stand (without their instruments), with their legs slightly spaced, and weight distributed equally and comfortably.

2. Place their hands on the area most students will consider their stomach (their diaphragm).

3. Have the students quickly exhale and clean out their breath completely.

4. Slowly and continuously have them inhale for five seconds, always trying to expand the area under their hands. (As they get better at this, increase the amount of time.)

5. Hold that air without any movement for five seconds. (Again, the amount of time can be extended with practice.)

6. Gradually and slowly, exhale for the count of five. (This will be especially difficult for some students since they will exhale too fast. One of the objects of this exercise is to develop control.)

7. Have the students place their hands on their waist with their fingers towards the back and do the exercise again. This time, they should try to expand in the area under their hands.

The elusive area of tonal quality comes from within the player him- or herself. Nobody can force another person to like or emulate another player. Nevertheless, your role should be to provide each player with the opportunity and incentive to listen to numerous fine musicians. That listening should take place with both recordings and live performances since there is a dramatic difference. Imitation is one of the essential activities young saxophonists should be developing.

In addition, stress to sax students that another way of developing a tonal concept is to listen to themselves. Long tones are an essential way of improving sound since the sound can be closely examined. The exercise in Figure 7-2 is used by flutist Moyse de la Sonante. Practice should include examples with and without vibrato and concentrating on matching the sound quality of each note to its preceding note. Repeat the sequence throughout the range of the instrument. Five minutes each day will allow your students to become more aware of the tone quality they are producing. Be sure that the exercise is taken slowly!

FIGURE 7-2

The use of vibrato in the jazz band sax section is one of those touchy subjects that is full of controversy since nobody seems able to agree. Usually, the section is expected to match the vibrato of the lead alto. Duke Ellington developed the concept of "harmonized unison" when each player used his own wide vibrato on unison lines. In a Basic-type swing chart, the vibrato is smaller and faster. This is closer to a "classical" vibrato in that it is continuous. Many jazz groups today (Ferguson, Herman, Rich, etc.) will start the tone straight and then add vibrato in a 50%–50% straight tone-vibrato ratio. No vibrato, which is indicated in the music as "N.V." or dead tone, implies a slight vibrato for warmth in the tone. It is often used when backing up a brass solo or brass soli.

Vibrato can be produced in a number of ways: diaphragm contractions, throat contractions, or movement of the jaw. Jaw movement is the most commonly used today. Dropping the jaw slightly (not back and forth) while keeping the embouchure pressure steady will produce a drop in pitch. Thus, the continuous process of dropping the jaw will cause the pitch to regularly drop below pitch and return to the proper pitch level. Figure 7-3 shows how correct and incorrect vibrato would look if diagrammed.

A correct vibrato would be represented like this where the vibrato starts at the note and then drops below it:

An incorrect or sharp vibrato would look something like this:

FIGURE 7-3. VIBRATO DIAGRAM

First attempts at teaching vibrato should be slow and exaggerated, sounding like a "sick" lawn mower. Once evenness is achieved, the vibrato can be accelerated. Avoid the "nanny goat" vibrato, that is, fast and narrow. Variation in the size of the vibrato can be manipulated with the use of different syllables. A "wah" or "yah" will tend to produce a large, open-sounding vibrato, while a "wee" will tend to produce a smaller, more closed vibrato. The following brief suggestions should be considered when dealing with vibrato:

- In fast passages, don't use vibrato.
- Always maintain sufficient embouchure pressure while using vibrato.

- Don't use vibrato during unison lines unless actually called for.
- When using a vibrato for a sustained note, make certain the vibrato doesn't end before the note.
- Higher notes can have a faster vibrato than lower notes.

Towards Good Sax Intonation

Sax sections are often notoriously out of tune, particularly during unison lines. Here are several common reasons:

- the use of vibrato *during tuning*
- dramatic embouchure differences among players
- improper breath support coupled with a lack of focus in the tone
- improper reed (too hard or soft) for the mouthpiece
- poor concept on the part of section members
- the mouthpiece
- the instrument is way out of tune on some notes

To check intonation trouble spots, try ascending and descending intervals using a strobe tuner in all registers. Generally, the upper register of the saxophone is built sharp and the lower is built flat.

Saxophone Articulation Techniques

When a saxophonist tongues, the tongue leaves the reed about ⅛th of an inch below the tip of the tongue. If the tongue touches below that point, it will tend to deaden the vibrations. The tongue should begin from a natural position in the bottom of the mouth. If it is pressed down into the mouth cavity, there will be too much space created with no resistance for the air coming from the windpipe into the mouthpiece. If the tongue is pressed too far up or down, it will create muscular tension in the throat muscles.

Most of the time, the sax section should employ a legato or moderately soft style of tonguing. The marcato (heavy) tongue should be reserved for use with accents. A major difference in tonguing between jazz and other styles is that a sustained softer tongue is used more frequently in jazz.

Two kinds of specialized tonguing are commonly found in jazz. These include the half-tongue and breath articulation. The half-tongue is a swing articulation produced by a narrowing or partial closing of the mouth cavity by the back of the tongue and slightly stopping the reed with the tongue, as in the syllable "um." This produces an articulation that is purposely not clear. Its most common use is for scale-wise or arpeggiated passages of consecutive eighth notes. In standard legato articulation (du, du), a stiff—rather than swing—feeling would result. Breath articulation is produced by a push or "huff" from the diaphragm with no tongue action at all. Frequent application is found in a sustained background figure for a brass solo.

Ghosting is an effect of fingering a note in a melodic line and half blowing it so that what comes out is not the true pitch, but rather a deadened tone without any definite pitch. This usually occurs in a pattern of eighth notes. The ghosted note still provides a rhythmic kick to the phrase even if its pitch and sound quality are indefinite because of its forward-motion feeling. When performing a phrase with ghosted notes, the student should think of the non-ghosted notes as the melodic line while the ghosted notes provide a subtle sense of interspersed silence. An example of ghosting is provided in Figure 7-4.

FIGURE 7-4

Special Baritone Sax Techniques

Your baritone sax player needs to be an extroverted player who isn't afraid to project forcefully and play at full volume while at the same time be willing to accept the position of a section person who must conform to the lead alto. The baritone player functions on several levels in a jazz ensemble.

- As the bottom voice in a sax section, the baritone sax follows the lead of the alto sax player.
- In a tutti passage that involves the entire band, the baritone follows the lead trumpet player.
- The baritone part is often written into trombone section voicings where the player must then think like a trombone player and match what is happening in that section.
- Sometimes, the baritone is expected to double the bass part and then concentrate on hearing the bass to match the sound.

To balance properly with the sax section, the baritone player must have a firm command of low register notes. Because the baritone often doubles an octave lower with the lead alto, it is necessary to pay particular attention to intonation. Because the instrument is so large, leaks are much more likely to happen. The high register will tend to thin out, but an open throat will help produce a fuller tone.

Encourage your baritone player to listen to some of the fine baritone sax players in jazz. Pay particular attention to Harry Carney (Duke Ellington), Pepper Adams (Thad Jones/Mel Lewis), Jack Nimtz, Bobby Millitello, and Bruce Johnstone (Maynard Ferguson), for big band playing, and Gerry Mulligan for solo and combo work.

Woodwind Doubling:
Concepts and Considerations

In today's professional music market, it is necessary for the woodwind musician to be a proficient doubler. A doubler is especially important in woodwind sections of the jazz ensemble. Many high school- and college-level jazz charts feature woodwind doublings written in the parts. In the school jazz program where participation becomes competitive, woodwind doubling can quickly become an important criterion for selection in the group.

The woodwind student can become a proficient doubler through the study of any of the woodwind instruments from a serious perspective. Each instrument should be approached like it is the student's major instrument, with one instrument mastered at a time. As each new instrument is mastered, certain techniques will be transferrable, but high standards of tone, intonation, technique, flexibility, and so on, should be maintained throughout. The student learning to double should not actually perform on the new instrument too early; basic fundamentals should be mastered, or the student will acquire a tendency towards bad habits.

Students should be encouraged to use the best possible quality instruments and equipment. If the instrument or equipment (mouthpiece, reeds, etc.) is inferior, the player will be handicapped and limited. Whereas this principle is generally taken for granted in the instance of a primary instrument, it is often overlooked when it comes to the doubled instrument.

Most woodwind doublers start with the clarinet or saxophone, progress to the flute, and finally master the double reeds. Although each of the saxes is somewhat distinctive, good saxophone players are usually adept at all of the saxophones. Whereas sax and clarinet are somewhat similar in embouchure, the flute presents a major change of concept in terms of embouchure and breath control.

The chart in Table 7-2 indicates the most frequent doubling demands for each of the standard parts found in the sax section. Flute and soprano saxophone are particularly called for in many of the more advanced charts.

Grade IV and V charts in the NAJE grading system for advanced high school and college groups call for extensive doubling. Professional charts (grade VI and VII) can require doubling on the more exotic instruments such as English horn, alto and bass flute, E^b clarinet, etc. In addition, pro-

TABLE 7-2. STANDARD WOODWIND DOUBLINGS

Part	Doubling Instruments
Alto I	flute, soprano sax, clarinet, piccolo
Alto II	clarinet, flute, soprano sax
Tenor I	flute, clarinet, soprano sax, oboe
Tenor II	clarinet, flute, bass clarinet, baritone sax
Baritone	clarinet, bass clarinet, bassoon

fessional charts require more of the woodwinds parts to double rather than just a few.

Frequently Used Special Saxophone Effects

A knowledge of special effects for the sax section will aid the players in producing those sounds that are unique to the style of jazz. The lead player and director should be particularly familiar with sax effects since they are not always notated for the sax section and must be tastefully supplied. As in so much about big band playing, the Count Basie band is especially useful to help understand how special effects *should* sound. Have your sax section listen to the Basie sax section for guidance and a model.

A bend does just what the word implies: it moves the pitch downward from a given note by a dip in the pitch and then returns back to the original level. This effect is usually accomplished by relaxing the embouchure and dropping the jaw rather than with the fingers. The speed with which the note bends depends on the tempo and the length of the note. Generally, the longer the note, the slower the bend. An alternative method is to play the initial note, slur to the note one-half step below, and then return to the original note.

An ascending smear or scoop is started below the pitch and slides quickly up to the given pitch with a delayed resolution. This is accomplished by the embouchure rather than with the fingering. The scoop starts anywhere from a half-step to a minor third below the final note, slides into the note and reaches it only at the last second while in no way affecting the value of the preceding note. Generally, the longer the note, the longer the scoop, but all scoops should have the feeling of being relaxed. A crescendo can be used to dramatize the effect of the scoop, but it should not be accented.

The descending smear is a relatively quick-sounding slide effect that usually does not exceed a quarter note in duration. The interval of this slide is usually a major third or less and involves fingering techniques rather than embouchure change. If the descending smear pitch is immediately preceded by a note above, begin the smear from that preceding pitch.

A fall-off is a quick descending slide from a given note that fades away. The length of the drop is determined by the length of the arched line from the pitch and the tempo. Most fall-offs are short and played by relaxing the embouchure for the drop in pitch. A long fall-off will be achieved by fingering a descending scale (usually chromatic) with a breathy tone quality. The long fall-off is indicated by a line extending across the measure or a long drop written in the part.

The doit (pronounced "doyt," not "do-it") is a pitch that slides upward and fades away, usually to a perfect fifth. This glissed effect should not be distinctly heard. It is an aggressive slide that includes a decrescendo that gradually cuts off the sound followed by a rest. Be sure to clearly sound the written pitch before sliding upward. The duration and interval distance of this effect varies widely and can include several beats in length over an octave. Short doits would be played diatonically and long doits chromatically. The inflected note is taken from the given pitch.

A gliss effect is similar to a drop, smear, or doit with the exception of one important characteristic—the gliss always ends on a definite pitch while the others fade away. This inflection usually includes a slightly delayed crescendo into the note, giving the feeling of a last second rush. If the interval of the gliss is a third or less, the notes are connected chromatically. If the interval is larger, the notes are connected diatonically. When executing gliss effects on the saxophone, consider the following:

- Glisses with a long line are usually diatonic, while a short gliss line is played chromatically. In either case, it must be smooth with *no* individual notes heard.

- A wavy line usually indicates a "notey" gliss (chromatic or diatonic in rapid succession). If the wavy line ascends, this gliss effect is called a lift. If the wavy line descends, this effect is called a spill. To achieve this action, rotate the fingers back and forth down or up a scale pattern. Be sure to use the fingering that will allow the greatest speed.

- Don't begin glisses across the break in the register.

- To lengthen a gliss, begin with embouchure inflection followed with finger assistance. This is accomplished by using a tightening embouchure when ascending and a loosening embouchure when descending.

- The length of a gliss depends on the tempo of a chart, length of the printed line, and good taste.

- Grace notes that are inserted at the end of a gliss are to be played clearly with a push.
- When a gliss connects the same two pitches (a reverse gliss), attack the first note, start a gliss about a third above or below the note, and then gliss into the second note.

There are three classifications of gliss effects used in jazz (see Figure 7-5).

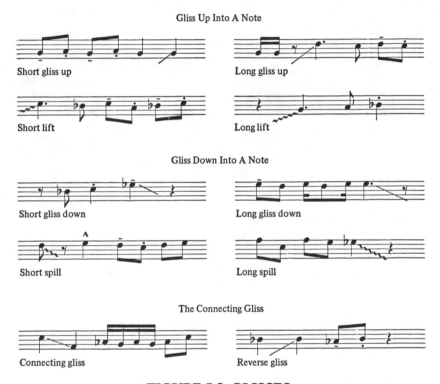

FIGURE 7-5. GLISSES

The flip is basically half of a classical turn or gruppetto between two notes, the second of which is always lower than the first. Slur up from the first note a 3rd or 4th with a slight crescendo and then gliss down to the second note. The flip does not begin any sooner than the last one-third of the beat. The highest note of the turn gets a little push and the last note is accented. The flip can be substituted for a downward gliss between two notes. If the tempo is too fast and the students feel uncomfortable, have them do a mordent in the classical style instead.

The shake consists of a trill-like motion between a given tone and a tone a 2nd or 3rd higher (never more than a 4th). It can be produced in two ways on the saxophone—as a jaw vibrato or as a slow fingered trill. The latter method is the more common. Generally, the slower the tempo, the wider the interval and the slower the speed of the shake. The reverse would, of course, hold consistent as well. Frequently, the end of a shake will gradually speed and crescendo as it nears completion. If the shake occurs in a sax soli, normal fingering will be used. If the shake occurs in a unison with brass, harmonic fingerings will be used to better match the intervals that the brass use. Brass players often use alternate fingerings for facility with the shake, and sax players may try to imitate that sound. Establish the written pitch, then begin slowly and gradually increase the speed between the two pitches.

Ghosting is caused by a slight interruption of the airstream (such as between the syllables "du-'n-du"), producing a deadened, indefinite pitch. These notes usually occur interspersed in a pattern of eighth notes. The ghosted note still provides a rhythmic kick to the phrase even if its pitch and sound quality are indefinite due to its feeling of forward motion.

Figure 7-6 shows musical examples of the effects described above.

FIGURE 7-6. SPECIAL EFFECTS

The Brass Section

The demands of jazz brass playing today are equal to those in the classical brass setting, requiring the same facility and attitude while demanding additional flexibility of repertory and expanded technique, projection, strength, range, and endurance.

The concept of jazz brass sounds has varied greatly over the years. Early dixieland bands generally featured a rough, almost crude brass sound. The swing bands brought a more finished sound with more emphasis on ensemble blend and clearer playing. Two schools of style emerged in the late 1940s and remain as major influences on brass players today: (1) a slight narrowing of tonal breath with an increase of brilliance, modeled after the playing of Dizzy Gillespie and Roy Eldridge, and (2) a widening of tonal breath with emphasis on interpretation and coloration, as performed by Miles Davis and Art Farmer. The current big band brass sound has more brilliance while combo brass players seek the mellower, more lyrical sounds of Woody Shaw and Freddie Hubbard.

THE BASICS OF JAZZ BRASS PLAYING

Tone Production Factors

As with woodwind instruments, there are two sets of factors that shape tone quality. The external factors include the instrument bore size and the type of mouthpiece. The effect of these factors is discussed in detail in Chapter 4.

The internal set of factors includes breathing techniques, embouchure, and tongue placement. Each of these factors can be modified, with the correct combination producing the desired tone quality.

The most important aspect of playing any wind instrument is to get maximum air through the horn. The most perfect embouchure/instrument/mouthpiece combination will not produce a full, mature sound if breath support is not correctly supplied. To quote the fine jazz brass pedagogist, Mike Vax: "The basic approach to playing a brass instrument is 90 percent air, 9 percent brains, and 1 percent chops." The main objective for tone production is to get the air through the horn by means of proper support and breathing. A brass player needs to concentrate on projecting the sound into the far corners of the room. *Keeping* the sound projected is equally important and requires consistent breath support. Consider the following breathing exercises as a means of helping students to breathe deeper and with more support.

Deep Breathing—Inhale on three levels of air intake. First, fill up the lower abdomen including the small of the back; next, fill the lower chest; and last, fill the upper chest, raising the chest (but not the shoulders) only slightly. Do this in three slow counts and then exhale in reverse order.

Yoga Breathing—Inhale in the same manner as for the deep breathing exercises, holding that breath for 30 seconds. Exhale the air in the same manner as the deep breathing exercise.

Listed below are a few hints to reinforce the students' breath support.

- Breathe through the corners of the mouth without disturbing the mouthpiece placement.
- Don't raise the shoulders while inhaling.
- Fill up an imaginary inner tube circled around the mid-section (front, side, and back).
- Maintain abdominal support at all times by flexing the muscle as though someone might hit you.
- Project the sound so that you think of it as moving out and away from you.
- Think of your throat as a large pipe that you're trying to fill with air as you inhale and exhale.

A brass player's embouchure includes the mouth, lip, and facial muscles. The lips function in two distinct capacities. First, they seal the point of contact between the lips and mouthpiece to insure no loss of air.

Second, they are a source of vibration which is amplified and projected through the instrument.

Because the rate of vibration has a direct bearing on the pitch of the note, it becomes clear that one of the embouchure's important functions is to change the rate of vibration to cover the highest to the lowest possible notes of the instrument. Proper development of the lips will allow them to vibrate freely in all registers with power, endurance, and flexibility.

Since no two players are physically alike, no attempt will be made here to generalize as to *where* to put the mouthpiece. Advise your brass players to use a natural placement. As long as it isn't too extreme, this is almost always the best solution.

The center of the lips is usually responsible for vibration (although some players naturally play off to the side) and so it is the focus of most attention in brass playing. The upper lip muscles should move towards the center, not toward the corners of the lips. The lower lip is responsible for adjusting the size of the opening or the aperture. As the pitch ascends, the lower lip will slightly rise in the center.

A brass player is sometimes found to have a too circular or highly arched aperture. The resulting sound can be described as a dull, hooty, and dark tone which is usually responsible for flat intonation. Check these remedies for the symptoms listed above.

- Check to see if the mouthpiece is placed too high, allowing very little lower lip available for aperture control and support. Difficulty will arise because the lower lip can contribute little to the work load and the upper lip will be subject to extra work.
- Check to see if the mouthpiece is placed so that most of the pressure is on the lower lip (the horn will usually be pointed downward). Get your students to play with their horns directed over the stand. *Pressure on the lips must always be avoided!*

There is some debate on whether brass players should play with dry or wet lips. With the demands that jazz playing makes on brass players, the wet-lip school is preferred by most players for the following reasons.

1. The mouthpiece can be more accurately positioned while playing to make minute adjustments easier.
2. The wet-lip system requires a player to develop the lip muscles in order to keep the mouthpiece stationed in a particular spot on the lips.

3. A student may begin using wet-lip first in the low and middle registers and then slowly move into the upper register. This will allow time to develop strength in muscles and help to establish control.

4. It is easier to play with wet lips if you are suffering from chapped lips.

5. Lip sores are less frequent with wet lips and usually can be treated without having to stop playing.

Facial muscles can provide valuable control in brass playing, particularly in pitch and embouchure flexibility. All facial muscles should be directed toward the mouthpiece. Firm corners help guide the air for proper playing. To form the correct facial feel, say the word "prune." While ascending to higher registers, the corners of the lips should pull together and down. For lower notes, the corners should relax without smiling.

The tongue is a major consideration for articulation. It holds back the air pressure and then simply drops to release that air pressure, acting as a valve releasing air and setting the lips in vibration. Generally, the back of the tongue should be kept down, out of the way while playing, using as little tongue as possible when articulating.

The tongue is kept basically flat in the mouth cavity while slightly arched in the center. For high notes, the tongue is in an "ee" position and for lower notes, it is in an "ah" or "oh" position. The tonguing process can thus be described as the tongue "floating" on the air stream. The tongue should feel as though it never really stops the air but simply makes a dent in it. This is the essence of legato playing and, if there is perhaps a secret to jazz brass playing, it is that there must be precise legato (never sloppy) playing from the brass. The student shouldn't attack the tone but rather dent the continuous air stream when releasing the tongue. If there is too much tongue motion and too strong an attack, the legato connection will lack speed and precision. Trombone players must work extra hard on this concept since their legato playing is based on the precise coordination of both articulation and the slide movement.

The explosive tongue is never to be used regardless of how heavy an accent mark or dynamic marking appears over or under the note. An accent should be produced by air-weight rather than a change of syllable articulation. Accents and louder dynamics imply more air (faster and harder), rather than a heavier tonguing action. The tongue should never be heard, even in accented and staccato passages. What makes these articulations work is not the attack but the use of a tongue cut-off. The student should use the tongue to stop the air by closing the air stream.

The tongue does more than stop and start articulations. It also creates the resistance that enables you to play higher, to do lip trills, and to maintain control over the instrument. A simple change of the tongue to the syllable "du" or "ah" will give better control in descending passages, and "wee" or "eee" when performing ascending passages. "Oh" will work well in the low register. For lip trills, there is no change in the lips, but rather in the tongue (ahh-eee, ahh-eee, ahh-eee, etc.). An ascending glissando will have more clarity if the syllables "oh" to "ee" are formed ("ee" to "oh" in a descending glissando). The precise angle that the tongue moves depends on the shape of the mouth and how high the note is. Care should be taken not to tighten the throat, neck, or chest muscles when arching the back of the tongue in the "ee" position.

The development of right hand finger technique on trumpet should not be taken lightly or left to chance. Likewise, the position of the right hand for the trombone player is one of the most important aspects of correct playing and is often overlooked.

For trumpet, the only way that finger dexterity can be developed is by proper practice. Consider the following advice.

- Keep right hand fingers in a natural, relaxed position. Do not over-arch the fingers.
- Let the fingers move with the valves as though they were attached. Push the valves down crisply like a typist rather than in a lazy fashion. The difference between a trumpet player who works at proper finger control and one who is lazy is very noticeable for speed, accuracy, and control.
- In jazz, the use of alternate fingering has wide application. Encourage students to develop skill and facility with alternate fingerings and they will produce better technique and speed in their overall playing.
- On trumpet, a false-finger trill can be an effective tension-guilding device. The slight intonation difference between two notes can create excitement if not overused.
- Alternate fingerings can help get around the problem of slurring over consecutive intervals where there is no valve change.
- Alternative fingerings can help smooth out awkward passages. Trumpet players will find difficult passages with many cross-valve combinations easier to play with, for instance, 3rd valve substitution for 1 and 2.

For trombone, too many trombone players ignore the function of the wrist in their use of the right hand. The wrist should work like a gate, with the right hand cupped and facing towards the performer. This allows maximum flexibility and movement of the wrist and will produce a shift from a note to another note one position away without the need to move the rest of the arm.

False positions are particularly important for trombone players. Flexibility and legato passages can be simplified with the appropriate false positions.

The left hand should function as the support base in holding the horn securely. Students should be encouraged to avoid producing pressure on their lips through excessive left-arm leverage. In order to prevent this tendency, squeeze the horn with the left hand firmly but maintain the sense that the horn is floating just in front of the embouchure.

The slur is accomplished by moving from one note to the next without breaking the air stream. The student should support (from the diaphragm) and set for the upper note rather than the lower note. The following checklist might prove useful to improve slurring on any brass instrument.

- The least amount of lip motion is the most desirable; this includes the jaw and the corners of the mouth.
- The slur should be played entirely by air, support, and syllable— "tah-eee" or "duu-eee" when ascending and "tee-ahh" when descending.
- Coordinate the syllable change and the finger or slide position change with a slight kick of the diaphragm muscle. Try singing slurs with a slight breath push or articulation (the syllable "th" does the best job since it breaks the air flow only minimally).

The use of pedal tone can add to becoming a well-rounded brass player. This can be a valuable practice technique in helping to develop the extreme registers of the instrument. Problems with the upper register resulting from too much mouthpiece pressure, too much tension in the lips, or not enough air can be minimized if the transfer of learning from pedal tone is applied to the upper register.

It is impossible to produce pedal tones if the performer is not relaxed, providing a good air flow, and avoiding the use of pressure. The notes just won't come out without the proper activities taking place for the brass player. Once the brass player has developed a good sound on pedal tones, range, tone, and support from the diaphragm should all be easily transferred. Proper practice of pedal tones can: (1) develop endurance, (2) establish a bigger sound in ALL registers, (3) develop freer vibration, (4) increase range, (5) improve tone, (6) provide more power, (7) minimize pressure, and (8) help keep everything relaxed.

Vibrato can be produced three ways on brass instruments: (1) by movement of the right hand, (2) with the use of lip vibrato, and (3) pulsations of the air column by rapid contractions of the diaphragm. Some professionals recommend that young players begin with a hand vibrato. This is accomplished with a slight back and forth movement by the right hand, which in turn creates the vibrato effect in the lip as pressure changes against the mouthpiece. While this is preferred for more inexperienced students since it is easier to control, hand vibrato can contribute to excessive mouthpiece pressure on the lips. Be careful to remain vigilant with any young players about any bad habits that could come from hand vibrato.

Lip vibrato is produced by a slight movement of the jaw and lips, which affects the lip pressure on the mouthpiece. This is more difficult for a younger student to control, and sometimes a thin tone will result from the use of a lip vibrato.

A good vibrato is one that the player has complete control over and is able to speed up or slow down according to the music. Longer notes should begin with a straight tone, establish the pitch using a solid sound, and then begin the vibrato. Each player should strive to match vibratos within any section and should practice one of the vibrato approaches until it is mastered.

The trombone vibrato is slightly different since it comes from the slide in most cases. The slide is moved smoothly and rapidly back and forth with a loose wrist. The tendency to move the slide too far can cause a wide vibrato that is especially damaging to the sax section. The trombone vibrato must be performed with moderation.

The tempo and style of the chart are the determining factors on how vibrato should be handled. Here are some general guidelines that will help govern general vibrato use.

- Vibrato is to be used sparingly in ensemble passages and more frequently in solo passages as a means of expression to warm the tone.
- A slower tempo uses a wider vibrato while a faster tempo uses less vibrato.
- The higher the note, the faster the vibrato.
- Straight tone is used in unison or in octave passages or when N.V. (indicating no vibrato) is written. Vibrato should only be used in harmony passages when indicted.
- In *tutti* passages, the lead trumpet is the only player to have the option to use vibrato on long tones. In *soli* passages, the lead player of the section has the option to use vibrato.

Warming Up: Don't Self-Destruct

Brass warmups should consist of sustained tones, flexibility studies, and tonguing exercises. It is important to stress that every brass player should devote some time to warming up, but that this time should be observed as just a warmup and not get over-extended so that the player ends up "burned out." Warmups are the musical version of calesthenics and help loosen things up to "get the juices flowing." Consider the following guidelines when using brass warmups.

- Begin in the middle register and work gradually towards each extreme of the range.
- Play five to ten minutes of long tones. Start with soft dynamics and gradually increase with the use of crescendos.
- Rest as much as you play. Brass players should be careful not to over-extend.

Developing the Upper Register

There's no shortcut to the development of the upper brass register. Since so many jazz charts demand playing in the upper register, it is most important to master this range and play correctly for jazz than any other style the young brass player encounters.

The proper use of the diaphragm is essential to the production of high notes. The diaphragm is a muscle and, for the upper register, the notes must begin with the "flexing" of the diaphragm to provide proper support. Many young brass players tense up in order to produce high notes and, though it may sometimes work, it will eventually prove damaging to use tension for the upper register. The player must remain relaxed, with a sense of openness for the entire air column. The corners of the lips should be pulled back and down. The lips will vibrate faster but there should be NO PRESSURE. The mouthpiece should remain lightly on the lips and the sound should come mainly from proper support and an open air stream. Lip flexibility slurs and pedal tones are excellent exercises to help prepare the student brass player to perform in the upper register better. It is important to transfer the techniques used in the lower ranges for these exercises to the upper register performance.

Towards Good Brass Intonation

Brass instruments are similar to all melodic instruments in that they have built-in intonation problems. The most important thing is for the student brass player to develop a concept of intonation so that there is some understanding taking place. Students should check their instruments with a strobe to find out which notes are the biggest problems. Part of the section concept where everyone is supposed to match the lead player includes proper intonation so students should strive to be as precise as possible in their effort to sound alike when working within the section.

There are certain situations where the intonation problems are built into the music. Crescendos and dimuendos will usually cause difficulty with intonation unless the student is aware that this is a problem. Loud dynamics can often cause problems, so brass students need to be particularly sensitive to very loud passages. Overblowing will create a tone that has lost its center and is much more susceptible to intonation difficulties.

Any section of the music that calls for mutes in the brasses will be difficult intonation-wise unless the students make adjustments to compensate for the mutes. It should be stressed to all members of the group that intonation is a full-time activity.

Perhaps the best focus and frame of intonation reference for the entire band is the bass part since the bass can provide real stability of pitch.

SPECIAL BRASS EFFECTS

One of the least understood areas of jazz brass playing is that of special effects. There are no in-depth sources to consult like those found in other areas of jazz technique. Special effects are a part of every style of jazz from dixieland through fusion and are just as common as the use of mutes. When students have developed proper tone quality, vibrato, register extension, and endurance, they should then be taught those special effects commonly written for jazz ensemble. These effects can also be extremely useful in adding nuances and expression to improvised solos.

The du-wah is the easiest special effect to perform on a brass instrument. It is executed in two parts as its name implies. First, there is the "du" notated by a plus (+) that indicates the tone is to be muffled. This is done by placing the left hand over the bell with the fingers slightly spread in the shape of a fan (a plunger mute or felt hat may be used for this purpose). The "wah" is notated by a circle (o) indicating removal of the hand after the "du" effect.

The plunger mute will give a tighter sound than the hand or hat and is preferred by many brass players. The hand is least desirable since it is inconsistent and can cause tone control and intonation problems within the section. The du-wah effect was very popular during the swing era and is still found in Basie-type charts.

The dip/bend sounds like the note is sagging in the middle. The note is usually longer than a quarter note and is attacked normally. In the middle of the pitch's duration, the note is dropped and brought back up. It is always bent down, never up. To produce this effect, the student should deliberately relax the embouchure to flatten the pitch and then bring the embouchure back to normal. The speed of the dip/bend should be proportionate with the duration of the note—the longer the note, the slower the dip/bend.

The smear/scoop is similar to the bend except the note starts well below the pitch and usually slides quickly to the given pitch with a delayed resolution. The interval of the smear/scoop is usually a minor third or less. To produce this effect, attack the given note by either relaxing the embouchure and dropping the jaw to start the note flat and then quickly adjust to a normal embouchure, or use the appropriate valve combination just below the note you want to play and squeeze this fingering about halfway down. The smear takes up most of the time value of the note and, generally, the longer the note, the slower the smear/scoop.

The fall-off is a special effect that falls or drops from the indicated note with a sliding (down) sound that fades away. The length of the drop is determined by the length of the arched line from the pitch. It can either be short or long. To accomplish this effect, attack the written note solidly, sustain it for approximately half of its value and then play the fall-off quickly in one of the following ways:

- Relax the lips and direct the pitch downwards.

- Allow the notes to descend with the aid of the valve or slide with a *subito* pp.

- Slightly depress the valves while simultaneously relaxing the lips. The length of the drop determines the speed of the drop—a longer drop would be slower.

The doit is an upward gliss from a given note following the same rules as a fall-off. After clearly sounding the written note, partly close one or more of the remaining valves and gliss upward while fading away. The length up is determined by the tempo of the tune and what follows the doit, as well as the flexibility of the player's embouchure and range extension. NOTE: whenever the valve is partly closed, more air will be needed to continue the sound. The phonetic vocalization of this effect is "do-weet."

A gliss is similar to a drop, smear, or doit with the exception of one important characteristic: the gliss always ends on a definite pitch while the other effects fade away. This inflection usually includes a slightly delayed crescendo into the note giving the feeling of a last-second rush. If the interval of the gliss is a third or less, the note is connected chromatically. If the interval is larger, the note is connected diatonically. When executing gliss effects of a brass instrument, consider the following.

- A straight line or smooth curve is produced by either the lips alone (by relaxing or tightening the muscles) or with the aid of half-valving. In either case, it must be done smoothly with no individual notes heard.

- A wavy line usually indicates a "notey" gliss (chromatic or diatonic in rapid-fire). If the wavy line ascends, this gliss effect is called a lift. If the wavy line descends, this effect is called a spill. To achieve this rapid-fire effect, flick the valves in a quick rotating motion starting with the third valve in a 3 – 2 – 1 progression.

- A full sounding gliss with half-valves requires good breath support and full air.

- The length of a gliss depends on the tempo of a chart, length of the printed line (up or down), and personal judgment.

- Grace notes that are inserted at the end of a gliss are to be played clearly with a push.

- When a gliss connects the same two pitches (a reverse gliss), attack the first note, start the gliss approximately a third above or below the note, and gliss back into the note.

Indicated in Figure 8-1 are the various types of gliss effects.

The flip is a variation of the classical gruppetto or turn (∞) but produced in a different manner. Obtain the flip by playing the first note nearly full value. Next, quickly reach for the highest, most easily obtainable harmonic above it while maintaining the same fingering, and then glissing down the harmonics to the original note with a crescendo. Do not change fingerings until moving to the next note. The higher one can play between the written notes, the more effective the flip. Flips can also be inserted as a substitute for a connecting gliss.

The plop ( ) is a rapid slide down the diatonic scale into the written note. It is similar to a flip except the first note is absent and the principal note is often short. Start about a 5th to an octave above the sounding note and slide down the diatonic scale to the written note, much like a grace note effect.

The ghosted note ( ) is played with a deadened tone on an indefinite pitch, which implies rather than sounds specific. On a trumpet, it is played with a half-valve technique (as if to throw the note away) and is usually played between two full-sounding notes. The ghosted note still provides a

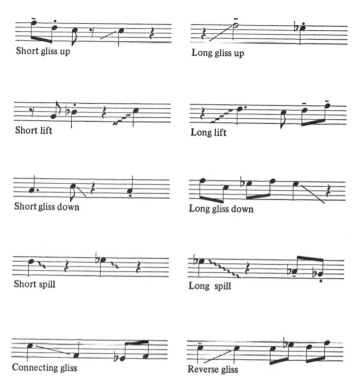

Short gliss up

Long gliss up

Short lift

Long lift

Short gliss down

Long gliss down

Short spill

Long spill

Connecting gliss

Reverse gliss

FIGURE 8-1. GLISS EFFECTS

rhythmic kick to the phrase even if its pitch and sound quality are indefinite. This effect is commonly found in Basie-style charts.

The shake is perhaps the most commonly used brass effect. It is similar to a trill but with a wider interval. The shake can also be described as an extension of the lip slur between a note and another note a major second to a perfect fourth above the note. It has the function of creating excitement on climatic notes. It is also the most difficult effect to master. A good deal of time and practice must go into developing a good shake and its mastery depends on frequent use for the band and lip flexibility for the individual. The notation used is a wavy line over the note. It can be played in one of three ways: (1) as a lip slur, (2) with the use of a hand shake, or (3) as a combination of both.

To begin the shake, play the given note and slur upwards to the desired interval or harmonic (often a third) that uses the same fingering and return to the original note. This process is repeated much like a trill and can be augmented with the hand moving back and forth towards the lip. Alternate fingerings for the initial note may be used to facilitate the production of the shake, but the player must be careful about intonation problems associated with alternate fingerings. One way to avoid this is to attack the note with the regular fingering and then switch to the alternate fingering as the shake progresses.

Or, try half-valving the note and using a lip slur at the same time. The use of syllables (du-ee or tah-ee) is helpful for some brass players, with speed coming with practice. A slow wide shake is characteristic of the Maynard Ferguson band, while a faster, more narrow shake is more common to Basie's band. Shakes are commonly found on notes lasting a half note or longer in the upper register where the tones are closer together and easier to slur. Shakes on lower tones are difficult because of the wider spacing of harmonics. If a shake is encountered on a lower note, it can best be simulated by using a wide vibrato on the written note.

JAZZ TROMBONE TECHNIQUES

The most demanding and important technique to master on the trombone is the coordination of the tongue and slide in order to produce a good legato sound. There are three types of slurs that may be used for trombone: (1) legato slur, (2) natural slur, and (3) lip slur. The legato slur can be described as a slur in which the slide moves in the same direction (up or down) as the note. This necessitates that the player employ a soft, legato articulation for each successive note in the slur (ta-tha or ta-da). The complete coordination of tongue and slide movement is essential for smooth and correct execution. The lip slur demands special attention for the trombone.

Against-the-Grain Playing

Against-the-grain playing or natural slur is a procedure that eliminates the need to tongue but still produces a legato sound. It is produced when the slide moves in contrary motion to the notes. No tongue action is required as long as the slide movement is brisk and accurate, so it is highly desirable for jazz trombone players to work on this type of slur. The advantages for against-the-grain playing are:

- It most closely approximates the smoothness of a trumpet valve sound.
- It provides speed and technique often not possible when using the legato or lip slur.
- Coordination is built into this technique so that the legato effect is produced automatically if it is performed correctly.

Encourage your students to make more use of alternate slide positions in scales, arpeggios, melodies, chords, and so on to help develop facility with the natural slur.

Special Trombone Effects

The glissando is natural to the trombone. The only limitation on the glissando is the range of a diminished 5th (1st to 7th position). A long drop or fall-off needs to be practiced since young trombone players have a tendency to hurry the gliss effect and finish too soon. The use of alternate positions can help create the maximum effect for a long gliss or a notey fall-off.

In order for a trombone section to approximate a trumpet section doing a long fall-off, have the section execute a long, notey fall-off with a defined dimuendo. Though the fall-off will not be as dramatic, it will produce the effect of matching the trumpet effect. Figure 8-2 outlines the long fall-off, as well as some other special effects.

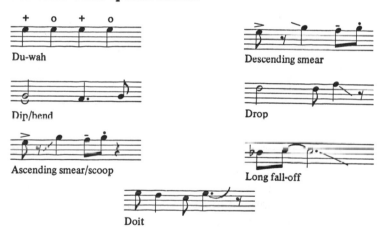

FIGURE 8-2. SPECIAL EFFECTS

A gliss into a note can be accomplished by starting beyond the natural position and playing up to the note by bringing the slide into the note. As long as the player starts below the indicated note (in the appropriate overtone series just below the note), this will always produce a gliss.

Ghosted notes cannot be done as easily as with the half-valve effect used by trumpets. On trombone, there are two approaches that can be used: (1) the dynamic contrast (play the note *subito pianissimo* and quickly crescendo, or (2) squeeze the embouchure as small as possible and then release the tension into a full sound. This technique of squeezing simulates a half-valve effect, but can be dangerous if used by young players who do not have a stable, mature embouchure. In using the first approach, a slight amount of air going through the horn will help maximize the effect by implying the note rather than actually playing it.

When playing a flip, do not change slide positions until after having slurred up (a 3rd or 4th). Then drop down to the next pitch in the normal fashion.

Pedal tones are in the repertory of the jazz trombonist and are frequently used. The corners of the mouth must be relaxed, with the center relaxed using the thicker part of the lip with a wider aperture opening. Response time is longer for pedal tones, so the trombone player must practice in order to learn to anticipate the attack time. Pedal tones for notes beyond 3rd position are particularly stuffy and difficult to get started. The key to proper pedal tone production is that the player must remain relaxed!

The Use of the Bass Trombone

The bass trombone is a valuable addition to the trombone section, not only because it can play more comfortably in the lower register, but also because its depth of tone is so magnificent (due to the larger mouthpiece, bore, and bell). A greater number of alternate positions are available to the player via the use of the thumb trigger. The most common bass trombone for public school use is the B^b tenor trombone with an F attachment. Professional bass trombonists frequently use a B^b bass trombone with double rotors, but this is not really necessary for school use. Because the F attachment adds length to the trombone when the trigger is depressed, the slide positions are farther apart, resulting in six positions rather than the standard seven. Adjustments must be made for intonation but the advantages include many more alternate positions, especially in the higher positions which facilitate faster technique, and extended range.

Since bass trombones are superior to the regular tenor trombone in the lower register, the full impact of the bass trombone can only be realized if the player develops an enormous resource of air, the appropriate use of support, and good embouchure control. Bass trombone playing demands special attention and has special needs. It takes time for a regular trombone player to adjust to bass trombone and, if the part is actually going to work, serious attention from the student needs to be focused on the special demands of the instrument.

PHRASING CONSIDERATIONS FOR THE JAZZ BRASS SECTION

In the brass sections, each part has its own responsibilities and, like a machine, if one part isn't doing its job, the entire section is affected. The first thing a brass player must learn is to develop good musicianship—tone, intonation, range, dynamic contrast, reading, and articulation must each be mastered before anything. Jazz specialization can come later. Many young players are too anxious to go too far, too fast, without spending enough time learning the fundamentals of both brass playing and musicianship. It is the role of a good teacher to help determine the young player's needs and help encourage that student to develop.

The Role of the Lead Player

Most of the success of the section and the ensemble rests on how responsibly and accurately the lead player fulfills his or her role. As the best overall musician, the student must display an interest in the details of phrasing and articulation; must be strong enough to be heard by the section; must be consistent to provide a solid foundation from which his or her section can work; must be sensitive to the music so that his or her interpretation is consistent with that of the director's and the composer's; and must be responsible enough to assume a leadership role for his or her section.

The lead trumpet assumes the role of lead player for the entire ensemble, while the lead trombone player must be careful to match the lead trumpet player (where he or she is also playing), yet be dynamic enough to lead his or her own section. An effective way to develop fine lead playing, especially for the lead trumpet, is to play the part in a jazz solo manner within the ensemble. This will give the ensemble a musical and effective sound by merely imitating the lead.

As the person responsible for the section, the lead player needs to communicate openly and take an interest in the other members of the section. Leadership qualities and a sense of comradeship can instill pride and a sense of team effort for all the members of the section.

Blending Volumes and Tone Quality

To achieve optimum sectional blend, consider tone quality in addition to sound volume. It is important for each member of the section to develop a good tone that will compliment the section, since its tone will only be as good as the weakest member. Generally, the lead player should have more edge in tone than the rest of the section, with the sound quality of the remaining players becoming progressively fuller and darker. Members of the section should be especially sensitive to unison lines and strive to match tone quality. For example, just one player with too much edge can distort the otherwise good unison blend of a section.

A frequent problem section players have is the skillful combination of tone quality and sound volume. To blend well within the section, a player must listen carefully to him- or herself and strive to match the section. The second or third trumpet should never play in an obtrusive manner so that the part intrudes or "sticks out" from the rest of the section. Nevertheless, if the part is played too softly, it will sound like the lead is too loud. A good rule for a section player is to play loud enough so that the lead player and the person on the other side of him or her can be heard. This blending technique is called *masking*. The sign of a good player is his or her ability to listen intelligently in addition to playing well.

Rotation of Parts

Rotating parts within a section can be used as an effective alternative method for developing a brass section. If the players are fairly well balanced in terms of skill, then the music can be passed out in a different order for each piece so that each member can experience all roles of the section. Students are often motivated by this challenge and become more sensitive to their work within the section. Be careful, however, not to put anyone on a part that is too high. Give everyone an opportunity to play some jazz solos, too, so that you will end up with a totally versatile section.

Regularly scheduled sectionals are important. Sections will work most effectively if you identify what needs work and hold the section leader accountable. There are a variety of techniques that can be used in sectional rehearsals.

- Augment the traditional sectional by bringing in the rhythm section. This will provide drive and enthusiasm in the section and will facilitate learning parts in the proper tempo.
- Record some sectionals for further analysis or for use in a conference between yourself and the section leader.
- Sectional rehearsals are an excellent time to listen to recordings, especially for specific details that are appropriate to a special problem within the section.

The Rhythm Section

THE ROLE OF THE RHYTHM SECTION

The rhythm section is the heart of the jazz band. While it may seem to be the "miscellaneous section" with its apparently dissimilar instruments, it must be the most well-rehearsed section—the most capable, dependable, and confident section to insure stability for the entire jazz ensemble. Too frequently, however, it is the weakest and most misunderstood section in the entire ensemble. While wrong notes or unmusical phrases can be obvious to spot and correct in the horn sections, it is often more difficult to specifically identify or solve problems within the rhythm section. In addition to the obvious difficulties of volume, playing together, or wrong entrances, you must be sensitive to the section when: (1) it doesn't swing, (2) it lacks drive, or (3) it just doesn't feel comfortable. In essence, if the rhythm section doesn't make it, the band will *never* swing together.

The prime function of the rhythm section is to keep time. Ideally, the rhythm section should be an energy force pushing the band ahead. In the best rhythm sections, each member is playing well enough to keep a strong pulse and the players are also listening to everything that is going on around them. Each player provides the pulse, meter, accents, rhythmic "swing," responsive balance, and harmony in a way best suited to his or her individual instrument. Nevertheless, each player is, *first and foremost*, a time-keeper. To stay together, the members must feel the pulse both physically and mentally. They should be encouraged to be independently strong and capable of staying on the beat without getting distracted by another player's playing. Perhaps the easiest way to point out the necessity of mental concentration and physical coordination is to have the rhythm section play stop time to the blues.

Playing stop time to the blues involves playing only on beat 1 every four measures or wherever the chord changes in the blues progression. Once the rhythm section has mastered this, have the entire band play one of the notes of the chord in the stop time figure. Everyone will quickly sense a need to keep the time and better appreciate the need to listen.

The second function of the rhythm section is to provide the proper feel in several different styles. Consider how ballad, swing, latin, and rock styles differ and you'll quickly realize that rhythm section players require careful assistance in order to express and cope with the entire style spectrum.

To discuss these various elements, the format of this chapter is in two sections. The first section will cover each rhythm section instrument separately, getting down to specific functions, basic techniques involved to improve each individual player, and musical concepts of what each instrument should sound like. The second part will treat the rhythm section as a unit, with emphasis placed on how to put it together in a rehearsal.

A FOCUS ON THE DRUM-SET

You should consider the drum-set player the focal point of the rhythm section. He or she provides the driving force by pushing the band, exciting the soloists, tightening ensemble passages, and setting up entrances. The way the drummer chooses to fulfill this role should be influenced and dictated by the style of music to be played.

Surprisingly in jazz, 70 percent of the drum-set performance is on the hi-hat and ride cymbal, with only about 30 percent on the bass drum, snare, and tom-tom. In rock, the ratio changes to about 50 percent each. If a drummer can get the correct proportions, he or she has mastered the first basic concept of jazz playing.

Developing Ride Cymbal Techniques

Contrary to popular belief, the drummer does not keep time with the snare and bass drum. The snare, bass drum, and tom-toms are reserved for accents, improvised ideas, or in accordance with the figures notated in the chart. Many drummers like to keep a steady, light beat on the bass drum while making the drum obvious only when accenting something.

The basic pulse of the drum-set is maintained by the ride and hi-hat cymbals. The drummer must be able to play a correct ride pattern. A basic "swing" is phrased in the eighth-note triplets. Nevertheless, the following ride pattern is played at various tempos and styles even though it is notated the same way for everything.

The most common mistake is to consider the interpretation as always being either a triplet (♩ ♪) or dotted eighth note feel (♫). The tempo should determine the proper pattern. The drummer should be aware of the different beat divisions as dictated by the style and tempo. Note that as a general rule, the faster the tempo, the more even the beat divisions, and conversely, the slower the tempo, the more uneven the divisions. This "laid back" delay of the second part of the beat is what helps give jazz its unique feel. Young drummers must work very hard to achieve this feel while not dragging the tempo, so encourage your drummers to listen to the Count Basie Band to get the right feel. Whatever the beat division, the ride rhythm must sound crisp.

Frequently, an inexperienced drummer will play a mushy ride cymbal due to a lack of intensity; this will tend to cause the band to wilt and result in no drive. The patterns indicated above will help sustain the drummer if he or she practices each of the tempos religiously and masters each level. The medium to medium-slow tempos are especially treacherous to sustain while maintaining a swing feel.

Every ride cymbal has several playing areas, with each area producing a different sound and volume. The ride cymbal will produce a high-pitched "ping" when it is struck near the bell and there will be few overtones or ring. When struck near the edge, the cymbal produces a sound with a lot of overtones and ring. The point midway between the edge and the bell of the cymbal is generally considered to be the best spot for producing ride cymbal rhythms. The actual spot will vary somewhat depending on the volume at which the cymbal is played, the size and tone of the cymbal, the type and size of the sticks used, and the individual touch of the drummer. Be aware that some cymbals have more than one good "playing spot."

Although a good ride cymbal should ring with overtones, it should be distinguishable when playing at full volume. It is recommended that the ride cymbal be heavy enough to penetrate the big band sound and yet have a center to the pitch. When playing in a "live" room where the ride cymbal rings too much, put some small strips of tape underneath the side of the bell of the cymbal. Later, the tape can always be removed and the cymbal will not be harmed.

Improving Hi-hat Techniques

In jazz, the hi-hat must accent beats 2 and 4 in a jazz swing style, which will compliment the ride cymbal pattern. The hi-hat can also be used on all four beats. Many inexperienced drummers produce a very stiff sound on the hi-hat. Like the ride cymbal, the hi-hat must produce a crisp, penetrating sound, best described as a hard "chick."

There are two ways the hi-hat can be played: (1) as soon as the cymbals have met, they are held together via foot pressure and then released, or (2) as soon as the cymbals have met, the pressure is immediately released. The first method is more common and has certain advantages. The heel *must* come off the pedal and the toe *must* dig in on each "chick" of the hi-hat (otherwise, a looser "ching" will be produced)—this rocking back and forth of the foot helps coordinate a steadier feel for the beat. The constant sound of the hi-hat on beats 2 and 4 is a prime element in producing the pulse which can cut through a band.

Beginners often encounter difficulty when trying to coordinate the cymbals as they are performed with the left foot and right hand. The drummer should try sitting at different distances from the hi-hat to find the most comfortable spot. The student should also experiment with the adjustable tension springs so that the amount of tension can be controlled. The tension spring controls the speed at which the foot board springs back.

The Correct Use of the Bass Drum

With the right hand on the ride cymbal and the left foot on the hi-hat both occupied with keeping time, the bass drum, snare drum, and tom-tom are free to play improvised accents or follow the written figures from the chart. In a big band setting, the bass drum is usually played very lightly on all four beats or on beats 1 and 3. If the bass drum is played on every beat, it must stay below the sound of the bass. The bass drum is supposed to support the bass without getting in its way. If the bass drum is played too loudly, it becomes too heavy (which often drags the tempo) and gets in the way.

On the other hand, no bass drum takes away from the feeling of depth in the rhythm section. When played correctly, the bass drum adds intensity and percussiveness to the bass part.

There are two ways to play the bass drum: (1) when the beater ball strikes the head, it is held on the head for a fraction of a second, or (2) when the beater ball strikes the head, it is immediately released. The first method deadens the sound by stopping the vibration of the head, while the second lets the drum head ring longer. Inexperienced drummers who try to use the first approach generally find their bass drum sound lacks precision, has a sluggish tone quality, and drags. The second approach, however, will normally improve the tone quality, speed, and control of the bass drum. Drummers should also experiment with the tension screws on the pedal for adjustment of reflex action, but care must be taken to avoid applying too much tension.

Getting the Most from the Left Hand

While the right hands keeps time, the left hand comps, accents, fills, and reflects the rhythms being played by the horns. Drummers with a rock background tend to restrict their left-hand technique to a repetitive, heavy back beat with the snare and hi-hat on beats 2 and 4 for everything they play, regardless of styles. The left hand for a developing jazz drummer, however, is typically more spirited and imaginative. It should always utilize creative comments in the style of the tune—simple comping for a laid-back swing, aggressive "chatter" for bebop, or a strong back beat for rock and soul jazz. It is the left hand that communicates musically with the other members of the band. Sometimes this communication is in the form of musical support to the melody and sometimes it is through counterpoint. The best way to develop these communicative skills with the left hand (besides lots of practice!) is to listen to recordings of such fine big-band drummers as Jake Hanna, Ed Soph, and Joe LaBarbera with Woody Herman; Butch Miles and Sonny Payne with Count Basie; Peter Erskine and Randy Jones with Maynard Ferguson; Sam Woodyard and Louis Bellson with Duke Ellington; Mel Lew; Buddy Rich; and Peter Donald with the Toshiko Akiyoshi/Lew Tabackin band.

Drum-Set Organization and Tuning

The usual drum-set is comprised of four drum sounds, using pitch levels distinct to each drum. These drums include: (1) the snare drum, (2) the small tom-tom, (3) the large tom-tom, and (4) the bass drum.

In addition, a drum-set includes cymbals of indefinite pitch: the hi-hat, ride cymbal, and, often, a crash cymbal. The position of this equipment for a right-handed player would look like the diagram in Figure 9-1.

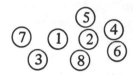

1. Snare drum	5. Small tom-tom drum(s)
2. Bass drum	6. Large tom-tom drum
3. Hi-hat cymbal	7. Crash cymbal
4. Ride cymbal	8. Throne

FIGURE 9-1. DRUM-SET DIAGRAM

The above would be reversed for a left-handed drummer's setup with the exception of the bass drum which remains in the center. The drum setup needs to be comfortable for relaxation and ease of movement, and efficient so that motion is never wasted.

While there is no standardized form of drum-set notation, the following is frequently used on a 5-line staff of manuscript.

Although much can be made of tuning, it is ultimately an item of individual preference. Here are a few guidelines.

• The bass drum should be tuned below the lowest string on the string bass (Great E). Great C is the approximate pitch. The actual pitch to use will depend on how much ring is desired from the bass drum. The heads should be tightened so that the front head is tighter than the batter head. To deaden the ring, a towel or rug can be put inside the bass drum. There should be no rattling due to loose drum heads. Count the turns of each tension rod as the head is tightened to ensure equal tension all around.

• There should be a contrast in the pitch between the large tom-toms of at least a third to a tritone above the bass drum. The batter head should be the looser head.

• The pitch of the drums should gradually ascend from the bass drum to large tom-tom to small tom-tom to snare. With three tom-toms, there should be five distinctive pitches.

• The snare drum should be tighter for the snare head than the batter head for a good crisp sound with a distinct quality which blends with the tom-toms and bass drum; not too tight and high-pitched, yet crisp enough for clarity.

Setting Up Accented Figures: Driving the Band

The kick is the means by which the drummer drives the band in a tutti passage. It is a well-placed drum phrase played simultaneously with the band, which accents the ensemble's melodic phrase. A kick in a tutti passage breaks into the ride cymbal's time-keeping pattern with a combination of two or more drums and/or cymbals. An effective way to play section figures is with the snare or bass drum while maintaining the ride cymbal with the right hand.

Short notes in the kick ($\hat{\varphi}$) can be played on any of the drums and/or the closed hi-hat, but are usually most effective when played on the snare or bass drum. Trumpet patterns are often copied on the snare because of the similarity of timbre and crispness. Trombone, tenor, and baritone sax lines are often played on the bass drum, again because of similarity.

Long notes in the kick ($\bar{\varphi}$) are most effectively played by hitting the ride or crash cymbal and bass drum together. The cymbal adds the sustaining quality that makes it feel like a long note and the bass drum adds the bottom strength to the accented figure. To gain an even sharper attack, the snare drum is often added.

Perhaps the best way to help your drummer with the location of kicks is to provide a lead trumpet part or a copy of the condensed score. The drummer can clearly see where to punctuate ensemble figures and releases.

A set-up is a short rhythmic figure played by the drummer that precedes an ensemble or section entrance and makes the entrance more accurate, together, and easier to identify. It communicates to the band the exact point of their entrance. The set-up figures end just as the band is entering in a style that is complimentary to what the band will play. In the drum part, the ensemble figure is generally written in cues above the staff. It might also be marked as "ensemble," "ens.," or "tutti."

Figure 9-2 shows typical set-ups.

A fill is a designated place in the music where the drummer is supposed to supply a short solo (usually between phrases). The fill must also set up

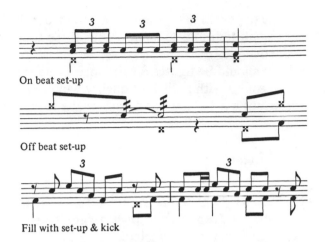

On beat set-up

Off beat set-up

Fill with set-up & kick

FIGURE 9-2. SET-UPS AND KICKS

the upcoming entrance of the band. This should not be seen as a spot to "show off," but rather a place to carefully solo as it is written specifically for the music. Since the fill is actually a very short improvised solo (seldom more than four measures), it should be carefully planned, compact, and appropriate to the style and what will be played immediately afterwards.

Playing Behind Soloists

The drummer must remember to play under or behind the soloists, particularly at the beginning of the solo. The soloist should have a chance to be the featured performer—the drummer should never intrude into the solo but, rather, try to complement the solo performance. The drummer keeps interest going during solos with comping techniques of the left hand. The drummer should be intensely sensitive to the soloist and learn to respond to what the soloist is doing. If your drummer is accountable (able to explain *why* any figure is played) it will show there is thought and awareness taking place. Drummers also should be responsive to dynamic changes from the soloists, and be especially aware of form and cadences. It is disconcerting to hear changed rhythm patterns in the midst of a solo unless it is appropriate to a new section in the form and/or follows something the soloist is doing. Likewise, cadences can be emphasized by indicating turnarounds with increased volume, syncopated rhythms, or drum rolls one or two measures before the next chorus begins. Drummers can also help a soloist by ending a chorus along with the soloist by changing style or a dimension in the playing for the new chorus.

Variations of Basic Beats

The need for a variety of basic beat patterns to be used while keeping time may not be glamorous but is essential to good playing (especially when backing up a number of soloists in one piece). It is also important to have a wide repertory of patterns for all the styles of jazz. Some of the basic beat patterns are indicated in Figure 9-3.

Ballad (R.H. either plays snare or ride cymbal)

Dixieland

Slow Blues

Bebop

Rock

Afro-Cuban

Standard Ride Beat

Boogaloo

Shuffle

FIGURE 9-3. BEAT PATTERNS

THE ROLE OF THE BASS

The rhythm section provides the heartbeat of the ensemble while it lays down a carpet of harmony for the soloists. The main purpose of the bassist is to pump a steady pulse through the ensemble. This focus on the beat is vital and without it, the group and the tune can come unglued. For the best results, the bass player should be set up very near the drummer's hi-hat.

Playing interesting melodic lines based on the harmony and chord progressions can provide a creative outlet for the bass player. There are some styles such as Latin and fusion in which more freedom is allowed in the bass line. Nevertheless, keeping good time is still the first priority. It is in the swing tune that the bass player becomes the lead player of the rhythm section.

Getting the Best Sound for the Bass

Quality equipment is essential to produce a desirable bass sound. A detailed description of bass, amplifier, and accessory equipment is presented in Chapter 4.

Given the proper equipment, the student should attempt to make the proper adjustments to gain a characteristically solid bass sound. There is a wide spectrum of bass sounds being recorded in various styles of music today. A good jazz bass sound lies somewhere in the middle of this spectrum. Set the controls of a bass guitar and amp at the midway point and then begin adding treble and decreasing bass until the desired sound is achieved. To achieve better volume control, set the amp in its lowest third of the volume range and set the instrument so that it is somewhere in the top of its volume range. For up-tempo charts, use more treble for better projection. The reverse is true for ballads—turn the treble down a bit.

The skill with which the bass player uses the right hand can also determine the quality of sound. The bassist should not play solely relying on the amplifier for power and volume. Bass pizzicato can project with either the "thumpy" style which produces a doo-doo-doo-doo sound or the "smooth" style which sounds like doom-doom-doom-doom.

Also consider the area where the string is played. On the acoustic bass, the midpoint of the fingerboard gives more bass to the tone. The bottom of the fingerboard produces a better tone for jazz with more definition. On the electric bass, the area nearest the fingerboard has more bass sound and the area near the tail gives more edge to the tone.

Understanding Bass Notation

Published jazz charts are often ambiguous when it comes to the bass part. Often, acoustic or electric is not specified and in addition, the notation is inconsistent from one publisher or arranger to the next. Some bass parts are completely written out with chord symbols optional. Sometimes, only the chord symbols are given (this is especially true for the more difficult charts). It is assumed that a bass player performing an advanced chart has the capability to read chord changes. Since all bass players must eventually learn to play with chord changes, it is recommended that the student begin as soon as possible.

Problem Solving:
Theory Via the Fingerboard

What many young bassists lack in theory, they attempt to make up for with their ears. There are, however, restrictions even to good ears. The problem is compounded by bass players who don't read music, fake, or misinterpret chord symbols. This situation is especially true for electric bassists who have had no prior exposure to school music programs or who lack any formal training.

It is important for the young bassist to become accustomed to playing whole and half steps over the entire fingerboard. Since learning chord symbols is essential, it is a good idea for bass players to be able to play all scales and modes accurately and intelligently, since these scales are the basis for walking bass style. Initially, the bass player should learn the major scales (see Example 1 in Figure 9-4); the Dorian mode, which is used with minor 7th chords (see Example 2); and the Mixolydian mode as applied to dominant 7th chords (see Example 3). Learning theory through performance practice is the answer for those bass players who view the traditional approach to learning unenthusiastically.

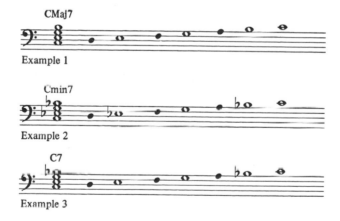

Example 1

Example 2

Example 3

FIGURE 9-4. SCALES TO LEARN CHORDS

A broad, step-by-step approach to building a walking bass line is provided in Figure 9-5. Each step should be practiced in several keys and mastered completely before moving on in the sequence.

FIGURE 9-5. DEVELOPING THE WALKING BASS

Identifying Some Special Sound Problems

Listed below are some special problems that might occur with your electrical equipment. Refer to this list often—it could save you both time and money!

Troubleshooting for the Bass*

PROBLEM	CAUSES & CORRECTIONS
Amplifier hum	Ground switch (polarity) needs to be reversed. If the amp doesn't have a ground switch, reverse the AC plug.
	Insufficient ground on the instrument. Check with a good repairman or add a wire from pickups to a metal part of the bass to ground it properly. Sometimes, just shifting the position of the instrument can correct the hum (especially when the amp and bass are too close together).
	Too close to fluorescent lights.
	Low-quality instrument pickups.
	It could just be the nature of the amplifier. The cause must be corrected by a good repairman.
Buzz	Too much high (treble sound) on amp.
	Ground needs reversing or there is a bad connection.
	Instrument volume knob might be loose.
	An amp tube may be blowing out or hanging loosely.
Crackling	Instrument cord may be bad.
	Amp tubes may be going bad.

Personally Yours by Carol Kane, GWYN Publishing Co. (exclusive selling agent is Warner Bros., New York) 1970, 22-23.

PROBLEM	CAUSES & CORRECTIONS
Crackling, cont.	Loose or dirty knobs on instrument. Use a cleaner to spray into potentiometers and tighten knobs.
	Loose pickup or loose wires in the instrument.
Distortion	Amp speaker may be tearing or blown completely.
	Strings vibrating too closely to the pickups. Raise strings and/or lower the pickups.
	Resistor in amplifier needs replacing.
	Front grill cloth on amp loose and vibrating.
	A short in the amplifier system.
	Speakers having caps need air holes.
	Nuts may be loose on speakers. Tighten, but not too much!
Rattles	*Amplifiers:* Grill cloth loose; face plates loose or ill-fitting; speaker nuts loose; cones in the speakers fluctuating; insufficient baffling and low amp wattage power in amp; tubes loose in sockets; filaments loose in the tubes (add springs or shock absorbers); replace tubes; cap the speakers with air holes drilled in the caps.
	Bass: Strings buzzing on frets or pickups on the instrument. Adjustment needed.
Note length	Take the bridge-cover off for a longer sound (it has a piece of sponge rubber glued in it). Obtain a longer sound by loosening the phillips-head screws slightly (these hold the bridge cover on). If the screws are loosened too much, it will cause the cover to rattle slightly. Tighten these for a

PROBLEM	CAUSES & CORRECTIONS
Note length, cont.	more muted (less overtones) sound. Recording sound requires an extra piece of felt muting to stop all overtones. Place it under the existing muting next to the strings. This can also be done for live performance.
General amp care	Do NOT use the standby switch or turn off amp to save tube-life between sets. Standby switches cause an overload of power which hits the tubes too fast. Ventilate tubes adequately. If tubes become too hot, turn off amp completely. Treat the amp gently—abuse produces cabinet rattles and ruined tubes. Don't poke holes in air-tight chamber amps just to add wheels—use a dolly. Add shock absorbers to protect tubes. Use a well-built case with good lining for extensive travel. Set amp on an even floor. Keep amp away from bass drums. Avoid drapes and walls which can deaden the sound. Too many amps have shorted out because of spilled coffee cups! If you smell smoke, unplug the amp.

THE ROLE OF THE PIANO

Unlike the drummer and bassist, the primary purpose of the pianist is not one of keeping time. While there may be ample opportunity to solo, much of piano playing involves comping. Comping is a word unique to jazz —it combines the two words "accompany" and "complement" to form a precise representation of the activity. The pianist is much like a painter who brings color and sparkle to an otherwise "black and white" rhythm section. The result adds character and style to the driving energy of the other two players. The role of the pianist in the jazz ensemble rhythm section probably requires more technical facility and theoretical understanding than any other member.

The style of a chart and frequency of the solo sections determine the demands on the pianist. Very little playing is needed in the full band sections of most standard jazz tunes. However, rock and Latin charts call for piano much more in setting the style and rhythmic concepts. The slower the chart, the more the demand on the pianist to hold the flow of the tune together as it moves through the solo sections.

Young pianists are often intimidated by the challenge of reading the piano part. Various publishers notate the part several different ways. Some piano parts only feature a single staff with chord symbols on the appropriate beats while others provide the entire part. Unfortunately for young players, jazz piano players are supposed to infer their part from the music rather than play it literally. When the part is written completely, it tends to make the player somewhat stiff and rigid. In addition, the piano player should be encouraged to "swing" along with the wind players in the ensemble.

The piano player should follow a sequence towards freeing the part from what is written. Make certain each step is mastered before moving on to the next.

1. Be able to alter the written rhythms and articulations with swinging eighth notes in both solo and comping sections.

2. Replace the traditional legato style with the more percussive style associated with jazz. With the exception of ballads, avoid the use of the sustain pedal.

3. Choose open, but original rhythms for comping. This may include the use of some written rhythms mixed with some original rhythm patterns.

4. Learn to play more "holes" in the music by not playing so much. This helps the young player to learn about balance and selection.

5. Develop short riffs and fills that can be placed in spots of the music where there is little else happening. This must be done with discretion or it will become monotonous.

Although listening is an activity that every member of a jazz ensemble should be encouraged to do, it is imperative that the pianist listen, know, and recognize the top pianists in the jazz field. Encourage the young piano player to listen specifically to style and solo techniques. The student should be particularly encouraged to reproduce chord voicings, comping styles, rhythmic patterns, and solo riffs of the top jazz pianists. Also, the student should listen to both combo and big band pianists. At first, the director should spend some time with the student to help point out what to listen for. Also, patience should be stressed—duplicating some of the more advanced and intricate piano techniques may take a long time. Nevertheless, the student should develop good listening habits from the start.

Interpreting and Reading Chord Symbols

At this point, the young pianist must develop facility with the chord symbols written above the music. First, the student may acquire a working knowledge of the circle of fifths by the use of seventh chords. Begin with a series of simple etudes which consist of playing through the entire cycle with the following voicings:

```
              5 |
3 |    7 |    3 |
7 |    3 |    7 |   R.H.
3 |    7 |    5 |
5 |    5 |    5 |
R |    R |    R |   L.H.
```

First, the chords should be played as major 7th chords, then dominant 7th chords, and finally as minor 7th chords. Once the basic patterns have been accomplished, the player should begin to develop speed, dexterity, and facility.

Understanding Chord Progressions

With good voice leading and smooth resolutions as a goal, the student may now begin to play simple two-note voicings of dominant 7th chords as indicated in Figure 9-6.

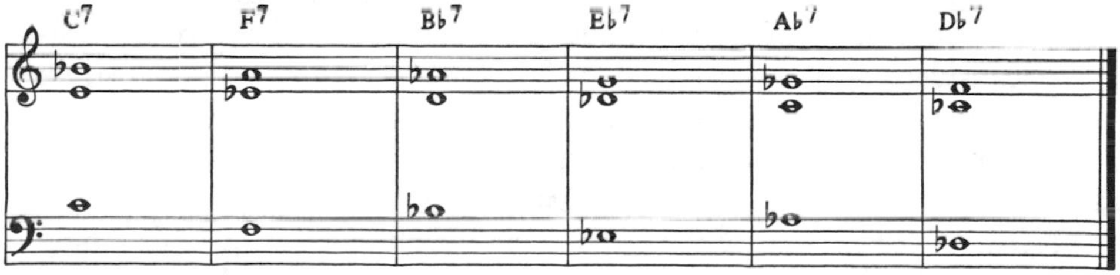

FIGURE 9-6. SIMPLE TWO-NOTE VOICINGS WITH ROOTS

Next, a slightly more complex voicing may be practiced. A sample of this voicing is indicated in Figure 9-7. Here, three- or four-note voicings may be used in the left hand while the right hand plays the appropriate scale to match the chord.

Initially, the voicing studies need only use whole notes. Once the student has accomplished facility with the progressions, rhythm patterns and comping may be applied to the progression.

The student should be thinking of progressions in the largest sense rather than just as a series of isolated chords. In particular, the student should begin to consider the cadential pattern of dominant-to-tonic (V-I). Next, this pattern can be expanded so that the pianist can play the pattern I-IV-V-I in all keys. This is the basis for the blues and prepares the pianist for the blues progression.

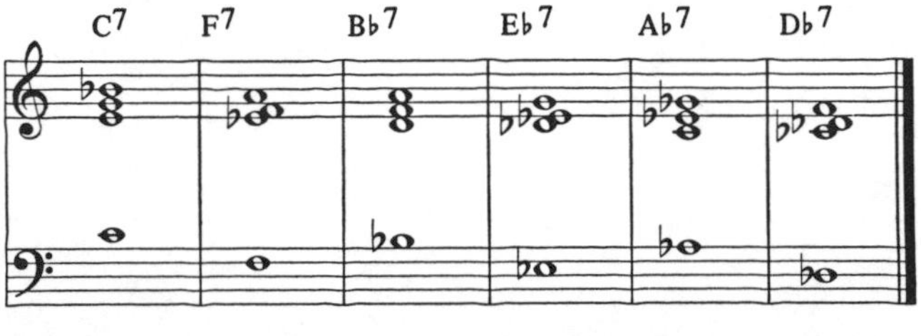

FIGURE 9-7. THREE-NOTE VOICINGS WITH ROOTS

Once the above patterns have been mastered, more complex progressions can be introduced with chord substitutions, added notes (9ths, 11ths, etc.), and new chords. The blues progression is basically a twelve-measure chord progression that utilizes three distinctive harmonic sections featuring tonic, subdominant, and dominant functions. Each harmonic section is four measures long. The first section is a tonic function. The second section is comprised of two measures of subdominant function and two measures of tonic or its substitute. The final section contains a cadence where the dominant function moves to the tonic for the last two measures. There is no single definitive blues progression due to a wide variety of chord substitutions. Consider the blues progressions indicated in Figure 9-8 to illustrate some of the possible variations available to the pianist.

It is important that the fifth measure with a subdominant function and that the cadence take place during measures 9, 10, and 11. The chords can be played in block style using the root, third, fifth, and seventh. Comping may be simple to begin, but the student should be encouraged to develop a comping "vocabulary."

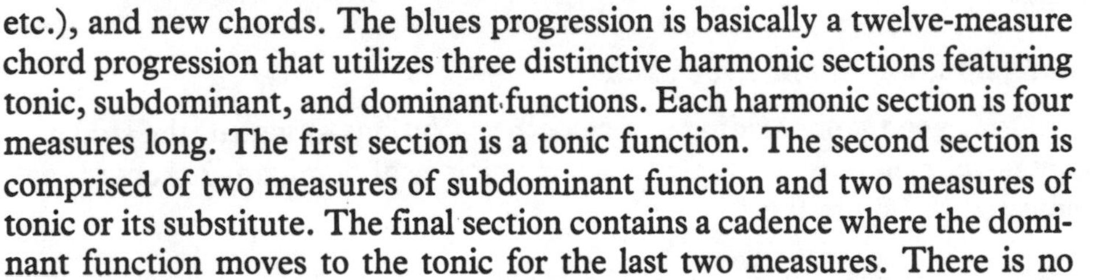

FIGURE 9-8. BASIC BLUES PROGRESSION
(ONE HAND VOICING)

The next example (Figure 9-9) demonstrates a subdominant substitution in the second measure and a change in the cadence. The most significant change takes place with the introduction of the II-V progression in measures 9 and 10. The II-V-I progression can easily be viewed as the most important progression in all of jazz since it establishes a strong impression of "key." This progression permeates almost all popular songs and standard jazz progressions. At this level, upper chord extensions are desirable. A good rule for chord voicing is to substitute the 9th of the chord and omit the root entirely.

Progression

measure:	1	2	3	4	5	6	7	8	9	10	11	12
chord symbol:	C⁷	F⁷	C⁷	C⁷	F⁷	F⁷	C⁷	C⁷	d–	G⁷	C⁷	G⁷

(Key of C)

(One hand comping)

(Have root played in left hand on first beat)

FIGURE 9-9. INTERMEDIATE-LEVEL BLUES

In the most advanced example of blues progression for piano included here in Figure 9-9, there is a great deal more chromaticism and more sophisticated harmony. This harmony might seem very complicated to the inexperienced pianist but if the student has really learned the earlier versions included above, the progression should make sense. As a result of the use of more II-V progressions, there is a stronger cadential resolution into measures 5, 11, and back into measure 1 of the repeated chorus.

Progression

measure:	1	2	3	4	5	6	7	8	9	10	11	12
chord symbol:	C⁷	F⁷	C⁷	g–,C⁷	F⁷	F⁷	C⁷	A⁷	d–	G⁷	C⁷	d–,G⁷

(Key of C)

(One hand comping)

(Have root played in left hand whenever chords change)

FIGURE 9-10. ADVANCED-LEVEL BLUES

Comping at this advanced level includes more varied voicings and more complicated chord progressions and substitutions. Rhythm patterns need not be complicated.

At this stage, the pianist should be able to compliment the soloist rather than simply play patterns against the solo. It is important to stress once again that the knowledge of chords and progressions alone will not produce an effective pianist. It is essential that the pianist *listen* to compliment the music and soloist.

The II-V Progression. The II-V progression consists of a minor seventh chord in a major key or a half-diminished seventh chord in a minor key built on the II chord followed by a dominant seventh chord, either a perfect fourth above or perfect fifth below the II chord's root. The II chord functions as a subdominant chord or "feeder" chord in the progression for the dominant chord that follows. The dominant seventh chord is a strong cadential function because of the tri-tone interval between the third and flatted seventh notes of the chord.

Turnarounds. Turnaround progressions are an important application of chord substitutions. The turnaround refers to a series of dominant seventh chords, occurring at the close of a section in a tune to function as an extension of a tonic chord. The turnaround provides relief from monotony while preparing for the repeat of another chorus. The turnaround is usually a two-measure phrase. In the blues, it occurs in the last two measures of the progression and clarifies the form by emphasizing the beginning of a new chorus since the resolution of the turnaround only comes on the first measure of the next chorus. The pianist should add turnarounds to the end of a chorus even when it is not notated.

The following turnaround in Figure 9-11 can be inserted into the blues progression in measures 11 and 12 to create a strong feeling of cadence and drive into measure 1 of the new chorus.

FIGURE 9-11. TURNAROUNDS

Voicing Techniques

There are three primary chord types and three secondary chords. The primary chords include major, minor seventh, and dominant seventh. The secondary chords are diminished seventh, half-diminished seventh, and augmented. The basic function of all these chords are unaffected by additional upper extensions of the chord (9th, 11th, 13th, etc.) or by alteration of certain chord members (5th).

Major chords tend to function as tonic chords or to establish a key center. These chords are relatively stable and do not need to progress to another chord type.

Minor seventh chords are simply minor chords with an added minor seventh interval. They are less stable than major chords and have more than one function. They can serve as a tonic chord in a minor key or as a supertonic, mediant, or submediant chord in a major key. This chord is particularly found in its application of a II chord in the much-used progression II-V-I.

Dominant seventh chords are still less stable and must resolve to another chord, usually either a half-step below or a perfect fifth below.

Secondary chord types provide harmonic coloration and more harmonic options. Diminished seventh chords are very unstable. Because the chord may resolve in so many ways, it is particularly appropriate for use in setting up modulations.

Half-diminished seventh chords are often used as substitution chords for dominant seventh chords where the root is omitted. They resolve and work just like dominant seventh chords in this setting.

Augmented chords are also substitute dominant seventh chords (only in this application, they utilize a raised fifth degree) and resolve to a chord a perfect fifth below.

A brief representation of each of the chord voicings is provided in Figure 9-12. The pianist should develop facility with the spelling and application of these chords so that they can be used in all keys.

Primary Chords

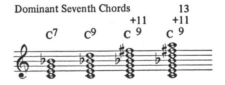

Secondary Chords

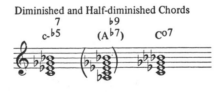

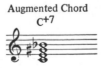

FIGURE 9-12. CHORD VOICINGS

Additional voicings of primary chords are provided below for both one- and two-hand applications. The voicings may be applied to all primary chord functions.

One-Hand				Two-Hand					
9	7	5	3	7|	9|	7|	7|	9|	
7	5	3	9	5	5	5	5	5 |	R.H.
5	3	9	7	9|	3|	3|	9|		
3	9	7	5						
				5|	7|	5|	5|	3|	
				1|	1|	1|	3|	7|	L.H.

THE ROLE OF THE GUITAR

The role of a guitar player in the rhythm section of a jazz ensemble is basically the same as the pianist's—to add rhythmic color to the steady pulsations of the beat. A guitarist is a time player, expected to help hold the band together. Since the function of the guitarist is so similar to the pianist, the guitarist must be extra careful about getting in the way.

Freddy Green, the guitarist who has been with the Count Basie for many many years, is generally acknowledged to be the finest rhythm guitar player ever. Even before the ensemble's first rehearsal, give your new guitarist a recording of Basie's band and point out how, although Green just uses an acoustic guitar and plays on the beat, he provides a solid and steady pulse that is both light and crisp. Encourage your guitarist to emulate the style and sound of Green. Electric guitarists need to play pianissimo at all times so that the guitar is *felt* rather than *heard*. If the guitar chords can be distinguished as guitar chords, then the guitarist is playing too heavy and too loud. The guitarist should always strive to lightly blend with the drummer's ride cymbal.

A second style of playing guitar is the jazz "comping" style. Here, the guitarist can interpret his or her part in a more rhythmically free manner. Usually, the written part will either provide only the most important rhythmic clues (with special figures) or by vertical slashes. In either case, the guitarist can add his or her own figures. NOTE: Care should be exercised not to overplay or get in the way of what the pianist is doing! The director should decide if he or she wants a Freddy Green type of accompaniment or a comping style. In rock-oriented charts, the rhythms are usually more complicated or active, so the guitarist is given more freedom.

Getting Control of the Guitar Sound

Since the electric guitar is an amplified instrument, there are many potential problems. These include: (1) worn or dead strings, (2) a pick that's worn, frayed, or the wrong size, shape, or thickness, (3) a faulty pickup, and (4) the amplifier needs proper tone adjustment.

The tone controls on the amplifier, in conjunction with those on the guitar, give the guitarist a wide range of tonal variation. Proper adjustment of the amplifier can be achieved in the following sequence:

1. Close all volume and tone controls on the amp.
2. Open the volume control on the guitar all the way.
3. For jazz, adjust the volume control of the amp for the proper volume (barely audible); for rock, a louder volume setting should be used so that the guitar can be heard distinctly.
4. Set the tone control on the guitar for the most natural sound of *that* guitar through *that* amp. (This is known as "flat-tone setting.") By experimenting with the amp's bass, midrange, and treble controls, the guitar can come up with a variety of sounds to be used for different situations. For a jazz style, use more lows on the amp to produce piano-like comping sounds. For rock, use more treble on the amp.

Some Fundamental Guitar Techniques

An important facet of rhythm guitar playing is right-hand technique. A straight flat pick should be used. This has several advantages over finger or thumb picks: (1) more speed in single string work, (2) more dynamic contrast is possible, and (3) more flexibility of articulation (legato, staccato, accented, etc.). There are a number of picking styles to use. The downstroke is indicated by a ⊓ and is the most frequently used. It provides the best fullness of sound, control, and volume. Up-picking (V) is used alternating with down picking in passages where eighth notes or fast rhythms are used. The guitarist should strive to obtain sound as even with both strokes as possible. Both up and down strokes should be balanced and matched so that alternated picking techniques are undetected. A mellow and sweet sound can be produced at the end of the fingerboard—it becomes more twangy as the pick moves toward the bridge.

Speed and dynamics are controlled by pressure of the fingers and wrist. More thumb pressure on the pick will increase the volume and intensity levels. Even though electric guitar is controlled by a volume knob, it is desirable to be able to naturally control musical dynamics through physical control while playing.

The production of a light, yet tight, rhythmic beat on the guitar requires precise coordination of both right and left hands. For a clean attack, the pick and left-hand fingers must meet the strings simultaneously. The preceding note, no matter how legato the passage, should not sound after the next note has been attacked. The sooner the left-hand fingers are relaxed after the note has been picked, the shorter sounding the note will be. This is most appropriate for jazz guitar playing and results in a "chunk-chunk" sound. At no time should the fingers be taken completely off the strings. When playing a chord, be sure to have a firm contact of the left hand with the strings being pushed. A weak left hand will contribute to a sloppy sound. Together, right-hand picking, left-hand technique, and deadening of unused strings will produce a more concise and solid-sounding beat. Rock styles tend towards longer sounds.

Special Guitar Effects

Guitar effects can be accomplished either on the amp or through modular units that connect between the amp and the guitar by a patch cord. These effects are more frequent and common to rock-style charts than those that are primarily jazz oriented.

Guitar amps usually have a tremolo effect control that is used to produce rapid changes of volume. One regulating control on the amp is for intensity and the other is for speed. The intensity control varies the volume range. The speed control lets the player vary the speed of the quiver from rapid to slow. A foot pedal is recommended since it enables the guitarist to turn the device on and off quickly. The tremolo effect simulates a vibration effect and can be used effectively if it is used sparingly.

A guitar amp also usually has a reverb control, which adds electronic reverberation to the amplified sound. The reverb effect adds depth and gives an illusion of sustaining the tone and sound color.

Auxiliary electronic equipment available for special sound effects includes fuzz-tone distortion devices, wah-wah pedal, volume pedal, tone-sustain box, the treble-bass booster, volume booster (pre-amp), tone dividers, echoplex, and other items.

With the use of patch cords, any of the above-mentioned equipment can be hooked up in a series between the guitar and amp. The result is an infinite number of special sound effects. There is no limit within the bounds of creativity.

The volume pedal makes it possible for an electric guitarist or bassist to freely and quickly change dynamic levels. Rapid fluctuations of dynamics on every note can be used to imitate a steel guitar effect.

A wah-wah pedal cuts out low and high frequencies at alternate positions of the pedal, thus creating a "wah-wah" sound effect. In addition, some pedals have a switch on them to change the color of sound produced.

The fuzz-tone device purposely distorts the sound of a guitar. Fuzz-tone and its many variant devices have become an important aspect of rock guitar playing. A foot pedal is used to greatly enhance the use of a fuzz-tone.

The tone-sustain box sustains a sound to the point of controlled feedback. It is distortion free and doesn't add any different color to the sound.

The treble-bass booster acts as a pre-amp and enhances either the treble or bass of the guitar sound.

The volume-booster is also a pre-amp and greatly boosts the gain from the guitar before it gets to the amp. Guitarists purposely plug this booster into a small amp in order to get planned distortion. This natural distortion, usually in funky and R & B blues is often preferred over the "fuzz" tone distortion device.

Tone dividers are octave doublers of one or more octaves below a played note. These are also popular for use with wind instruments.

The echoplex was made popular by Don Ellis. This device is a tape recorder with an endless tape loop that makes it possible to accompany yourself and use creative unusual effects.

Guitar Chord Notation Simplified

The guitar is tuned in perfect fourths, except between the second and third highest-sounding strings, where the interval is a major third.

If the guitar fails to stay in tune after it has been tuned, it may be due to one or more of these causes: (1) old or defective strings, (2) bridge improperly located or set upright imperfectly, (3) instrument neck warped, and (4) tuning keys slip (due to wear or defectiveness) allowing string tension to release.

Many arrangers will write chords for the piano to play and then automatically give them to the guitarist to play also without realizing how hard they are to play idiomatically on the guitar. For example, Thad Jones' charts sometimes have four or more chords per measure; these are much more difficult to voice on guitar than at the piano. Simplify the process by eliminating some of the chords (at least two per measure). Another solution is to eliminate some of the upper extensions and alterations if they are complicated.

For function of chord types, chord symbols and interpretation, and chord substitution, see the piano section under the appropriate heading.

Voicing Techniques

Since the guitarist should be felt rather than heard, voicing techniques are rather restrictive. Three- or four-part chords played in a Freddy Green style (chunk-chunk) are more desirable at a pianissimo dynamic level because they blend better and are clearer sounding. An important concept for a guitarist playing in a jazz style is to use the lower sounding strings since they give the chords a darker, less conspicuous, better blending sound.

Though barre chords are very important in blues and rock, they are not as important in jazz styles and should usually be avoided. A barre chord uses one finger extended over a few or all of the strings, allowing the guitarist to move the chord up or down the fingerboard to any fret without changing the fingering.

It is recommended that beginning and intermediate guitarists in the jazz ensemble play three-note chords rather than four-note chords because (1) three-note chords penetrate the band easier; (2) three-note chords allow better voice-leading, and (3) three-note chords are easier to play.

Few guitar books make any reference to three-note voicings. Three-note chords usually have the root, third, and seventh (or sixth) with the fifth dropped. Sometimes, the fifth will replace the root. To achieve the desired sound, it is required that the three-note chords be open-voiced on the sixth, fourth, and third strings. The player should simplify all higher-numbered chord extensions (ninths, elevenths, thirteenths, and so on) to a seventh chord. By voicing on these strings, the chords will be naturally open-voiced with the root or fifth in the lowest string and the seventh or third on the highest sounding strings. In addition, there will be a sixth or seventh interval between the lowest two-chord members, which helps to project a fuller sound. Close-voiced intervals are used sparingly for solo work rather than rhythm guitar playing.

The guitar voicings for the three-note chords of major, minor, and dominant seventh chords are listed in Figure 9-13 as a guide. Since the guitar has a fretted keyboard, each voicing can be instantly transposed to eleven other fret positions without changing the relative fingering pattern.

Dominant Seventh

C⁷   D♭⁷   D⁷   E♭⁷   E⁷   F⁷   G♭⁷   G⁷   A♭⁷   A⁷   B♭⁷   B⁷

Major Seventh

CM7   DbM7   DM7   EbM7   EM7   FM7   GbM7   GM7   AbM7   AM7   BbM7   BM7

Minor Seventh

c-7   d-b7   d-7   e-b7   e-7   f-7   g-b7   g-7   a-b7   a-7   b-b7   b-7

FIGURE 9-13. THREE-NOTE CHORD VOICINGS

As in piano voicing techniques, the guitarist should try to retain common tones between different adjacent chords. Eliminate large shifts by using chord types that maintain common tones. Observe the blues progression in Figure 9-14.

FIGURE 9-14. THREE-NOTE BLUES PROGRESSION

Four-part open-voiced chords are recommended for some intermediate and advanced guitarists in the jazz ensemble. Four-part chords are always played on the sixth, fourth, third, and second strings. The fifth and first strings should be muffled by the fingers playing other notes. The blues progression in Figure 9-15 is provided in four-part open-voiced chords.

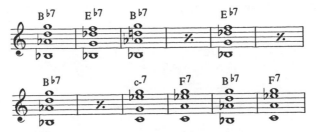

FIGURE 9-15. FOUR-NOTE BLUES PROGRESSION

Comping Behind a Soloist

Comping behind a soloist is more difficult than playing straight rhythm guitar. Use chord voicings taken from the higher strings (fifth, third, second, and first) of the guitar. These chords get a lighter sound than the heavily voiced chords whch use five or six strings. In comping, it is always better to play too little than too much. If the piano player is comping, either lay out completely or just play straight rhythm guitar. Another good effect is for the piano player and guitarist to work out some kind of a figure they can play together. At other times, the piano player can lay out and let the guitar do all the comping. The piano and guitar should never comp at the same time behind a soloist since this results in a confined sound.

PUTTING TOGETHER THE FOUR-PIECE RHYTHM SECTION

As previously indicated, the rhythm section provides the heartbeat of the jazz ensemble. When its members play well together and are sensitive to each other and to the needs of the entire group, the music comes alive. A working knowledge of each instrument in this section by the director is essential in order to know how to put the section together musically. Consider the following areas of concern for your rhythm section: (1) tempo, (2) dynamics, (3) balance, and (4) comping style.

If the tempo in your group ever starts to fall apart during a performance, the rhythm section should immediately look around at each other and have one player cue the others so that it comes together. When in trouble, the drummer needs to simplify playing and get the hi-hat clicking tightly on beats 2 and 4, while getting the ride cymbal cooking in straight fours. Don't allow the bass drum pedal to be used as a timekeeper because it tends to slow down the tempo. It is the bass player's primary function to keep a pulsating, rhythmic beat, so the drummer must not conflict with the time set by the bass player. The hi-hat should follow the bass player's beat. Rushing or dragging the tempo puts undue strain on the beat of the rhythm section and the band. Be sure the bass sound has enough treble definition and edge. Generally, bass players tend to drag tempos due to lack of control or from tension. Be alert to these problems.

The rhythm section actually has control over the volume of the entire band. A loud rhythm section will strain brass players and make lead players uncomfortable. Good brass "chops" can be worn out quickly when they are forced to play too loudly just to be heard. Good rhythm sections can play with just as much intensity but at a softer level. Directors should require all rhythm section players to mark dynamics in their parts to correspond with the band or soloists. When the rhythm section is felt rather than heard, the balance across the band will improve immediately. It may not be easy to have a rhythm section with such flexibility in adjusting to dynamics, but it is well worth the effort. A general rule is: solo, soli, and unison passages should all be played softer than tutti or short passages written in harmony.

For rhythm section balance, any player having trouble hearing the other players in the section should automatically play softer. This is particularly important in the rhythm section where certain players will often try to dominate the section.

Comping is the most sophisticated area in which a rhythm section has to coordinate their efforts. It can be defined as the ultimate art of the rhythm section to accompany a jazz group or soloist in a manner that is complimentary in style and presentation. An insensitive rhythm player can easily negate the rest of the section and stifle the creativity of the entire ensemble. Each player must clearly understand the specific responsibilities of his or her position and must be a good listener to the other rhythm players, to soloists, and to the entire band.

It is the director's responsibility to fully understand the role of each of the players in the rhythm section and to be able to communicate any remedial steps that need to be taken. It is very much in the director's best interest to convince the rhythm section members to develop excellent listening skills. A wise director will take the time to select various recordings that feature the desired way a rhythm section works, or at least the correct manner of performance of one element in music. It is then not enough to expect the rhythm section members to just hear the music—the director should focus the members' attention to the specific details that are most crucial. Finally, the director should encourage the rhythm section to perceive themselves as a separate combo from the remainder of the ensemble; the tighter the rhythm section plays together, the tighter the entire ensemble performs.

THE USE OF AUXILIARY PERCUSSION

NOTE: The authors want to thank Pat Hanley, 8673 Litzsinger, Brentwood, MO 63144, for assistance in the preparation of this section.

The present role of the jazz band percussionist is always expanding. In addition to drum-set and vibraphone, it is common to use auxiliary percussion. Besides involving another percussionist in the program, it also adds many new and exciting tone colors to the music. The best philosophy is that: "The auxiliary percussionist is an integral and meaningful member of the ensemble, not just an extra added attraction." Playing correctly on all of the instruments within the auxiliary percussion domain takes as much skill as for any other member of your group. The following lists include the most practical instruments for most school situations.

Auxiliary Percussion Basic Equipment

Traditional Latin Instruments

Conga Drums

Bongos

Timbales

Claves

Maracas

Guiro

Large and Small Cowbells

Suspended Cymbal

Jazz-Rock Fusion Instruments

Conga Drums

Tambourine (with head)

Triangle (standard and glissando)

Cabasa/Afuche

Large and Small Cowbells

Agogo Bells

Wooden Agogos/Reco Reco

Suspended Cymbal

Shakers:
  Tuba/Ganza (metal tubes)
  Caxixis (wicker with handles)
  Homemade

Instruments That Are Used as Colors

Vibra-Slap

Flexatone

Samba Whistle (multi-pitched
  police whistle)

Bell Tree

Wind Chimes (metal/glass/bamboo/shell)

Piccolo Wood Block

Finger Cymbals

An indication of the importance of auxiliary percussion can be seen in the number of professional studio percussionists working on recordings. The auxiliary percussionist has also become an integral part of various contemporary jazz groups such as Spyro Gyra, Pat Matheny, Lee Ritenour, Bob James, and so on.

At first glance, the cost of auxiliary percussion might seem prohibitive for some directors. For around $200, you can equip an auxiliary percussionist with everything except the conga drums. Of course, you may have to make some of the instruments, shop at an import store, and/or take a trip to the junk yard. One good source for these instruments is:

> Brazilian Imports of Santa Cruz
> P.O. Box 1454
> Santa Cruz, CA 95061

Since many of these instruments are fragile, it is important to take care of them to minimize replacement The less breakage you have, the more you can spend on new additions to your auxiliary percussion collection. You must instill pride in the player and provide a good safe place for storage so that the instruments are not used as toys by non-percussionists. It's a good idea to wrap the more fragile items in old towels after each use for protection.

Conga Drums

Used wisely, the conga drum can add polyrhythms and textural variations to the rhythm section. It can accentuate the feeling of the hi-hat or, if used continuously, the conga drone under the band sounds like a heavy bass drum.

Conga drums are made in three sizes. The smallest drum is called the "quinta," the middle-sized drum is the "conga," and the largest is called "tambodora." The most popular sizes range from $22'' \times 8''$ for the quinta to $30'' \times 12''$ for the tambodora. Most conga players use two drums, with the smaller drum placed on the player's left.

There are three types of conga drum construction: (1) wooden body with no tension rods, (2) wooden body with tension rods, and (3) fiberglass body with tension rods. Because they provide the more natural sound of native drums, congas without tension rods are more authentic-sounding for accompanying interpretive dancers who perform the traditional dances of Africa, Cuba, Haiti, and other Caribbean islands. Congas with tension rods are easier to tune and are usually preferred for jazz use. These drums should be tuned a perfect fourth apart in pitch, with the heads on the tight side for more projection without too much force needed. The heads should be loosened after each use to avoid stretching. Fiberglass drums are used primarily in the big band setting because of their powerful resonance. Wooden body drums, usually more expensive and providing a more natural sound, are particularly versatile.

From all the percussion instruments that can be added to the rhythm section, the conga drum requires the most attention to details. It is not mere brute force that produces the correct sound, but a combination of correct hand and finger positions complimented by striking the skins with the appropriate speed. For short sounds, strike near the edge of the drum with the palm of the left hand. For deeper, booming sounds, strike in the center of the drum with the palm of the right hand. Do not allow the fingers to remain on the head after hitting the drum as this will deaden the tone. The fingers should remain straight but without tension.

There are two basic striking areas on the conga drum and each results in its own distinct tone. The illustration in Figure 9-16 shows the location of the striking area and its resultant tone.

Strike the shaded area to produce an open tone.

Strike the shaded area to produce a closed tone.

FIGURE 9-16. CONGA STRIKING AREAS AND TONE PRODUCTION

Conga drums can be played in either a standing or seated position. A conga drum mounted on a stand has greater volume since the sound can be projected from the drum bottom. This position also permits the auxiliary percussionist to have freer access to other instruments. It is possible to obtain a greater variety of tones by playing the conga seated because the feet can raise or lower the drum as it is struck. To play the conga in the seated position, the drum must rest off the floor, on your feet, and tilted slightly forward. If the floor is carpeted, the congas can sound muffled. To correct this, place a wooden board under the drum(s) to produce more projection and sound.

The right hand produces open and closed tones on a conga drum. The open tone is a full, unmuffled, true sound produced by hitting the edge of the drum. This technique requires that the hand be removed quickly after striking the head. All the fingers, except the thumb, strike the head in a flat position.

The closed tone is produced by hitting the center of the drum with either a full cupped hand or the palm of the hand. The palm of the hand produces a slap effect while the full cupped hand gives more of a thud effect. These are done quickly and result in a pitch considerably higher than the open tone sound. By keeping the left hand on the drum head, the pitch can be made even higher. In the open tone, the fingers bounce off the head, while in the slap sound, they grab the head.

The left hand is used for accents. The heel of the hand and the tips of the fingers are used for basic types of left-hand strokes. The left hand should slide across the surface and not be lifted off at all.

There are two basic styles of conga playing—South American and Afro-Cuban. The South American style stresses the use of cupped hands to produce high sounds and emphasizes the open and closed sounds with the use of cupped or flat hands. Prominent performers of this style include Mongo Santamaria, Airto, and Ray Barretto.

In the Afro-Cuban style, the higher closed sounds are produced by leaving the fingers flat. The open sounds are produced with the fingers across the drums. Afro-Cuban conga players include Joe Montego, Ralph McDonald, and Ramon Lopez.

Students should be encouraged to listen to all of the above performers and develop skill in both styles. Listening is especially important for accurate conga performance. When playing correctly, these drums can really enhance a performance, but when played inaccurately, they have a tendency to just get in the way.

The basic rhythm patterns for various styles are provided below. Some of the variations can be used by themselves or in conjunction with other percussion instruments. Abbreviations and symbols used for conga drums are provided for reference in Figure 9-17.

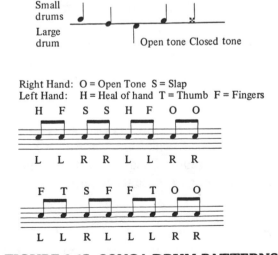

FIGURE 9-17. CONGA DRUM PATTERNS

Tambourine

The tambourine has several different applications in the jazz ensemble. When playing eighth or sixteenth notes in a rock chart, the tambourine should be held in the right hand, striking against the lower left palm for accents. Sustained rolls can be played for special effect. The tambourine can also be struck against the player's knee or more simply by laying it flat on the trap table. The shake roll is frequently used for rock type charts.

A bossa nova effect can be achieved by waving the tambourine back and forth on a straight eighth-note pattern. This creates a "jingle" sound. Just like in concert band, the tambourine should be held at chest level for maximum projection and clarity. Figure 9-18 shows several tambourine rhythm patterns.

Medium Rock:

+ = Palm of Left Hand

Light Rock:

Slow Rock:

Wave Motion: Bossa Nova

Disco:

Balance on knee & play on rim with fingertips.

Samba:

Hold tambourine in right hand with edge down.
K = hit edge on knee
H = hit with hand or fist inside tambourine

FIGURE 9-18. TAMBOURINE RHYTHM PATTERNS

Cowbell

The cowbell is held flat by the thumb and little finger. The other three fingers are placed on the back to aid muffling. If more muffling is needed, you may wrap tape around the mouth of the bell. The stick ought to be short and thick. The bell faces away from the player with the seam side up. The open sound is used for accent notes and is made by striking the edge of the bell. All other notes use a closed sound made by striking halfway down the bell. Care should be taken not to interfere with the drummer's rhythm patterns. Figure 9-19 illustrates some cowbell rhythm patterns.

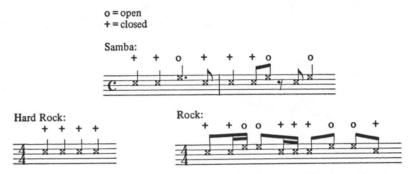

FIGURE 9-19. COWBELL RHYTHM PATTERNS

Claves

Claves are a pair of sticks generally made of rose wood that form the basis for most Latin music. The pair comes in two pitches, the lower of which is usually held in the left hand. For best resonance, the left hand is cupped and the clave is placed on top of the fingers. The right clave strikes the left and produces the higher pitch. Several clave rhythm patterns are shown in Figure 9-20.

FIGURE 9-20. CLAVE RHYTHM PATTERNS

Triangle

The triangle is held palm-down in the left hand by the first finger around the holder or clip. In this way, the triangle can be muffled by the palm and second and third fingers. The triangle is played with the beater striking the inner sides of the triangle and each note is played on a different side. Usually, the first note is played on the bottom side. More delicate bell-tones, however, are produced closer to the top. A triangle with ridges cut in one side is also available to provide a glissando effect. The triangle is a possible wind chime substitute. Figure 9-21 shows four triangle rhythm patterns.

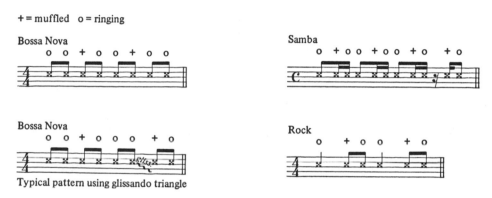

FIGURE 9-21. TRIANGLE RHYTHM PATTERNS

Shakers

Tube-type shakers are best held parallel to the floor and grasped with the palm faced upward and the thumb wrapped on top of the shaker. It is best to move the shaker forward and backward so that the beads strike the front and back in a steady rhythm. Wicker shakers are held upright and played by hitting the bottom on the palm of the hand.

Many studio percussionists make their own shakers from such items as soda cans, panty hose plastic containers, and film canisters. They fill these items with gravel, popcorn, rice, and so on, for a variety of tone colors.

Cabasa/Afuche

This is a valuable and frequently used auxiliary instrument. It is often played in a "twist" motion (see Figure 9-22). The instrument is held in the right hand while the sphere is rotated against the palm of the left hand. The beads should only come in contact with the middle three fingers.

FIGURE 9-22. CABASA/AFUCHE RHYTHM PATTERNS

Other effects include the "shake" and the "disco gallop." For the shake, the instrument is held in one hand which thrusts it in a back-and-forth direction. For accents or louder passages, the thrust is lengthened. In the disco gallop, the left·palm is hit by the cabasa on the eighth note and the two sixteenth notes are played by two quick up strokes in the air. This works best when the player waits until the last second before lifting the cabasa from the hand.

Guiro

The guiro is a hollo gourd-like instrument with ridges cut in a row along one side. Traditionally, the guiro is held in the left hand perpendicular to the floor. A thin wood stick is wiped across the ridges and all playing is done with a down stroke.

Maracas

Maracas are basic to Latin rhythms. Several techniques have evolved in their use. For single notes and accents, a full stroke can be used in which the beads alternately hit the top and the bottom of the gourd as a group. By holding the gourd in one hand and hitting it with the index fingertip, the beads will only bounce on the bottom of the gourd to produce a "dry" sound.

Rolls can be produced by a full shake or swirl in which the gourd is held upside down with the handle held between the two palms and turned repeatedly in a circular motion.

Full Stroke   Finger Stroke

The use of auxiliary percussion can either add a dimension of excitement to the rhythm section or clutter up the chart. Consider the following guidelines in making the choice of the appropriate instruments.

1. The style of the chart should be the prime consideration. The instrument should complement the style no matter what it is.

2. The instrument's characteristic sound should fit the intensity and mood of the chart. For example, the cowbell adds power and drive to a rock chart, the tambourine would fit into something with less intensity, and a cabasa could be used in a light rock chart.

3. The decision needs to be made about the *function* of the instrument. Do you want timekeeping or a color?

4. The percussionist should stay on one instrument within a chord cycle and avoid changing a timekeeping instrument within a chorus.

5. As an integral part of the percussion "team" and rhythm section, the auxiliary player should be careful not to get in the way of the drummer or soloist.

6. Avoid continuous use of auxiliary percussion throughout the chart. It's a good idea to provide "space" within any chart.

7. Try to use a tasteful combination of time and color instruments. A variety of texture can enhance the character of a chart.

8. Always strive to exercise good taste and moderation!

Table 9-1 lists the albums of several well-known recording artists who have made use of auxiliary percussion instruments.

THE ROLE OF THE VIBRAPHONE

Although the vibraphone is not considered a newcomer to jazz (it has been used for over sixty years!), it is not usually viewed as a standard instrument in school jazz groups. Its strength is in a unique tone color different from any other instrument. Also, it can be used for solos, as a double for other melody instruments, and/or as a harmonic instrument similar to the guitar or piano. Vibes are particularly effective when doubled with flutes, guitar, or muted brass. The biggest problem usually encountered with vibes, however, happens when the piano, guitar, and vibes comp at the same time. Just like when a conflict occurs between guitar and piano, the best solution

TABLE 9-1. AUXILIARY PERCUSSION DISCOGRAPHY

ALBUM	*ARTIST*	*LABEL & #*	SIDE & TRACK	INSTRUMENTS
Free	Airto	CTI/CTC 6020	S2/T1 ("Free")	Flexatone Wood Agogos Shakers Cowbells
Free	Airto	CTI/CTC 6020	S1/T1 ("Return to Forever")	Picc. Wood Block Shaker Agogo Bells Wind Chimes
Morning Dance	Spyro Gyra	Infinity INFC 9004	S1/T1 ("Morning Dance")	Congas Shakers Steel Drum Triangle Picc. Wood Block
"	"	"	S1/T3 ("Little Linda")	Bongos
"	"	"	S1/T4 ("Song for Lorraine")	Agogo Bells
The Path	Ralph MacDonald	Marlin Mar 2210	S2/T2 ("Feels So Good")	Congas Cowbell
"	"	"	S2/T3 ("Smoke Rings & Wine")	Finger Cymbals
Carnaval	Spyro Gyra	MCA/MCAC 5149	S1/T4 ("Cachaca")	Guiro Flexatone Shakers Castanets Agogo Bells Cowbell Congas
"	" "	S2/T4	("Carnaval")	Triangle Samba Whistle Cuica

is to alternate comping instruments behind different soloists and thus provide more variety and contrast to the rhythm section.

Vibes players need to be proficient in both two- and four-mallet technique since the vibes part often calls for large intervals and double stops in one or both hands. Choice of appropriate mallets is important to ensure that the right timbre is effected.

As a solo instrument, one or two mallets are often used. This technique does not overly tax students with previous keyboard experience, and a smooth transition is common. As the vibes player becomes more adept and skillful, the use of three or four mallets grows more appropriate.

Dampening and pedaling techniques contribute to the phrasing of musical lines. These techniques are particularly important when three or four mallets are used where notes can ring and overlay. The pedaling technique on the vibraphone is similar to that of the piano. By depressing the pedal, any note struck is sustained. This is usually indicated by a slur marking. Phrasing and blending on vibes can be improved during pedaled passages with the use of dampening. Mallet dampening is accomplished by striking a note, dampening that note by pressing the mallet head on the tone bar while another mallet strikes the next note, and then continuing the process. The final result is a smooth line with certain notes dampened and other notes (or chords) sustained.

Currently, vibrato is limited on vibes to better emphasize clear tones. When the vibrato is not in use, the fans in the resonators should be vertical (facing straight up and down) so that the sound will have maximum projection. When vibrato is used, the speed should match the desired effect of the composition. Medium and slow vibrato speeds are often used too infrequently. While a fast vibrato can be effective, it can also become trite if overused.

The vibes should be placed near the piano. It is usually necessary to amplify vibes to produce clarity in the jazz ensemble setting. Some companies (Deagan and Musser) manufacture pick-ups that can be attached to the vibes and can then be plugged into any system. Otherwise, it is necessary to use microphones (two are best) mounted on boom stands.

Even with beginning vibes players, chord voicing techniques should be considered. Of the four notes found in 7th or 6th chords, the two most important notes are the third and seventh (or sixth). These notes determine the quality of the chord. The notes are commonly guide tones or color tones. The vibes player should become sensitive to these particular chord tones so that movement of chord progressions will be easier. For more details concerning two-, three-, and four-part voicings, read about the piano. When playing three- and four-note chords, add the root and do not substitute the ninth for the root as is commonly the case with guitar voicings. For best voice leading in four-part open chords, keep the guide tones in one hand and the fifth and root in the other. When more tension is desired, add the ninth, flat ninth, or sharp ninth and leave out the root of the chord. You may also elect to add the eleventh, sharped eleventh, or thirteenth, and omit the fifth of the chord. Closed chords (when the notes of the chord are voiced directly beneath one another) are easiest to play and voice. Playing open voiced chords provides a warmer, more legato sound and is particularly suitable for backing up a soloist.

10

The String Section

Today's jazz includes an expanded use of string instruments. Not only are strings being used for studio orchestra settings or the occasional jazz combo, but jazz ensembles are featuring string sections with many arrangements specifically designed to take advantage of the string section sound as distinctively as the sax, trumpet, trombone, or rhythm section sound. Whether you want to offer one string player the chance to sit in with the group occasionally or maintain a complete string section full-time, you are encouraged to "think strings" when it comes to performing jazz.

THE MANY APPLICATIONS OF STRINGS IN JAZZ PERFORMANCE

The use of string instruments is, of course, dictated by the musical setting and circumstances of availability. Each type of group offers special demands and opportunities.

Strings in the Jazz Combo

In this situation, you may approach the combo setting from two entirely different points of view—the combo setting which utilizes one string player, or the string combo (a "wire choir" comprised of a string quartet or more hooked to amplification is a popular example of this), with added rhythm section.

A jazz string combo is, to be sure, an ambitious undertaking. There are not as many arrangements specifically written for such a group (although the area is rapidly expanding) and there are few models to emulate. Nevertheless, this type of setting is especially well suited for an educational experience for all involved since (1) the group can learn jazz style and concepts as a unit, (2) there are no built-in performance demands (at least until your first performance), (3) distraction is limited to the rhythm section (which provides lots of attention to the special needs of the string players), and (4) the potential of creativity is extremely high.

You may choose music specifically written for string combo (unfortunately, much of this is very demanding and requires first-rate players) or you may choose to substitute easy charts originally written for jazz combo where you rewrite the parts for the various string players. In many cases, any talented and motivated student can easily develop some basic writing and arranging skill by doing this work for you. Since there are many similarities of ranges and parts, the transposition is fairly straightforward. The standard transpositions are provided in Figure 10-1.

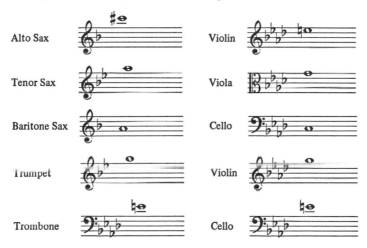

FIGURE 10-1. STRING TRANSPOSITION

If you only have one or two string players capable of performing jazz, encourage them to sit in with your combo. Since most combos deal more with very informal charts or head arrangements, the string player need only learn the lead lines and any backup riffs behind soloists. Emphasis should be on fitting in with the group so that the string instruments match the style, articulation, rhythm, and so on of the others without intruding. The string student can really focus on the most noticeable jazz characteristics—inflection, feel, and concept—at a more rapid pace since the other members of the combo help serve as a model.

Strings in the Jazz Ensemble

A jazz ensemble can be represented by a whole new dimension with the addition of a string section. For balance considerations, it works best if you add equal multiples of the standard string quartet: two violins, one viola, and one cello. Other combinations are possible but prove unwieldy. The diagrams shown in Figures 10-2 and 10-3 show a jazz ensemble with an amplified string quartet and an ensemble with three players on each part. Two strings on each part tend to create intonation problems. In each diagram, it should be noted that all wind players are standing, and that a large stage area is necessary for such an ensemble. String players (with the exception of cellos) may, of course, stand, but if they are amplified, there is much more wear and tear on the equipment and string players are usually less used to playing while standing than are wind players.

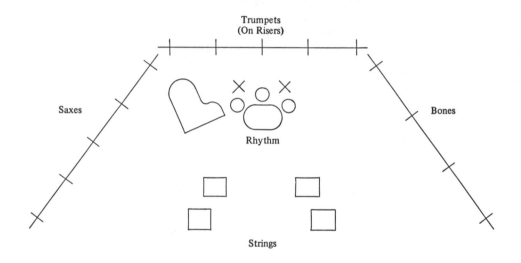

FIGURE 10-2. JAZZ ENSEMBLE SETUP WITH AMPLIFIED STRING QUARTET

There are many outstanding arrangements specifically designed for the jazz ensemble that use a string section. Some of these charts are very demanding on the string players, but represent a real showcase for that section. Charts that do not include parts written for strings can be turned into an asset by your enlisting members of the jazz ensemble to work closely with you to write special parts that allow the string section to perform the music with the ensemble, while not "getting in the way" of the original arrange-

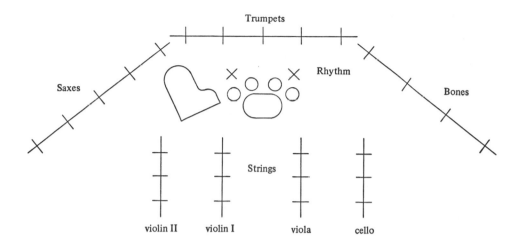

**FIGURE 10-3. JAZZ ENSEMBLE SETUP
WITH 12-PIECE STRING SECTION**

ment. The student arranger can learn a great deal about voicings, range, and selectivity by using a full score and taking advantage of your guidance. String parts can double any of the sections, cover a guitar or vibes (this is especially nice if you don't already have the player), or be featured in place of an open piano line. In any case, the string players will be a productive part of your group and your students are encouraged to eventually complete full arrangements and compositions.

Larger String Orchestras

Whereas the first two ensembles described above start with the jazz group and add strings, the studio orchestra offers string players an opportunity to play essentially within the context of the regular orchestra setting. Instead of having to deal with a new style and a new environment, the players are able to focus on style from within a familiar atmosphere. There are many fine arrangements designed for the studio orchestra at all levels. The music runs the gamut of popular styles from ragtime to jazz/rock and can easily become a part of any orchestra's repertory. Since that repertoire is probably comprised of more traditional compositions, it is recommended that the orchestra begin this repertory development with something familiar to players and audience before moving gradually to the less familiar areas such as bebop or early jazz.

Sources for Jazz String Materials

There are various publishers today who are addressing the specific needs of strings in the jazz setting. The following list comprises a number of such publishers:

William Bolthouse
P.O. Box 55
Monterey, CA 93940

Creative Jazz Composers
P.O. Box T
Bowie, MD 20715

Etoile Music, Inc.
Shell Lake, WI 54871

Charles Hansen
1860 Broadway
New York, NY 10023

Kendor Music
Delevan, NY 14042

Lantana Music Publishing
22118 Lantana Court
Castro Valley, CA 94546

Edgar Redmond
1609 Third Avenue
Los Angeles, CA 90019

Young World Publications
10485 Glennon Drive
Lakewood, CO 80226

Campus Music Service
P.O. Box AA
Hawthorne, CA 90250

Ellis Music Enterprises
c/o Pete Lengyel
Eastfield College
3737 Motley Dr.
Mesquite, TX 75150

Jazz Education Press
P.O. Box 802
Manhattan, KS 66502

Laissez-Faire Music
810 N. Cumberland
Lebanon, TN 37087

Ladd McIntosh
7712 Alcove Avenue
North Hollywood, CA 91605

Steve Wright Music Endeavors
15631 Lexington Circle
Minnetonka, MN 55343

AMPLIFICATION OPTIONS FOR STRINGS

The biggest problem associated with the use of strings in jazz is the lack of volume. In any jazz setting, an acoustic violin doesn't have a chance to be heard. The symphony orchestra's solution to this problem is to use a very large string section, but this proves impractical for the jazz educator. There are two approaches to amplification—the use of a pickup or microphone—but each solution shares one common problem: an amplified string instrument produces an inferior quality sound. You must work very hard with the players and sound system to try to develop the best possible tone quality. The sound coming from an amplifier will never sound like its acoustic source, but it can be developed into something appropriate for jazz.

The most popular kind of pickup used by string players is the transducer. The most popular brand is made by Barcus-Berry in the shape of a "T" and is attached with adhesive to the bridge. As an alternative, you may also choose to use a simple phonograph needle assembly or Radio Shack's glass-like harmonica pickup. Obviously, these devices are not specifically designed for strings, but they are less expensive, though more fragile, and with experimentation, can produce an adequate sound.

A wire then leads from the pickup to the amplifier (some string players prefer the use of a pre-amp, but it is optional and up to the director). The wire is very light, so students must be cautious in their movements when they play.

There are other pickups specifically designed for use with string instruments (a list is provided at the end of this section), and you may want to experiment to see which you prefer. The advantage of using a pickup is the direct sound produced by an element that actually becomes a part of the instrument. The disadvantage is the inherent fragility of the equipment.

The use of a microphone with a string instrument provides volume without many of the immediate tone production problems built into a pickup system. In many cases, no special equipment is needed if you already have a system, and none of the equipment is so delicate.

Microphone amplification is particularly desirable when only one string player is to be added to an ensemble. The string player must concentrate on keeping the instrument very near the microphone (this is often awkward), which sometimes produces a "stiffness" in the playing of the string player.

Difficulties are compounded, however, with the use of more than one string player. Because of the limited control associated with the use of a microphone (or microphones), balance and volume become major concerns.

Electric string instruments are available, though they are much more expensive than amplification systems. The electric instruments are created out of standard wooden bodies that are then covered with a very glossy lacquer specifically designed to improve the amplification. The instruments are the same size as conventional instruments, but heavier. The pickup is built into the bridge and a volume control knob is built near the chinrest. The main advantage is that the instrument is inherently stronger and specifically created for use as an amplified instrument.

Sources for String Amplification

The following list includes just a few names of companies that build equipment specifically for string amplification.

Acoustic Amplifiers
Acoustic Control Corp.
7949 Woodley Ave.
Van Nuys, CA 91406

Frap Pickups
1061 Fulsom
San Francisco, CA 94140

Barcus-Berry Transducers
  & Pre-Amps
5461 Springfield St.
Long Beach, CA 92649

Polytone Pickups & Amplifiers
1261 N. Vine St.
Hollywood, CA 90038

JAZZ ARTICULATION TECHNIQUES FOR STRINGS

Jazz bowing demands a different approach than found with the traditional "up-bow, down-bow, detaché" focus. The jazz string player must learn to be more concerned with expressing the music, so phrasing should become the primary principle. Since a rock beat is usually more even and straightforward, the string player with a traditional background will initially feel more comfortable by making the transition to rock or fusion charts as a first step in developing a jazz repertoire. The string player needs to listen closely to jazz phrasing and work towards imitating the articulation and rhythm concepts found in jazz. This requires using a non-traditional approach by bowing with a relaxed, irregular bow stroke. The string player will want to make use of the entire bow whenever possible to avoid a "choppy" sound. Working with a jazz string player does not mean starting over with bowing techniques; it is merely a practice of modifying bowing according to stylistic demands.

Although pizzicato is a powerful musical device, it is most often used by the cello and bass. There is a volume problem associated with pizzicato that amplification does not completely solve. Nevertheless, in the right musical conditions—a *piano* preparation so that the audience can pay attention for instance, with amplification so that all the strings can be heard—pizzicato can sound most impressive (see Don Ellis's "Strawberry Soup" on the Columbia Album *Tears of Joy*). Facility in pizzicato passages can be achieved by alternation of fingers whenever the notes cross the string or where there is a consistent rhythm pattern. Some young players may find pizzicato easier if the violin or viola is held like a guitar or ukelele; this is especially true if there is a very fast passage. In addition, guitar-like "strum" can be achieved where there are chordal passages.

Vibrato is one of those areas of flag-waving proportions in jazz controversy. Nothing draws attention to "poor concept" in performance quite as fast as inappropriate vibrato. In string playing, there is usually one vibrato applied to all music in general. In jazz, most players have a wide repertory of vibrato, with variety of speed, width, and placement according to the demands and style of the music. String players should be aware of this variety and strive to imitate jazz vibrato concepts. On the other hand, a good general "rule of thumb" is—when in doubt about vibrato, *use less!*

JAZZ STYLES IN STRING PERFORMANCE

Because of the paucity of string players in jazz, it is possible to isolate these few performers and make some general comments about their style. Since young string players interested in playing jazz have few models to emulate, this means that the few artists who do exist should be listened to most attentively. The young jazz string student should be encouraged to imitate and reproduce the solos and styles of these artists.

The style concept of the swing player is consistent, regardless of instrumentation. Students may emulate Stephane Grappelli, Ray Nance, Ray Perry, Stuff Smith, and Joe Venuti for their tone and style, but because swing emphasizes the *music* rather than the *instrument*, the student may choose any swing musican and develop the appropriate style and concept.

Although the post-bebop string player approaches the music in much the same fashion as any other jazz musician, there is growing emphasis on making the instrument speak its unique language. String players have begun to utilize those aspects of their instruments that are distinctive: tone, technique, and range, in addition to such special effects as pizzicato, double stops, glisses, and tremolos. The full spectrum of the entire string section is now represented with performances by the cello and bass (used now as a *solo* instrument rather than just a part of the rhythm section). Stephane Grappelli and Jean-Luc Ponty on violin are joined by David Baker, Ray Brown, Ron Carter, and Oscar Pettiford on cello; and Ray Brown, Ron Carter, Paul Chambers, Percy Heath, Milt Hinton, Charlie Mingus, and Leroy Vinnegar on bass (the bass is the fastest-growing solo instrument in jazz with incredible facility demonstrated by numerous others). Since the instrument is emphasized (in bebop), the music sometimes suffers; there are few examples of string players mastering the bebop and post-bebop styles for this reason. Young string players should listen to these string players for instrumental concepts but also listen to top horn players and singers to better understand and master the musical concepts.

The examples of jazz string players performing *avant-garde* jazz is characterized by incredible fluency on the instrument. Ornette Coleman and Jean-Luc Ponty on violin, and David Baker, Ron Carter, and Joel Friedman on cello, are joined by the bass performances of Ron Carter, Richard Davis, Charlie Haden, Charlie Mingus, Steve Swallow, and Wilbur Ware. Nevertheless, the source for all the inspirational performances of today reflects directly back to the work of Jimmy Blanton.

Jimmy Blanton was the bassist for Duke Ellington during the 1930s. Had he lived, it is impossible to project where his creative ability might have led. In much the same manner that all wind players should be aware of the earliest jazz influences for their instrument, string players should listen to Jimmy Blanton and be aware of all the musicians who have performed on string instruments in a jazz setting.

ADVANTAGES TO YOUR PROGRAM
WHEN YOU ADD STRINGS

Since this book is concerned with jazz *education*, the string student who lacks exposure to jazz is getting an incomplete education. Even the string player who only has an isolated experience with jazz is being cheated, so it is important for *all* music students to have a full understanding of this music.

There is evidence that string players who participate in jazz performance bring a more assertive and confident approach to the remainder of the playing. In addition, where there has been a consistent use of string players within a jazz setting, enrollment has increased for all performance groups. Finally, the use of strings is highly appealing to the audience from both a musical and visual perspective.

Putting It Together

11

Budgeting and Funding: Survival of the Fittest

PUTTING TOGETHER THE BEST BUDGET

The complete jazz program doesn't stop with an emphasis on technical fluency and aesthetic progress. Budget "savvy" is essential for the jazz educator in order to systematically have the means to develop a jazz program to its fullest. There are three main aspects to successful budget mastery: insight, consciousness, and strategy. You need insight to understand the workings and mechanisms that make up a budget; consciousness is essential 100 percent of the time; and strategy is needed to insure an intensive, comprehensive, and systematic budgeting program designed to reflect your needs and goals to the fullest.

As soon as possible, make it a point to confer with the person in your school or school system who deals most directly with your budget. Find out how the budget works for your system. You will want to know if there are any ways for you to increase your budget if you add new course offerings; whether you can purchase big items and have them paid for over three or five years; general procedures concerning bidding, purchase orders, etc.; and if there is extra money left over for a special purchase (rare, but not impossible).

Once you understand how your budget works, start a needs inventory. It is assumed that you already have a working inventory, but unless it specifically takes depreciation into consideration, you might want to use a special "depreciation inventory" available from the C. G. Conn Company, 2520 Industrial Parkway, Elkhart, IN 46516.

A needs inventory should include everything you feel your program is lacking. Since it is important to be efficient and systematic when dealing with your budget, list your needs according to categories: instruments and equipment, music, repairs, audio-visual, textbooks, and library needs. You should be concerned at this point with *what* you need, not how you will get it.

Be sure to include everything you *want*, but indicate priority according to the above categories by listing your needs first and wants last. At the end of this process, you should have a complete idea of what you have, should have, and would like to have.

Make certain that all the exotic instruments somewhat unique to jazz, such as soprano sax, flugel horn, electric piano, and conga drums, are included. Mutes, dance band stands, lights, music folders, mouthpieces, and travel cases should also be listed under this category.

Now is an excellent time to take a "condition inventory" where you check all the instruments and equipment to ascertain which instruments need to be repaired. Instruments and equipment that don't work don't count in your regular inventory since they can't be used. The key to a full working inventory is anticipation—a minor problem with an instrument will almost always develop into a disabling one if it's ignored.

There is no bigger waste of money than music that is purchased, rehearsed a couple of times, and then never looked at again. Care and attention to selection of music is something that should be a primary and constant process. Keep a list of charts you like performed by other groups, and make certain an arrangement will work for your group! Listen to promotion records and tapes provided by publishers. Get on mailing lists by writing to publishers and asking for study scores, records, or tapes (see Chapter 4). Learn the name of your favorite writers and arrangers so that if a new chart comes out and it is not recorded, you will know from experience the quality and basic concept of the arrangement.

Take advantage of the reviews of jazz charts found in each issue of *The Instrumentalist* and *Jazz Educators Journal*. These reviews include all pertinent information and can be invaluable.

Although curriculum is generally the main criterion for any textbook, do not be limited by lack of curriculum! Even if you are not offering courses in improvisation, jazz history, jazz theory, jazz arranging, orchestration, and jazz appreciation, there should be books available for your students to use. These books, with their focus on "how-to" aspects of jazz, should be in the domain of the music department and not the library.

Improvisation books should include a variety of approaches, including the use of records and tapes. Try to develop an entire series—the *Jamey Aebersold Series* is a primary example—so that the aspiring student can complete his or her knowledge on an individualized basis.

Try to develop a balanced and comprehensive set of textbooks—half should deal with improvisation and the other half should deal with those subjects that you feel will be of most interest and benefit to your students. The main idea of developing a textbook library within your department is to directly benefit your students. These books should always be in use!

The following list includes recommended textbooks on theory, arranging and composition, and jazz history.

Theory

Baker, D. *A New Approach to Ear Training for Jazz Musicians.* Lebanon, IN: Studio P/R.

Curtis, W. *First Steps to Ear Training.* Boston, MA: Berklee Press.

Dunbar, T. *System of Tonal Convergence for Improvisors, Composers, and Arrangers.* Kendall Park, NJ: Dunte Publishing Co.

Grove, D. *Fundamentals of Modern Harmony.* Studio City, CA: Dick Grove Publishing.

Kvam, A. K. *Rutgers University Music Dictation.* New York, NY: Music Minus One Corporation.

LaPorta, J. *Ear Training Phase I.* Boston, MA: Berklee Press.

Minasi, D. *Musician's Manual for Chord Substitutions.* Maspeth, NY: Sunrise Artistries, Inc.

Mymit, C. *Contemporary Harmony I* and *Workbook.* Merrick, NY: Five Towns College Press.

Rizzo, P. *Ear Training Based on 12 Tones.* Los Angeles, CA: Palisades Publishing.

Sandole, A. *Music Primer.* New York, NY: 1619 Broadway, Room 605.

Stanton, K. *Introduction to Jazz Theory.* New York, NY: Crescendo Publications.

Arranging and Composition

Bockholt, R. *Arranging Contrapuntally; Arranging for Small Ensembles; General Arranging Principles.* Las Vegas, NV: 2600 Arville Street.

Delamont, G. *Modern Arranging Technique; Modern Contrapuntal Technique.* Delevan, NY: Kendor Music.

Deutsch, M. *Encyclopedia of Arranging.* New York, NY: Charles Colin Music.

Kami, G. K. *Arranging Popular Music: A Practical Guide.* Downey, CA: Yamaha International.

Kerr, A. *Voices.* Melville, NY: MCA Music.

Leckrone, M. *Quicksteps to Arranging.* Lebanon, IN: Studio P/R.

Mymit, C. *Introduction to Small Band Arranging.* Merrick, NY: Five Towns College Press.

Principato, J. *The Arranger's Dreambook.* Monterey, CA: J. D. Music Publishing.

Rizzo, P. *Spread Chord Voicing.* Los Angeles, CA: Palisades Publishing.

Russo, W. *Jazz Composition and Orchestration.* Chicago, IL: University of Chicago Press.

Salat, H. *Arranging Made Simple:* West Babylon, NY: Harold Branch Publishing.

Spiegl, S. *Basic Theory and Arranging for Stage Band.* Orange, CA: Spiegl Music Publishing.

Taylor, B. *Jazz Combo Arranging.* New York, NY: Charles Hansen.

Jazz History

Berendt, J. *The Jazz Book.* New York, NY: Lawrence Hill and Co.

Berendt, J.(ed.) *The Story of Jazz.* Englewood Cliffs, NJ: Prentice-Hall, Inc.

Case, B., and S. Britt. *The Illustrated Encyclopedia of Jazz.* New York, NY: Harmony Books.

Collier, J. L. *The Making of Jazz.* Boston, MA: Houghton Mifflin Co.

Coryell, J., and L. Friedman. *Jazz-Rock Fusion.* New York, NY: Dell Publishing Co.

Erlich, L. *What Jazz Is All About.* New York, NY: Simon and Schuster.

Feather, L. *The Book of Jazz.* New York, NY: Horizon Press.

Feather, L., and I. Gitler. *The Encyclopedia of Jazz in the Seventies.* New York, NY: Horizon Press.

Hentoff, N., and A. McCarthy. *Jazz*. New York, NY: DaCapo Press.

McCarthy, A. *Big Band Jazz*. New York, NY: G. P. Putnam's Sons.

Schuller, G. *Early Jazz*. New York, NY: Oxford University Press.

Stearns, M. *The Story of Jazz*. New York, NY: Oxford University Press.

Tanner, P., and M. Gerow. *A Study of Jazz*. Dubuque, IA: William C. Brown Co.

White, M. *The Observer's Book of Jazz*. London, England: Frederick Warne.

Williams, M. *Jazz Panorama*. New York, NY: Collier Books.

Although audio-visual needs are dictated by diverse situations according-ing to the individual school, you should make certain that you always have access to recording equipment, your own set of tapes, and a sound system.

Your music library should include a tape of every concert you have per-formed and have the appropriate equipment so that you or your students may refer to that tape at any time. The tape recorder also serves as a helpful teaching aid in rehearsal situations. You can immediately point out prob-lems or use it for analysis after a rehearsal is concluded.

The NAJE annual conventions have had all clinics and performances taped for instructional reference since 1976. The following list indicates where you can purchase these valuable sources of information designed to help virtually every aspect of the jazz program.

1976 NAJE Convention Tapes
ASAP
13033 Ventura Boulevard
North Hollywood, CA 91604

1977 NAJE Convention Tapes
Sea Bird Recording Studio
415 N. Ridgewood Avenue
Edgewater, FL 32032

1978 NAJE Convention Tapes
Mother Dubbers, Inc.
2537 Carlisle
Dallas, TX 75201

1979, 1980, 1981, 1982, 1983, and
    so on NAJE Convention Tapes
Mark Educational Recordings
10815 Bodine Road
Clarence, NY 14031

Make certain you always have good-quality tapes available for recording your concerts. You will want the tape to hold up over the years, you may want to use it as a master tape to make a record, or you may want to use it as an audition tape for a national convention or some other major event.

There are some fine audio-visual aids specifically designed for jazz education. The following list of records and films represents what you may choose from until you build a really comprehensive and extensive collection.

Records

History of Jazz Series
Folkway Records
New York, NY

Jazz Education Packages
Follett Publishing Co.
Chicago, IL

The Smithsonian Collection of Jazz
Smithsonian Institute
Washington, DC

Educational Record Sales
157 Chambers Street
New York, NY

Films

(These films should be available from your local film rental agency.)

*African Soul Music, Past
and Present*
Carousel Films

Black Music in America
Indiana University

Blues
Oregon State University

*Duke Ellington Swings
Through Japan*
CBS-TV

The Jazz of Dave Brubeck
C.C.M. Films, Inc.

Manne and Jazz
University of Southern California

The Story of a Jazz Musician
ZIV–United Artists

Anatomy of a Hit
University of California
Extension Media Center

Black Music in Transition
Holt-Rinehart

Blues Like Showers of Rain
Impact Films

Jazz Is My Religion
Impact Films

Jazz—The Intimate Art
Robert Drew Associates

Mingus
Impact Films

If there has ever been an occasion when you needed a sound system from your school and it wasn't available, you may want your own individual system. If your school provides a completely satisfactory audio-visual service for all your needs, please remember to always be cooperative and appreciative—you have a rare and wonderful bonus in your school!

Don't ignore or neglect the library aspect of your needs. Use the library to complete a more general listing of books at the biographical level, make certain your library has at least one pictorial history book on jazz, and be aware of those books dealing with jazz on a level that would be of interest to the casual or non-musical student.

Encourage the library to carry a complete listing of jazz periodicals. *Jazz Educators Journal, The Instrumentalist, downbeat,* and *Billboard* magazines are all excellent sources for the library. Encourage your students to use the library for periodicals and, if there are periodicals that the students request, make sure the library gets them, too.

Many libraries include records in their catalogue. Start with those records that include arrangements your group will be playing, developing a complete jazz record collection that encompasses all styles and types of ensembles.

FINDING THE FUNDING

Statistics taken from a recent poll by *The Instrumentalist* indicate that over 50 percent of all music budget money comes from some sort of fund raising. With money getting tighter, the competition for each available dollar is certain to get even more intense. There are many fund-raising strategies, and the wise director is always open to all the creative possibilities. Fund raising need not be limited to door-to-door candy sales—in many instances, there are grants and benefits available through industry and organizations, as well as projects that can capture the attention and imagination of a community while bringing in money.

The National Endowment for the Arts has a specific section for jazz. This area is further divided into categories for professional groups, single performers or composers, and schools. While the requirements for acceptance are quite stringent, it is possible for any school system to qualify for an NEA grant with careful planning and preparation. Since the application must usually be submitted in June but can't actually be used before March or April of the following year, much thought, anticipation, and preparation should be applied. After the initial application, it is possible to maintain a schedule for each successive year; but it should be understood that, initially, the application process can be very time-consuming.

The majority of NEA grants available to schools are under the matching grant category. This means that the school provides x number of dollars for an event and the NEA matches that amount. This process, in effect, cuts your expenses for a big event (such as a clinic, concert, workshop, or artist-in-residence) in half.

NEA grants are particularly appealing for an artist-in-residence event. Having a jazz musician available for your school for an entire week or longer may seem inconceivable under normal circumstances, but an NEA grant makes such a situation more reasonable. The main point of acquiring an NEA grant should be to make an "impossible" event more likely.

The Music Performance Trust Fund (MPTF) has allocated large sums of money to NAJE in recent years. These funds are passed along to NAJE members for the employment of professional jazz musicians in an educational environment. This outright grant is available on the basis of payments to musicians directly at the local American Federation of Musicians' scale.

The requirements and conditions for eligibility are: the performance must be free and open to the general public, it must be *advertised* as free and open to the general public, the trustee's (that person in charge of allocating funds) credit line must be used in all press releases, programs, posters and other public announcements, and the performance must be in conjunction with an NAJE function.

MPTF application forms are available from NAJE, P.O. Box 724, Manhattan, KS 66502. The processing of applications usually takes 45 to 60 days. Once all requirements are complete, payrolls for the performance will be mailed to the leader of the requested group. This allows the director to be concerned with the logistical concerns of the performance and free from any of the financial concerns or considerations.

Since MPTF grants are provided in conjunction with the American Federation of Musicians, they are an excellent vehicle to provide support for your local professional musicians, expose your students to the performance and existence of local jazz musicians, strengthen public relations, and generally enhance your jazz program. Of course, the ultimate benefit is that there is no cost to your school or program!

Although they differ for each state in name, design, stated purpose, and area of application, there is some type of arts council in practically every state. Contact your state information office to find the name of the director of the council, a toll-free number, if there is any, for more specific information, the accurate title of the council, and the address. Apply immediately for all pertinent information and application forms. Find a time when you can devote yourself entirely to these forms without interruptions, since they are often like income tax forms—if they are not completed accurately, they are either returned to you or you do not receive your benefits. In addition to completing the form accurately and correctly, make certain all your information is very clear and that the form is submitted well before the application deadline.

Be prepared for an extended time-gap between the submission of your application and the actual implementation of a grant. There are often hundreds of applications and the council is charged with dispersing funds very carefully.

Since each state differs, you must investigate the guidelines outlined by your state to see how a grant can best be applied. You should examine every potential aspect of a state arts council grant with its specific relationship to your program.

There is a possibility that your state arts council can be of no help to you, so it is important for you to find out if their guidelines can be altered in the future. If you are unsuccessful with a state arts council application, do not give up; persist and keep in touch so that eventually you are in a position to benefit from a grant. Think of the money available through your state as rightfully being yours and continue to persevere! Design events that will conveniently fit precisely into your council's guidelines. With imagination, there are ways you can tap even the most stubborn state arts council.

Private sources are often overlooked or ignored as a provider of funds. Businesses located in your area are often willing to help underwrite your costs. In many instances, a parent of one of your students can provide contact with the person best able to help you.

Private sources can include businesses, industries, or individuals. They will all contribute to your program if you can convince them that your success will directly help them in some fashion. In some instances, a private source can provide your group with funding and in turn, your group can provide a performance for a special event or a special mention in your next concert. In all private grant situations, you must be careful to stay within the bounds of ethics and good taste. A grant from a controversial organization could in no way be deemed as in your best interest.

One specific way private sources can help underwrite your group expenses is by selling ads in a concert program. Divide the pages into eighths, quarters, halves, and whole-page offerings. Set up your program so that each increment is slightly more of a bargain per size of ad. A typical breakdown might look like this:

$ 35	1/8 page ad
$ 60	1/4 page ad
$100	1/2 page ad
$150	whole page ad

While the rate for a whole page ad doesn't match a whole page of 1/8 page ads (8 × $35.00 = $280.00), it is much more convenient to get one ad than eight. If you do use this method to solicit support from private sources, don't ignore a listing of patrons. Thus for a $5 or $10 donation, the patron has his or her name listed in the program and your group is directly underwritten. It is quite possible to have at least 100 names listed on a standard concert program-sized paper. This converts to over $500 in revenues.

The main elements for a successful concert program that uses ads are organization and time. It will take time to put together such a program, so you will need additional time to get it printed in advance of the performance. Nevertheless, the hard work is well worth the effort. As the breakdown of ad rates indicates, it is quite possible to make an average of $1,000 per open page (four sides of ads) without including patrons.

To some people, fund raising can be a terrifying experience and not worth the effort. In most cases, these persons have had exposure to a fundraising experience that has been unsuccessful. Here are a few simple rules that should serve as a guide for any fund-raising event.

- BE CREATIVE. Don't resort to the same fund-raising device as everyone else does in your community. Use your imagination to offer something everyone will want but is not offered by anyone else.
- BE CONSISTENT. If you find a fund-raising event that is creative and successful, make it an annual event! Have this event at the same time each year (perhaps linked with a holiday) and keep it at a consistently high level to ensure that members of the community will look forward to being your "customers."
- PLAN AHEAD. If you want to raise a large sum of money for a trip or some other big item, use a number of diverse projects rather than one "do or die" project. Plan the various projects so that you can reach your goal in plenty of time.
- GET EVERYONE INVOLVED. First, make certain that you share your goals with your band's parents. Be sure they agree with you about how to implement your plan, and then use their services so that the work load is evenly distributed. Don't be afraid to ask for help from anybody who can possibly be of assistance, such as your school art department or printing department.

The Instrumentalist provides a listing in each August issue of organizations that specialize in fund raising. Use this list for ideas and don't be afraid to interview numerous representatives to find and obtain the product and situation that is best for your group.

Broaden your creative horizons for fund raising by offering something other than a door-to-door campaign; a car wash, flea market sale, special meal, or movie can provide income for the group; an added advantage is that there is usually no overhead expense associated with these types of activities.

Though not necessarily a source of income in the fund raising sense, your group can gain over $100 in charts simply by having an NAJE 100% club. This simply involves getting every member of the group to enroll as a student member of NAJE. In this way, you have the use of more than $100 that you would have spent on the purchase of new music.

If you have an NAJE student chapter (and if you have a 100% club, you must have a chapter), the chapter can also sponsor special events to help underwrite your ensemble. Since membership in an NAJE student chapter is not restricted to just jazz ensemble members, it is possible to have a much larger chapter, with more students willing to help in their support of the jazz ensemble program.

A final area of fund raising for your jazz ensemble involves the most direct aspect you can offer: performance. While you don't want to do anything that is professionally unethical, you may accept donations for your performances, so that while your group is performing, it is also providing income. You might, for example, want to sponsor a dance for both the students and the parents. Make the evening a "bobby socks" night with music and clothes from the 1940s and 1950s, and you have the ingredients for an evening of fun and profit.

12

Promoting Your Program Through Special Activities

It's possible today to have one of the finest jazz programs anywhere and yet have it be a "best kept secret." Promotion is the life-giving breath necessary for your musical program, because without promotion, the best materials, work, and plans cannot achieve their full potential. Careful promotion not only adds a new dimension to any program, it can offer new opportunities and possibilities to your group.

In order to utilize promotion to your best advantage, it is important to first analyze your situation. Does your community have a television station? Which newspaper is read by the most people you hope to attract? How do your goals and objectives fit into the national picture? the statewide picture? the regional picture?

HOW SUCCESSFUL IS YOUR P.R.?

A simple questionnaire (Figure 12-1) should help you be prepared to use the right promotion techniques for your program.

I want my group to receive the attention due it with more exposure at the:

____ Community level, with the desired objective being larger audiences, easier budgets, and better community support.
____ Statewide level, with our group performing at special state events, highlighted in statewide magazines, and with appropriate media coverage (which I know will also help out at the community level).
____ National level, with the opportunity to perform at national conventions, attain a national reputation and generally enhance our overall program.

My best promotion skills are:

____ Writing, so I will work at developing a promotion package through my articles and letters.

____ Public relations, so I will work at developing contacts with people who can help promote our program.

____ Organization, so I can develop a promotion team to ensure meeting our objectives efficiently.

____ Administration, so I can manage and direct a group of persons who will each contribute his or her strengths towards our mutual success.

The group's best resources are:

____ Parents, who have shown a willingness and ability to help out with the program in any way they can.

____ Students, who are willing to make extreme sacrifices in order to achieve our common goals.

____ The school administration, which has consistently indicated a willingness to do whatever is necessary for the program.

____ The faculty, who have given support and aid to the band program at many levels, with many dimensions.

Given the above information, you should have some initial ideas about what you would like to see happen and where the strengths lie in your program. Now let's see *how* to implement this knowledge.

FIGURE 12-1. A PUBLIC RELATIONS SELF-EVALUATION

MAKING USE OF THE MEDIA

Often, a director will only think of the media when it comes to advertising a concert (and sometimes, not even then). Perhaps you use an ad or announcement occasionally through your local media, but only on an irregular basis. Now is the time to start developing good habits in using *all* media resources available to you.

Newspapers

Most newspapers are always looking for interesting copy. With a little imagination, many of the seemingly mundane events associated with the jazz program can be turned into an article for the newspaper. The article, however, must be of interest to readers. It's not the event that the newspaper will be interested in so much as some special dimension of that event that makes an article appealing to any newspaper. Don't just list an upcoming concert with the attendant "name, time, place, date, and admission price information" (although each of these pieces of information is necessary for a good article). Instead, select what you think makes this event unique or special and stress that aspect above everything else, almost as if the performance information is incidental. Prepare your performances to take advantage of this "special feature" interest—make sure each concert highlights a guest performer, presents a new work commissioned by your group, spotlights an award presentation (a built-in annual event of real journalistic interest), features an entire evening of the music of some famous jazz composer or period, and so on. Use your school photographer or an interested parent to take action shots that feature a soloist or combo as they perform (to be used after the performance) or a posed shot (done well in advance), to be used in coordination with an article. If your group has a logo (a distinctive trademark or emblem), always try to get it into the picture. Make an attempt to avoid "portrait" pictures where everyone is just standing around; posed shots are most suitable when someone is "doing" something like checking out a score or being given an award.

Become familiar with your newspaper and find out about deadlines, needs, and requisites. Prepare your copy by making certain that *all* information is included. If your copy is well prepared, it is much more likely to get into the paper than something that has to be completely reworked, so take your time to assure the quality of your article. Try to develop a schedule so that there are regular articles printed about your group, but keep a sense of balance—too much material might turn a newspaper off. Finally, don't just use the largest area commercial newspaper as your sole source; take advantage of the small "shopper" papers and your school newspaper. Often, you can receive coverage in these types of papers that far exceeds in size what the larger papers might be willing to provide.

The following guidelines should be followed when preparing copy for any newspaper article.

Copy
- Always type your copy with no errors or erasures evident.
- Use standard-size white typing paper, preferably bond.
- Only use one side of paper.
- Double space your article.

- Make certain that all spellings (especially names and places) are accurate.
- Be sure your article has answered Who? What? When? Where? Why?
- If possible, use your letterhead and provide your home phone number in case there are any questions.
- Keep your information brief and interesting!

Photos
- Submit glossy, black-and-white photos.
- Be careful to identify individuals in the photo correctly. Avoid confusing layouts where it is hard to keep track of who's who.
- Choose a photo that is clear with clean contrasts.
- Try to limit the number of persons in the picture to a maximum of five.

Radio

There are two ways to take advantage of your local radio stations—with public service messages and ads, or with interviews and performances. It is important to assess a radio's programming to find out if any station that programs live music would be interested in your group. A radio station that features jazz is more likely to conduct interviews with you, your students, or your guest performers about your program. If you are going to be interviewed on the air, have some idea of what you want to say, and have all pertinent information ready at hand so that you sound comfortable, in command, and at ease on the air. Be sure to *practice* before going on the air.

A radio station will accept a tape of a performance or do a live performance if you can show how it will be of benefit and interest to their listening audience.

Radio stations provide public service announcements for no charge. While you have no direct control on when or how often your announcement (perhaps concerning an upcoming concert, for instance) will be aired, you can prepare your own tape. Take advantage of your school's resources to the fullest; use media class, communications class, audio-visual personnel, and your school's public relation's representative (if you have any of these) to help you with a tape. Get someone with a good voice to read your prepared copy over a recording of your group playing something that would be appealing and easily recognized by the general audience. Consult with your local radio stations to find out what format (usually 8-track) is acceptable. These spots may consist of 10- to 30-second segments (again, according to the station's requirements).

If you plan to have a jazz celebrity perform with your group, radio stations will be especially interested. If there is time and the performer agrees, contact local disc jockeys and arrange an interview as part of your regular promotion for your concert.

Give your local announcers the opportunity to work as voluntary masters of ceremony for your concert. Many of these people are very knowledgeable about music and are always interested in being in front of a live audience. Get them excited about your program and they will promote your events on the air much more readily.

Television

If you live in an area where there is a local television station, there are many ways you can utilize its services. Any time you use a famous jazz musician as a clinician, guest soloist, or featured performer, a television camera crew is more likely to show up at your school. Anything that is visual and/or unusual will be considered by a television station. Timing is also an important factor. When there are few crimes, fires, accidents, events, etc., a station is more available and likely to shoot your story.

Many television stations offer opportunities to perform through interview shows, telethons, or special features. If you have a cable TV station, it is often especially interested in showcasing local talent.

If your school has video tape equipment, you can use television as a learning experience to help the members of your group deal with an important aspect of their performance: their appearance. Recognizing how they appear to others can bring about changes with your group that will carry over into the sound aspects as well. Posture, poise, setup, mannerisms, apparel, and demeanor can all be improved once members of a group see themselves the same way an audience does.

Other

And then there's paraphernalia. There are many items that can be used to provide your group with greater visibility and identity. Since being in the public's awareness is beneficial, these items are subtle reminders of the existence and function of the group.

Bumper stickers are an inexpensive example of paraphernalia-media as well as a handy way to help raise money. Not only can they appear on car bumpers, they can also be placed on windows, notebooks, instrument cases, luggage, and music folders. The message on a bumper sticker should be easy to read from a distance. There is a "bumper sticker psychology" that assumes the more exposure the average citizen has to a bumper sticker, the more familiarity with the subject, and ultimately, an implication of success about that subject is assumed. REMEMBER: In all forms of promotion, a positive image is basic and essential.

If you have a talented artist available (or have your art department sponsor a contest), try to develop the design or a logo for your group. This simple device can then be placed on anything associated with the group and eventually come to signify the group itself. Bumper stickers are the most obvious place for a logo, but don't forget banners, music stands, equipment stencils, stationery, posters, shirts, jackets, decals, and so on.

Stationery provides a positive, professional, and organized image of your group. In addition to a logo, stationery should include the director's name, name and address of the school, telephone number (be sure to include your area code), and the special name for your group if it has one. Some groups use regular school stationery with additional information printed in the same color ink as the original. If your school has its own printing department, it may be possible to have this important part of your image done for free; otherwise, a ream of stationery can be handled very inexpensively by a local firm.

Posters can provide short-term or full-year service as reminders to the public. If you have planned your concert schedule a year in advance (an excellent idea!), posters can present all pertinent information for the year at once. This method saves the expense of more than one poster being produced per year and serves as a constant reminder to the public. Single posters for events or special presentations should be more vivid since you have less time to catch the public's attention. Posters can be laid out by printers or created by an artist first and turned over to the printer for offset process. (Check with your printer first for special requirements; they are few but important.) The poster should contain all important information—Who? What? When? Where? Why—not be too wordy, and be immediately attractive to the eye.

A poster is useless if it is not well distributed. Music stores, record stores, libraries, malls, ticket offices, and anywhere there is pedestrian traffic are just a few places you will want to have posters.

T-shirts are items that can be used to remind the public about your ensemble, while providing your group with a means for raising funds. Some groups wear special T-shirts for their performances. Most T-shirts include a logo, name of the group, and (sometimes) the player's name. T-shirts are popular with students and can help bring attention to the program while instilling pride for the members of the ensemble.

Although the use of paraphernalia media might seem "lightweight," any device that focuses positive attention on a group should be seen as important and beneficial to that group.

Sometimes, the personal touch is the very best type of public relations. Whether your concerts are free or not, compose a list of people you specifically want to be your *guests*. This group should include administrators, area music teachers, media personnel, and, perhaps most importantly, your community's elderly citizens. Centers for the aged are natural places to issue special invitations for the residents to be your guests. Even if you charge admission for your events, free tickets do not cost you—they are a valuable part of promotion and, consequently, will end up to your benefit.

USING EVENTS TO GAIN ATTENTION

There are many experiences that can be offered to the members of an ensemble that will enhance their playing, give them experience with jazz, and develop consciousness and awareness that can't be covered just in rehearsal or performance. Listed here are some of these activities.

NAJE Student Chapter

Develop an NAJE student chapter. The National Association of Jazz Educators has long been identified as the most important organization to encourage youth to participate and appreciate jazz. While any student can qualify as a student member and join NAJE for a nominal fee per year, it only takes 12 students to have an official NAJE student chapter. The chapter qualifies for a $1 rebate per member, which creates an instant treasury for the chapter. The students do not have to be jazz performers to belong—anyone interested in the future of jazz education (or just supporting your program) is welcome. Membership offers the official NAJE magazine *Jazz Educators Journal*, which is full of information that can be used by students. The student chapter can provide opportunities for field trips, sponsor special jazz events, and provide a forum for members to discuss material that would be otherwise neglected and ignored concerning the historical and biographical aspects of jazz.

Here is a brief summary of the benefits of having an NAJE student chapter.

Why should a student join NAJE?

- Interest in jazz
- Interest in education

- Wants to support the jazz program
- *Jazz Educators Journal* benefits
  —Chart sources
  —Clinician sources and interviews
  —"How to" articles

Why should you form an NAJE student chapter?

- Listening to jazz in a group is beneficial
- Central fund raiser
- Group can provide promotion in the community:
  —Each member is assigned an area school
  —Each member has a specific activity (posters, tickets, programs)
- NAJE chapters provide an opportunity to get involved regardless of whether or not student plays in a group

What are some of the goals of existing student chapters?

- Promotion of jazz performance on and off campus
- Various projects
  —Jazz scholarships
  —Jazz trips
  —Bringing artists/clinicians to perform on campus
  —Commission new works
  —Develop a record collection
- Become acquainted with new artists, groups, recordings, etc.
- Weekly listening sessions

Record Club

Often, a school can provide the students the opportunity to share their hobby. If a record club already exists in your school, it's possible to introduce jazz recordings. Jazz discography is a relatively new but fast-growing field. Perhaps you could arrange for a discographer to speak or present some of the basics of what a jazz discographer does. In addition, early recording techniques utilized by some of the first jazz records might be of special interest to a record club.

Where it's not possible to fit a new course into the curriculum, a club might be the perfect setting for combos to be offered. Since the combo setting is so different from that of the big band, you can attract new participants and focus on areas that are impossible anywhere else. Combos are excellent for teaching improvisation and "head charts." In addition, a wider variety of styles is available to combos than anywhere else.

MAKING THE MOST OF PERFORMANCES

There are numerous performance opportunities available to the ensemble other than just the occasional evening concert. If the director looks upon these as opportunities of great potential, they can become one of the greatest assets of a program.

Public Events

Since being visible is vital to public relations, careful selection of public events can be especially helpful. Often, the group will come in contact with sectors of the public that would never have had the opportunity to hear them otherwise. Since you never know who might be in your audience, *every* performance should be viewed as being important.

Since the group is achieving new exposure and providing a public service, which is ideal for extra media coverage, each member should understand the importance of public behavior. Nothing can ruin an outstanding presentation faster than immature and irresponsible behavior in public by members of the performing group. A few simple rules should be established by the director (or the director and group together) that outline some basic guidelines for behavior in public. Language, dress, smoking, and noise are all elements that can be offensive to the public, so it is important that everyone understands about proper public behavior.

While participating in community events is commendable, it is important for the director to have some criteria defined in advance concerning the choice of performances. Before making a decision about any potential performance, the director should know:

- the "newsworthiness" of the event
- the size of the anticipated audience
- how interested the audience will be in jazz
- the environmental aspects of the performance
  acoustics
  available electrical outlets
  stage size
  seating capacity
  convenience for unloading equipment
  security area for cases, purses, etc.
  protection from weather (for outside performance)
- who is sponsoring the event
- whether the performance is ethical

There are some community performances that can almost be scheduled on a regular basis. Performances at feeder schools (those schools that eventually send you their students) help ensure interest and participation from younger students. School open houses, senior citizen centers, some prisons, and hospitals are all places that offer opportunity for your group to perform, provide a public service, and benefit from media coverage.

Jam Sessions

Jam sessions, where a group of outside musicians are invited to join with members of your ensemble, can be an exciting experience for your students. Area jazz musicians can be encouraged to come and "sit in" in an atmosphere that is not threatening to the young improvisor. Try to schedule jam sessions on some sort of regular basis (weekly, monthly). Good supervision is essential since these sessions do have the potential of attracting problems if they are too unstructured. Check with your administration to make certain that there are no restrictions or difficulties.

Jam sessions provide an opportunity for all participants to trade solos. A tune is chosen that is familiar to all (this is one of the reasons listening is so important) and the group plays the "head" together. Each soloist takes a turn at a prearranged number of choruses while the rest of the participants listen. Sometimes, a "riff" background is provided by the rest of the players behind a solo. A riff is a short phrase that fits well behind what the soloist is playing to add more excitement and impetus to the music. At the end of the arranged choruses, another soloist starts the entire process over until everyone has had a chance. The head is taken one more time with all the participants playing out to the end.

Clinics

An excellent means to establish identity as a school with a multi-dimensional jazz program is to sponsor clinics. These events can often be subsidized by instrument companies, record companies, publishing companies, and/or the media. In addition, a big-name musician is sometimes available for a minimal fee if that person and his or her group are on tour with an open date. The clinician comes into the school and offers first-hand techniques and insights that students can adapt quickly and easily. Clinics can offer intensive learning experiences to students.

Keep in contact with the person or group who will provide the clinic, and make certain you know about any special needs in advance. Be aware of the clinician's schedule so there is plenty of time between estimated time of arrival and the beginning of the presentation. Be a gracious, considerate host by providing refreshments, privacy (if requested), and security.

Sources for clinicians include any area college that has a successful jazz program (you should always consult with these clinicians before anyone else because they are usually free and most convenient) and the following sources. These sources utilize talent available from representatives and contributors to their product.

W. T. Armstrong
P.O. Box 963
Elkhart, IN 46515
(219) 295-0079

Kayne & Kayne Mgt.
275 E. Lake Boulevard
Lake Mahopac, NY 10541
(800) 526-1363

G. Leblanc Corp.
7019 30th Avenue
Kenosha, WI 53141
(800) 558-9421

Music Matters
15130 Ventura Boulevard
Sherman Oaks, CA 91403
(213) 783-7564

The Selmer Co.
P.O. Box 310
Elkhart, IN 46515
(219) 264-4141

C. G. Conn, Ltd.
2520 Industrial Parkway
Elkhart, IN 46516
(219) 522-3392

King Musical Instruments
33999 Curtis Boulevard
Eastlake, OH 44094
(216) 946-6100

Hal Leonard Publishing
8112 W. Bluemound
Milwaukee, WI 53213
(414) 774-3630

Roger Drums
1300 E. Valencia
Fullerton, CA 92631
(714) 879-8080

Yamaha Musical Products
P.O. Box 7271
Grand Rapids, MI 49510
(616) 942-9223

Other Elements

Whenever possible, link your clinic with a performance by your group because it can make a dramatic statement about your program. If the clinician is to perform with your ensemble, ensure that everything is prepared in advance so that your group is at its finest. Often, a clinician will attract new members to your audience, so this is your chance to convince these people to return for your next performance.

Too often, directors ignore some non-musical dimensions that help create the very best possible concert. Don't make the mistake of thinking that just because your group is playing the right notes, your concerns are over. Every aspect of the performance should be considered. Staging, lighting, programs, sound, announcements, and presentation should all be prepared in advance. Television has influenced audiences today so that they are much more sophisticated and demanding. Although some educators see the word "entertainment" as undesirable, their attitude is ultimately self-defeating. Moderation and good taste can serve as the foundation for a presentation of entertainment without compromising the quality of the performance. Your concert performance is your main instrument for public interest and support. With a little creativity and imagination, each of the following elements can assist you in presenting a performance that will inspire your audience to go out and tell others how exciting your concerts are (and *that's* public relations!).

For lighting, make certain that you: (1) turn down the houselights to a level that you can barely see the audience from the stage, (2) use a spotlight on soloists (whenever possible, lower the remaining stage lights so that the soloist is even more isolated, (3) lower the stage lights during announcements and introductions (but not so low that band members have a difficult time refocusing their eyes for the next number), (4) don't allow lighting to become too active or stagnant, and (5) occasionally (with moderation) use special lighting effects such as mirrored balls, strobe lighting, blackouts, and color changes as long as they compliment the music and don't interfere with the performer's ability to read music.

With a well-designed, organized, and artistic program, a number of statements can be made about your performance even before the first note of music is heard. Include what you will play, the order of the music, the names of the performers, who wrote the music, and who helped contribute to the overall effort. In addition, a program makes a positive statement about the organization and efficiency of your group. Programs may be completely hand-designed or program covers may be ordered from groups who specialize in concert program covers.

No matter who serves as master-of-ceremonies to introduce the music, it should be done in a professional manner. The presentation should be smooth, clearly articulated, factually correct, and interesting. The length of introduction for each new piece of music should be long enough so that the group can get ready for the next piece, but short enough so that the audience doesn't become bored. Regardless of who announces the numbers, it should be prepared in advance and contribute to the general flow and pace of the program.

While a good sound system can easily enhance a group's soloists, poor sound can also ruin a program. The group should rehearse with a system in the actual performance hall so that all acoustical and balance problems can be solved in advance. One of the final rehearsals should focus exclusively on the sound system. In addition, many young players are initially inhibited with microphones, so take steps in advance to overcome this problem.

A successful concert is comprised of many components, some obvious and some invisible. The following guidelines represent some factors that can help make any performance outstanding. REMEMBER: A really outstanding concert will leave the audience *breathless.*

- "Always leave your audience wanting more!" is a good rule for the length of your concert. Nothing is worse than losing an audience because of boredom.
- Variety is the spice of life and, in a concert, your music should include ballads, repertory pieces (Basie, Ellington, classics, etc.), vocals, combo works, and more.
- Timing is essential and in a good concert, *pacing* is the essence of timing. The performance should hook the audience with a solid opener, keep interest high with the use of variety, and build momentum towards a dramatic ending.
- Jazz is emotional music so don't be afraid to get your audience involved (clapping in time or acknowledging soloists immediately after their performance) with the mood of the music. You should want a "spirited" audience.

HOSTING A JAZZ FESTIVAL

Jazz festivals are a sure-fire method to bring other ensembles to your school, offer observers the chance to make comparisons, and provide a healthy exchange of ideas. If organized and prepared correctly, a festival can be an event that is viewed as worthwhile and positive by all involved.

Initially, you must decide what type of festival to have, either competitive or non-competitive. Administrative decisions must be made early, with plenty of time in advance to know: (1) the date of the event, (2) the maximum number of participating groups, (3) the length of each performance, (4) the budget considerations, (5) the names of adjudicators and type of adjudication sheet to be used, (6) the awards to be presented, (7) publicity considerations, and (8) general logistical problems. A good festival should have sufficient communication between the festival director, administrator, and participants so that all questions are anticipated before the event.

The following guidelines are provided by the National Association of Jazz Educators and represent a comprehensive indication of what a successful festival should *minimally* contain.

Mandatory Guidelines
a. Minimum of three qualified judges.
b. Sight reading (usually requires a fourth judge).
c. Use of official NAJE Adjudication Form.

d. Use of official NAJE Talent Citations.

e. Piano tuned to A-440.

f. Sufficient stage lighting, acoustics, risers, P.A. system, music stands, electric outlets, etc.

g. Consistent scheduling of groups by classification such as AAA, AA, A, etc. (All one classification of performing group should be scheduled consecutively.)

h. A person to serve as liaison between judges and stage area.

i. A seating plan of each group showing names, instrument (or part), year in school, etc.

j. Music scores—preferably full scores—for all adjudicators.

k. Clear and concise rules, regulations and other information made available to participating groups well in advance.

l. Signature of a school authority to verify that each student is eligible to perform in the group.

m. Eligibility status of the group to receive NAJE Talent Citations and/or Scholarships.

Suggested Guidelines

a. Minimum of 30 minutes for each group (including on and off time).

b. Clinics/workshops by qualified people.

c. Scholarships for students and educators.

d. Judges to include brass specialist, woodwind specialist, and a rhythm specialist.

e. Use of tape or cassette for judges' comments.

f. Photograph and/or tape for each group.

g. Invitations to administrators and other guests.

h. Complete coverage by all news media.

i. Trophies/plaques.

While the NAJE guidelines are important for festivals wanting to take advantage of being designated "NAJE Approved," they are also helpful for the novice festival director since they help to define values and establish some priorities for the new festival. It is sometimes easier to decide what you don't want or what you think is most important when you are provided with a list of what already exists somewhere else.

In planning a festival, consider the facilities available in your building. Each participating group should have a secure room for equipment and coat storage. Bathrooms should be accessible and clearly marked. There should be adequate space for unloading buses and vehicles without causing any traffic problems. There should be sufficient custodial help, lighting in all corridors or rooms to be used, and unlocked doors for all rooms to be used. Like all areas of good management, the key is preparation and anticipation —a smooth-running festival is achieved if problems are anticipated.

A JAZZ WEEK FORMAT

For the ambitious director, a jazz week can serve as a spotlight on your program and help attract new audiences. Presented during an entire week, you can provide a multitude of events that includes jam sessions, clinics, festivals, concerts, jazz films, panel discussions, and performances by famous musicians. One real advantage to a jazz week is the possibility of having an artist in residence for the entire week. This person can serve the jazz week in such functions as clinician, guest soloist, adjudicator, panel member, lecturer, and performer with his or her own group.

A jazz week can be an exciting event that offers infinite variety from one year to the next. It offers complete media coverage possibilities and creates an aura of success about your program. An excellent place to get ideas about what should happen during your jazz week is the annual NAJE convention. Its diverse activities offer something for everyone and can help you to decide which activities you want for your own event. The convention is also the ideal place to line up many of the participants for your jazz week.

CONCERT TOURING

One of the big inducements directors can offer music ensemble members is travel. Students enjoy the mystery and experiences associated with touring. A jazz ensemble particularly lends itself well to travel since the costs are somewhat minimized by the size of the group. Whether you choose to take your group on an extended tour of more than three days or on a brief tour, the following considerations should be examined.

- Always take a first-aid kit with your group.
- Always have permission slips signed by the parent indicating:
  - where YOU will be (include telephone numbers wherever possible)
  - your complete schedule including estimated times of arrival
  - what activities will take place
  - any potential medical problem the student might have that you should know about

—telephone numbers where one of the parents can be reached at all times

—the name of the transportation carrier(s) (for the parent's reference) including flight numbers, routes, etc.

- Establish rules of conduct well in advance of your trip with clearly stated options outlined for those who don't follow any regulations. Be prepared to stick to these rules and options.
- Provide plenty of supervision (one chaperone for every ten students is a good ratio).
- Provide sufficient protection for instruments and equipment so that there is no damage during travel.
- Make sure to "count heads" after each rest-stop or before beginning the next part of your trip so that you don't leave anyone behind.

Touring can involve many activities, ranging from exchange concerts to extended tours. There are advantages and problems for any type of tour. As usual, being prepared and organized will provide the most efficient and fulfilling results.

Exchange Concerts

Exchange concerts involve performances at some school that is usually within a 500-mile radius of your school. The students have an opportunity to become friends and learn a great deal from their exposure to another school. Exchange concerts can offer such multiple performance opportunities as: (1) guest school performs at host school, (2) guest school and host school perform together at both schools, or (3) all-star group is formed from guest and host school ensembles to perform at both schools in addition to the other two arrangements. Since the exchange concert situation usually involves staying overnight with a family from the host school, there is a period of time where direct supervision of your students is lost. With anticipation and good communication to the host parents, this need not pose any problem.

Extended Tours

A great deal of planning is necessary for any extended tour. Since an extended tour is so demanding, it is usually a good idea to schedule this activity once every three or four years. Every minute should be accounted for and planned in advance. Since extended tours are very expensive and usually need at least nine months to prepare, consult with travel agents who specialize in group tours. They can be very helpful in procuring hotels, restaurants, and travel carriers that fulfill your special needs. Extended tours are easiest to design if you have a big event to center your activities around, such as a performance at an MENC or NAJE national convention.

A very helpful aid in preparing for any type of tour is a flow chart, which is simply a form of calendar where you can see at once deadlines for each step of preparation.

Travel can be very hard on equipment, so it is important to have hard cases for all instruments. Your local music store can often provide large packing boxes used to deliver instruments and equipment. Your group's smaller cases can then all fit into the one large packing case. Equipment (microphones, cables, extension cords, stands, etc.) that normally has no case may be packed in any sturdy trunk or crate. Check airline requirements for size and weight restrictions in advance. All music folders should be kept in one suitcase or container with the same person responsible to check all the music after each performance. All equipment and instruments should be kept in place with foam rubber to avoid damage, with all cases and crates permanently labeled for easy identification.

When a group performs out of the country, it is important to find out all details as far in advance as possible. Passports, inoculations, and customs requirements are just a few of the problems found in international travel. Since each country has its own rules, it is recommended that a representative from that country be contacted before a final decision on the trip is made.

Remember to take full advantage of media interest for your tour. Let your television station know when your group will be leaving. If there is a talented writer in the ensemble, have him or her arrange with the newspaper to put together either short daily articles or a diary of the entire trip that can be printed when you return. Take advantage, too, of the media at the other end of your trip wherever practical by notifying them of your activities. Your school paper is certain to show interest with either an interview or diary account. As a travel activity, have all members of the group write a brief summation of their experiences and most enjoyable moments for use as a newspaper article or as part of a summary report submitted to your board of education. Tours are also rich opportunities for photographs and movies to be taken, and parents will especially enjoy seeing the tour as recorded on film. Since parental support is so important, these pictures can serve as a testimony to the success of your tour and give them satisfaction and reassurance. In addition, movies or video-tapes of your tour can be displayed before or during your next concert. Candid photos are ideal for a variety of uses: newspaper articles, magazine reviews, scrapbooks, a display on a bulletin board near the band room or in the library. REMEMBER: A picture can make a quick and powerful impression on the public.

SPECIAL PROGRAMS TO HELP DEVELOP PUBLIC AWARENESS

Capitalize on the interaction between the public and your jazz program. Whether the public is an active or passive partner, the important thing is that many people have some idea that something is *happening* in your program. With this awareness, the public is much more likely to be supportive.

Night-School

One means of involving the public is to invite them to participate in a night-school jazz ensemble (if you have a night-school program in your system). The course can be a fun-oriented group where everyone gets together for personal enjoyment and satisfaction. If instrumentation is incomplete, you can fill in with members of your day group, but the focus should be on the "public" performers. Because you are providing a service and the participants want to play together, this type of event takes little time other than for organization. Once the problems associated with logistics (who, when, where, etc.) are worked out, the program is fairly straightforward.

Summer School

While summer school programs don't usually offer the general public an opportunity to participate, it does give the jazz program a chance to expose new students to a jazz ensemble experience in a relaxed, non-threatening manner. The main emphasis should be on learning rather than preparing for a performance. Summer school is perhaps the best environment to offer a solid foundation to students with little jazz background. There are few distractions and demands placed upon the student normally associated with regular school activities. In addition, students who already belong to your ensemble can take the summer to concentrate on improvisation or learning a new instrument for doubling. Your lead players can be enlisted to help out as aides to work with the newcomers or develop student arrangements.

Typical course offerings for summer school should include those courses not yet in the regular curriculum. Beginning and advanced jazz ensemble, combo(s), and improvisation should all be included for any summer-school setting.

A FINAL WORD

In short, the use of public relations is essential to a strong program. Whatever your program involves, make certain the public sees:

- there IS a program
- what the program DOES

- the BENEFITS of the program
- the DESIRABILITY of the program

During every one of your performances, take a moment to urge your audience to write letters of support and approval to whomever they feel needs to know how they appreciated your program. For each performance, seek new members in your audience, and keep close relationships with the media. Learn to develop "media events" by creating new events to interest unexposed sectors of the public. If you don't make the effort to promote your program, there may be no program to promote.

Have I Been Successful? A Self-Evaluation Checklist

This section is designed for you to use as a self-evaluation *and* reference guide. Any area that shows a weakness or problem can be resolved by reading the indicated chapter. Since more than one chapter may be useful to solve a problem, all relevant chapters are indicated. Those few questions that do not include a chapter reference are designed purely as evaluative, so answers should be self-explanatory.

INSTRUCTION

Has your band been adjudicated? (6)

Have you worked on indicated weaknesses and followed suggested solutions? (6)

Do you regularly play recordings for your students? (3, 5, 7–10)

Do local professional jazz musicians get to hear your group and make comments or suggestions? (12)

Do you use different setups for rehearsals and concerts? (3, 6, 10)

Have you experimented with setups? (3, 6, 10)

Are you aware of local private teachers who teach jazz? (5)

Do you introduce your students to specific materials such as: (a) play-along records, (b) pattern books, (c) chordal/scalar books, (d) ear-training materials, (e) theory/arranging/composition, and (f) applied techniques? (7–10, 11)

Do you make recordings for improving individuals/ensembles? (4, 6, 12)

Have you ever evaluated your students and made specific recommendations about what they should do? (3)

Do you understand some of the idiomatic jazz techniques for each instrument: woodwinds, brass, all rhythm, strings? (7–10)

Do you recognize the different jazz styles and feel comfortable to teach all of them? (5)

Do you stress the importance of listening? (7–10)

Do you feel able to teach jazz articulation and rhythms? (3)

Can you deal with incomplete instrumentation? (3)

CURRICULUM

How much of your band's repertory is found in each of the following styles: swing, rock, Latin, ballad, other? (6)

Do you have a feeder school system? (3, 12)

Does your feeder system have complete course offerings, repertory, instrument inventory, clinics/concerts, assemblies/field trips, in-service training? (2, 3, 11, 12)

Does your ensemble regularly perform at your feeder schools? (12)

Do you have combos in your program? (2, 12)

Do you ever use strings in your program? (10)

Do you teach improvisation, theory, jazz history? (2, 11)

Do you ever sponsor jam sessions? (12)

Have you ever recruited players from outside the traditional music department enrollment? (11, 12)

Do you encourage your students to double to cover an unusual part? (6, 7, 9)

BUDGET

Do you have funds for purchases of textbooks, audio-visual, library materials, field trips, tours, festivals? (2, 11, 12)

Have you been able to purchase any new equipment? (4, 11)

Have you applied for a grant from MPTF, NEA, NAJE, private sources, local and state arts councils? (11)

Does your program include an NAJE student chapter? (11, 12)

Do you qualify for the NAJE 100% club? (11)

PUBLIC RELATIONS

Do you have high attendance for your events? (6, 12)

Do you have a close relationship with your local media? (12)

How much media coverage do you receive for your program? (12)

Has your group recently performed on local TV or radio? (12)

What percent of your instrumental students are involved in the jazz program? (2)

Have you ever presented a 1940s dance? (11, 12)

Have you ever hosted a jazz week? (12)

Bibliography

Note: The bibliography is listed in numerical order for your convenience. Any number that appears twice refers to the previously mentioned title with that same name.

CHAPTER 1

Books

1 Baskerville, D. *Music Business Handbook*. Denver, CO: Sherwood Co., 1979.

2 Leonhard, C., & W. House. *Foundations and Principles of Music Education*. New York: McGraw-Hill Book Co., 1972.

3 Mark, M. L. *Contemporary Music Education*. New York: Schirmer Books, 1978.

4 Tanner, P., & M. Gerow. *A Study of Jazz*. Dubuque, Iowa: Wm. C. Brown, Co., 1973.

5 Tellstrom, T. A. *Music in American Education: Past and Present*. New York: Holt, Rinehart and Winston, Inc., 1971.

Periodicals

6 Bash, L. "Jazz Education Given a Third Wave Perspective." In C. Brown (ed.), *Proceedings of the Ninth NAJE Convention*. Manhattan, KS: National Association of Jazz Educators, 1982.

7 Choate, R. A. (ed.) *The Tanglewood Symposium—Music in American Society*. Washington, DC: Music Educators National Conference, 1968.

8 Culver, D. "Jazz Education: We've Come a Long Way, Maybe." *The Instrumentalist*, August 1978, 33.

9 Ferguson, T. "Stage Bands Under Fire." *The Instrumentalist*, May 1980, 77–79.

10   Hall, M. E. "How We Hope to Foster Jazz." *Music Educators Journal*, March 1969, 44–46.

11   Hall, M. E. "NAJE—Starting Its Fifth Year." *The Instrumentalist*, June 1973, 58.

12   Marowitz, D. R. "Is Jazz an Art Form?" *The Instrumentalist*, April 1980, 116.

13   Suber, C. "First Chorus." *downbeat*, April 12, 1973, 4.

14   Tanner, P. "A Jazz Curriculum." *The Instrumentalist*, March 1974, 84–85.

15   Wheaton, J. "Jazz in the Schools—Why?" *The Instrumentalist*, April 1976, 58–60.

16   Wheaton, J. "Future of Jazz Education." *Musical America*, February/March 1977, 13–15.

17   Whitelegg, C. "Jazz in Music Education." In M. L. Raiman (ed.), *Midwest Symposium on Music Education* (Vol. I). Tulsa, OK: United States Jaycees, 1978.

18   Wiskirchen, Rev. G. "What's Right/Wrong with Jazz Education Today?" *Selmer Bandwagon*, No. 80, 33–35.

19   Wright, R. "The Future of Jazz Education." *Musical America*, February/March 1977, 17, 46.

Dissertations

20   Ferriano, F. *A Study of the School Jazz Ensemble in American Music Education.* Columbia University, 1974.

21   Hepworth, L. *The Development of a Course of Study in Stage Band Techniques.* University of Utah, 1974.

22   Herfort, D. A. *A History of the National Association of Jazz Educators and a Description of Its Role in American Music Education, 1968-1978.* University of Houston, 1979.

23   Wheaton, J. *The Technological and Sociological Influence on Jazz as an Art Form in America.* University of Northern Colorado, 1977.

CHAPTER 2

Books

24   Ferguson, T., & S. Feldstein. *The Jazz Rock Ensemble.* Port Washington, NY: Alfred Publishing Co., 1976.

25   Kolnut, D. *Instrumental Music Pedagogy.* Englewood Cliffs, NJ: Prentice-Hall, Inc., 1973.

26   Wiskirchen, Rev. G. *Developmental Techniques for the Jazz Ensemble Musician.* Boston: Berklee Press Publications, 1961.

27   *A Handbook for the Development of the Band Program.* Austin, TX: Texas Education Agency, 1975.

28   *Music in the High School.* Albany, NY: The University of the State of New York/The State Education Department/Bureau of Secondary Curriculum Development, 1972.

Periodicals

29   Allen, L. D. "The Total Music Program." *NAJE Educator*, April/May 1973, 6–8, 19–20.

30   Bash, L. "Jazz Is the Vehicle for Enthusiasm." *NAJE Educator*, February/March 1977, 23, 29.

31   Colnot, C. "One Means to an End—The Jazz/Rock Ensemble." *The Instrumentalist*, May 1974, 63–65.

32   Colnot, C. "Programming for the Jazz Ensemble." *The Instrumentalist*, December 1975, 80–81.

33   Delp, R. "The Jazz/Rock Percussion Ensemble." *NAJE Educator*, April/May 1973, 5, 22.

34   Jones, M. "The Organization of the High School Jazz Band." *The Instrumentalist*, September 1972, 70–73.

35   Kuzmich, J. "Jazz in the K-12 Curriculum." *NAJE Educator*, April/May 1976, 14–15.

36   Kuzmich, J."Jazz in the K-12 Curiculum (Part 2)." *NAJE Educator*, February/March 1977, 13–14.

37   Kuzmich, J. "Jazz in the K-12 Curriculum (Part 3)." *NAJE Educator*, April/May 1977, 13, 46, 51.

38   Papke, R. E. "The New Breed of Band Director . . . Think Comprehensively." *Music Educators Journal*, November 1970, 40.

39   Wiskirchen, Rev. G. "The Roots of Excellence, or, 'Bird' Who?" *Selmer Bandwagon*, No. 73, 28–31.

Dissertations

40   Disierio, A. R. *Teaching the History of Western Music Through Instrumental Performance in the Secondary School.* University of Southern California, 1966.

CHAPTER 3

Books

24   Ferguson, T. & S. Feldstein.

41   Henry, R. *The Jazz Ensemble: A Guide to Technique.* Englewood Cliffs, NJ: Prentice-Hall, Inc., 1981.

42   Kenton, S. "The Stage Band." In K. L. Neidig (ed.), *The Band Director's Guide*. Englewood Cliffs, NJ: Prentice-Hall, Inc., 1964.

43   LaPorta, J. *Developing the School Jazz Ensemble*. Boston: Berklee Press Publications, 1965.

44   Lawn, R. *The Jazz Ensemble Director's Manual*. Oskaloosa, Iowa: C. L. Barnhouse Co., 1981.

45   Lehman, P. (Chairman). *The School Music Program: Description and Standards*. Reston, VA: Music Educators National Conference, 1974.

46   Sherman, H. *Techniques and Materials for Stage Band*. Los Angeles: Creative World Publications, 1976.

47   Taylor, G. H. *High School Stage Band*. New York: Richards Rosen Press, Inc., 1978.

48   Wheaton, J. *How to Organize and Develop the Stage Band*. North Hollywood, CA: Maggio Music Press, 1975.

Periodicals

49   Delp, R. "Adding Extra Percussion to the Stage Band." *The Instrumentalist*, December 1972, 54–55.

50   Levey, J. "Beginning a Jazz Program." *The Instrumentalist*, October 1973, 65–68.

51   Morsch, R. "Jazz Band Rehearsal Techniques." *The Instrumentalist*, October 1975, 65–68.

52   Prebys, S. J. "The Vibraphone in the School Jazz Ensemble." *The Instrumentalist*, September 1978, 63–67.

53   Purcell, R. "Improving Ensemble Sound." *The Instrumentalist*, February 1978, 69–70.

54   Rader, D. "On Playing in the Jazz/Rock Ensemble." *NAJE Educator*, December/January 1973, 6–7, 18, 29, 32.

55   Wiskirchen, Rev. G. "Jazz in the Concert Band." *Selmer Bandwagon*, No. 81, 14–18.

Dissertations

21   Hepworth, L.

CHAPTER 4

Books

56   *Acquisition Power*. Elkhart, IN: Selmer Company, 1974.

Periodicals

57   Edwards, J. "Choosing the Right Microphone." *The Instrumentalist*, October 1981, 93–96.

58   Edwards, J. "Some Sound Advice." *The Instrumentalist*, September 1981, 119–122.

59   Gerber, T., & A. Kefower. "Don't Be Confused by Wow and Flutter—A Consumer's Guide to Audio Equipment." *Music Educators Journal*, October 1976, 66–75.

60   Gill, J. "Recording Tips for Band Directors." *The Instrumentalist*, January 1980, 20–21.

61   Hawes, C. B. "Gadgets for the Sound System." *The Instrumentalist*, January 1980, 14–17.

62   Hawes, C. B. "Sound Systems Outdoors." *The Instrumentalist*, January 1980, 21–22.

63   Neidig, K. L. "1982 Survey of School Instrumental Music Budgets." *The Instrumentalist*, August 1982, 12–17.

64   "Survey of Sound Equipment." *The Instrumentalist*, January 1980, 24–27.

65   "What's Wrong with a Lot of Public Address Systems?" *The Instrumentalist*, January 1980, 17–19.

66   "Buyer's Guide." *The Instrumentalist*, July 1982, 22–36.

67   "Associate Members." *Jazz Educators Journal*. April/May 1982, 88–90.

68   "Patron Member Directory." *Jazz Educators Journal*. April/May 1982, 94–95.

CHAPTER 5

Books

69   Coker, J. *The Jazz Idiom*. Englewood Cliffs, NJ: Prentice-Hall, Inc., 1975.

70   Coker, J. *Listening to Jazz*. Englewood Cliffs, NJ: Prentice-Hall, Inc., 1978.

24   Ferguson, T., & S. Feldstein.

41   Henry, R.

71   Hewett, P. W. *Essential Techniques for the Development of a Stage Band Program*. Harris Music Publications, 1970.

43   LaPorta, J.

44   Lawn, R.

72   Ostransky, L. *Understanding Jazz*. Englewood Cliffs, NJ: Prentice-Hall, Inc., 1977.

46   Sherman, H.

73   Strommen, C., & S. Feldstein. *The Sound of Jazz.* Port Washington, NY: Alfred Publishing Co., 1976.

48   Wheaton, J.

26   Wiskirchen, Rev. G.

Periodicals

74   Arnn, J. M. "Rehearsal Techniques for Tighter Ensemble Playing." *The Instrumentalist*, December 1978, 71–73.

75   Colnot, C. L. "Understanding Jazz-Rock Articulations." *The Instrumentalist*, March 1975, 103–106.

76   DiCioccio, J. "Swing to the Shuffle." *The Instrumentalist*, March 1981, 72–73.

77   Garrett, G. "The Do's and Don'ts of Jazz Band Conducting." *The Instrumentalist*, November 1978, 62, 64–66.

78   Kistner, K. "Jazz Interpretation for the Traditionally Oriented Teacher." *The Instrumentalist*, November 1971, 26.

79   Lawn, R. "Jazz Articulation." *The Instrumentalist*, January 1982, 78–81.

80   Matzke, R., R. Ramsdell, & B. Smith. "Secrets of Successful Jazz Ensemble Directors." *The Instrumentalist*, March 1980, 41–43.

51   Morsch, R.

81   Owen, H. S. "Jazz Ensemble Sight-Reading." *The Instrumentalist*, September 1977, 86–87.

82   Sherman, H. "Jazz Phrasing and Articulation." *NAJE Educator*, April/May 1977, 48–51.

83   Slone, K. "Good Time." *The Instrumentalist*, April 1981, 58–62.

CHAPTER 6

Books

84   Leach, J. *Chart Sources.* Northridge, CA: Studio 4 Productions.

85   Voigt, J. *Jazz Music in Print.* Boston, MA: Hornpipe Music Publishing Co., 1978.

48   Wheaton, J.

Periodicals

86   Bash, L. "Jazz Festival Directory." *Jazz Educators Journal*, December/January 1982, 88–89.

87   Blackley, T. J. "Selecting Music for Jazz Contests." *The Instrumentalist*, February 1973, 58–59.

88   Colnot, C. "Programming for the Jazz Ensemble." *The Instrumentalist*, December 1975, 30.

89   Everett, T. G. "Literature for the Jazz Ensemble (Part I)." *The Instrumentalist*, January 1975, 62–64.

90   Everett, T. G. "Literature for the Jazz Ensemble (Part II)." *The Instrumentalist*, February 1975, 29.

91   Grashel, J. W., & M. J. Bergee. "P.E.R.T.: Help in Planning." *The Instrumentalist*, July 1982, 8–9.

92   Marcone, S. "Choosing a Set." *NAJE Educator*, December/January 1976, 13.

93   Band Aids. Every issue of *Jazz Educators Journal* and *NAJE Educator*.

94   Choral Aids. Every issue of *Jazz Educators Journal* and *NAJE Educator*.

95   New music reviews. Every issue of *The Instrumentalist*.

CHAPTER 7

Books

96   Bay, B. *Flute Improvising Workbook*. Pacific, MO: Mel Bay Publications, 1980.

97   Bay, B. *Jazz Flute Studies*. Pacific, MO: Mel Bay Publications, 1980.

98   Ellis, D. *Quarter Tones*. West Babylon, NY: Harold Branch Publishing, 1975.

99   Gerard, C. *Improvising Jazz Sax*. New York: Consolidated Music Publishers, 1978.

100   Jones, T. *Lead Sax Book*. Delevan, NY: Kendor Music, 1979.

101   Kynaston, T. P. *Circular Breathing*. Lebanon, IN: Studio P/R, 1978.

102   Lang, R. *Beginning Studies in the Altissimo Register*. Indianapolis, IN: Lang Music, 1971.

43   LaPorta, J.

103   Nash, T. *Studies in High Harmonics*. New York: Leeds Music, 1956.

104   Niehaus, L. *Basic Jazz Conception for Saxophone*. Hollywood: Professional Drum Shop, 1966.

105   Niehaus, L. *Intermediate Jazz Conception for Saxophone*. Hollywood: Professional Drum Shop, 1964.

106   Northway, E. *Guide to the Saxophone*. Salt Lake City: NC & A Press, 1979.

107   Opperman, K. *Handbook for Making and Adjusting Single Reeds.* New York: Chappell, 1956.

108   Rascher, S. M. *Top-Tone for the Saxophone.* New York: Carl Fischer, 1942.

109   Seckler, S. *Take the Lead.* Iowa City, Iowa: Phantom Music, 1977.

110   Terry, C., & P. Rizzo. *The Interpretation of the Jazz Language.* Cleveland: M.A.S. Publishing Co., 1977.

111   Teal, L. *The Art of Saxophone Playing.* Evanston, IL: Summy-Birchard Co., 1963.

112   Viola, J. *The Technique of the Saxophone (Scale Studies).* Boston: Berklee Press, 1965.

113   Viola, J. *The Technique of the Saxophone (Chord Studies).* Boston: Berklee Press, 1963.

Periodicals

114   Allison, E. "Advice for the High School Jazz Saxophonist." *The Instrumentalist*, December 1974, 29.

115   Cochran, A. W. "Lead Alto Player." *Jazz Educators Journal*, 62–65.

116   Farrell, J. "Playing in a Section." *Selmer Bandwagon*, 1971, 12–14.

117   Foster, G. "The Toshiko-Tabackin Sax Section: Woodwind Doubling." *NAJE Educator*, October/November 1979, 60–62.

118   Foster, G. "Thoughts on Woodwind Doubling." *NAJE Educator.* December/January 1979, 70–72.

119   Fowler, W. L. "How to Hit the High Notes—on Sax" *downbeat*, November 6, 1975, 40–41.

120   Hahn, R. R. "The Flute Embouchure and the Soda Straw." *The Instrumentalist*, October 1975, 46, 48–50.

121   Hummel, G. "Classical Playing Techniques in Jazz Flute Performance." *The Instrumentalist*, February 1979, 38, 40–41.

122   Muro, D. "Amplifying Traditional Instruments." *NAJE Educator*, December/January 1977, 66–68.

123   Pemberton, R. "The Craft of Lead Alto Sax Playing." *NAJE Educator*, April/May 1978, 57–58.

124   Pemberton, R. "Saxophone Section Problem Solving." *NAJE Educator*, February/March, 1977, 45.

125   Prince, B. "Woodwind Doubling." *NAJE Educator*, April/May 1979, 11–12.

126   Ricker, R. "Woodwind Doubling." *Woodwind World*, September 1973, 10, 13, 22.

127   Richmond, K. "Woodwind Doubling." *The Instrumentalist*, January 1979, 54–56.

128   Runyan, S. "High Notes for Saxophone." *The Instrumentalist*, December 1974, 29.

129   Seckler, S. "Balancing and Blending in the Sax Section." *Musical America*, January 1977, 6–9.

130   Seckler, S. "Saxes Overshadowed." *Musical America*, February/March 1977, 10–12.

131   Seckler, S. "Vibrato." *Musical America*. December 1976, 18–21.

132   Suber, C. "Jazz Flute." *The Instrumentalist*, November 1972, 36–37.

CHAPTER 8

Books

133   Ballentine, R. *The Science of Breath*. Glenview, IL: Himalaya International Institute of Yoga Science.

134   Baker, D. N. *Contemporary Techniques for the Trombone, Vols, I & II*. New York: Charles Colin, 1974.

135   Baker, D. N. *Jazz Styles & Analysis: Trombone*. Chicago: Down Beat Publications, 1974.

136   Bay, B. *Jazz Trumpet Studies*. Pacific, MO: Mel Bay Publications, 1979.

137   Farkas, P. *The Art of Brass Playing*. Bloomington, IN: Brass Publications, 1962.

138   McNeil, J. *Jazz Trumpet Techniques*. Lebanon, IN: Studio P/R, 1976.

139   Malone, T. *Alternate Position System for Trombone*. New York: Synthesis Publications, 1974.

140   Panico, F., & Rev. G. Wiskirchen. *A Manual for the Stage or Dance Band Trumpet Player*. Boston: Berklee Press, 1964.

141   Stuart, G. *The Art of Playing Lead Trumpet*. Redondo Beach, 1974.

142   Winding, K. *Mr. Trombone*. Pacific, MO: Mel Bay Publications, 1979.

143   Zorn, J. D. *Exploring the Trumpet's Upper Register*. Delevan, NY: Kendor Music, 1975.

Periodicals

144   Baker, B. "Trombone Talk." *NAJE Educator*, December/January 1972, 15–16.

145   Baker, B. "Trombone Talk." *NAJE Educator*, October/November 1972, 18.

146   Baker, B. "Trombone Talk." *NAJE Educator*, April/May 1973, 21, 30.

147   Baker, B. "Trombone Talk." *NAJE Educator*, December/January 1974.

148   Baker, B. "Trombone Talk." *NAJE Educator*, April/May 1974.

149   Baker, B. "Trombone Talk." *NAJE Educator*, December/January 1975, 41.

150   Brownlow, A. "The Mute in Contemporary Trumpet Performance." *The Instrumentalist*, May 1979, 52, 54–55.

151   Ernest, J. S. "Clinic Comments from Maynard Ferguson." *The Instrumentalist*, November 1974, 40–41.

152   Gibson, R. "How the Professionals Play Double High C." *The Instrumentalist*, December 1974, 29.

122   Muro, D.

153   Purcell, R. "Playing Trombone in the Stage Band." *The Instrumentalist*, June 1977, 60–63.

154   Shew, B. "Big Band Lead Trumpet Playing." *NAJE Educator*, December/January 1979, 86–88.

155   Shew, B. "A Positive Approach to Practicing." *NAJE Educator*, December/January 1980, 78–79.

156   Shew, B. "General Information on Mutes." *NAJE Educator*, October/November 1980, 66–69.

157   Vax, M. "Questions Frequently Heard at Clinics (Part I)." *The Instrumentalist*, October 1975, 93–94.

158   Vax, M. "Questions Frequently Heard at Clinics (Part II)." *The Instrumentalist*, November 1975, 75–77.

159   Wiskirchen, Rev. G. "Anima Musicae." *Selmer Bandwagon*, No. 69, 18–21.

160   Wiskirchen, Rev. G. "Good Brass Playing Is Good Brass Playing." *Selmer Bandwagon*, No. 88, 15–18.

Pamphlets

161   Bloomquist, K. *Higher and Louder*, Elkhorn, WI: Getzen Co.

162   Bloomquist, K. *Pedal Tone Study for Trumpet*. Elkhorn, WI: Getzen Co.

163   Gordon, C. *How to Practice to Develop Your High and Low Ranges*. Eastlake, OH: King Musical Instruments.

164   Neilson, J. *Warm-Up Procedures for the Brass Player*. Kenosha, WI: G. Leblanc, Corp.

165   Sautter, F. *Yogi Exercises and Breath Control*. Elkhorn, WI: Getzen Co.

166   Severinsen, C. *Why Warm Up?* Elkhorn, WI: Getzen Co.

CHAPTER 9

DRUMS

Books

167 Burns, R. *Cymbals.* Rockville Centre, NY: Belwin, 1964.

168 Chapin, J. *Advanced Techniques for the Modern Drummer* (Vol. I).

169 Chapin, J. *Advanced Techniques for the Modern Drummer* (Vol. II).

170 Cusatis, J. *Rhythm Patterns.* Melville, NY: Belwin/Mills, 1963.

171 Cusatis, J. *Rudimental Patterns.* Melville, NY: Belwin/Mills, 1968.

172 Dahlgren, M., & E. Fine. *4-Way Coordination.* Melville, NY: Belwin/Mills, 1966.

173 Davis, M. *Basic Beats for the Working Drummer.* Lebanon, IN: Studio P/R, 1974.

174 Dawson, A., & D. DeMichael. *A Manual for the Modern Drummer.* Boston: Berklee Press Publications, 1962.

175 Feldstein, S. *Disco Drums Handy Guide.* Sherman Oaks, CA: Alfred Publishing Co., 1979.

176 Feldstein, S. *Drum-Set Handy Guide.* Sherman Oaks, CA: Alfred Publishing Co., 1978.

177 Fink, R. *Drum-Set Reading.* Port Washington, NY: Alfred Music, 1973.

178 Fink, R. *Latin American Rhythms for the Drum Set.* Port Washington, NY: Alfred Music, 1975.

179 Herrick, J. *Contemporary Drum Solos.* Winona, MN: Hal Leonard, 1979.

180 Igoe, S., & H. Adler. *Drum Breaks and Fill-Ins.* New York: Belwin/Mills, 1959.

181 Jerger, J. *Complete Instruction in Jazz Ensemble Drumming.* Lebanon, IN: Studio P/R, 1977.

182 Kettle, R. *Drum Set Reading Method.* Rockville, NY: Belwin, 1968.

183 Lambert, J. *Drum Improvising Studies.* Pacific, MO: Mel Bay Publications, 1979.

184 Lamond, D. *Design for the Drum Set.* Rockville, NY: Belwin, 1966.

185 Lewis, M., & C. DeRosa. *It's Time.* Delevan, NY: Kendor Music, 1978.

186 Mintz, B. *Different Drummers.* New York: Amsco Music, 1975.

187 Perry, C. *Introduction to the Drum Set.* Melville, NY: Belwin/Mills, 1966.

188   Perry, C. *Rockin' Bass Drum.* Port Washington, NY: Alfred Music.

189   Pickering, J. *The Drummer's Cookbook.* Pacific, MO: Mel Bay, 1979.

190   Pickering, J. *Stage Band Drummers' Guide.* Pacific, MO: Mel Bay, 1976.

191   Pickering, J. *Studio/Jazz Drum Cookbook.* Pacific, MO: Mel Bay, 1979.

192   Piekarczyk, J. *The Drumset Exerciser.* Northbrook, IL: Opus Music, 1978.

193   Rothman, J. *Phrasing Rock Breaks.* New York: J.R. Publishing, 1972.

194   Rothman, J. *Take a Break.* New York: J.R. Publishing, 1974.

195   Spera, D. *Blues and the Basics (drums).* Winona, MN: Hal Leonard Publishing, 1976.

Periodicals

197   Barr, W. "The Salsa Rhythm Section." *NAJE Educator*, December/January 1980, 15–18, 58–59.

33   Delp, R.

198   DeRosa, C. "Becoming a Jazz Drummer." *Selmer Bandwagon*, No. 83, 5–6.

199   Fink, R. "What to Tell Your Stage Band Drummers." *The Instrumentalist*, December 1975, 77–79.

200   Galm, J. K. "How to Perk Up Percussion." *downbeat*, December 4, 1975, 36–37.

201   Henry, D. "Rehearse Your Rhythm Section Before You Rehearse Your Jazz Ensemble. *NAJE Educator*, October/November 1974, 13.

202   Pierkarczyk, J. "Drum Set Basics." *The Instrumentalist*, November 1979, 54–58.

203   Prebys, S. J. "Choosing Percussionists for the High School-College Jazz Ensemble." *NAJE Educator*, December/January 1975, 50.

204   Soph, E. "Drummer Confidence." *The Instrumentalist*, February 1978, 70–71.

205   Soph, E. "Big Band Drumming Basics." *The Instrumentalist*, December 1979, 38–41.

206   Wiskirchen, Rev. G. "Drummers Are Too Musicians." *Selmer Bandwagon*, No. 74, 24–26.

BASS

Books

207 Bredice, V. *Basic Impulse Bass.* New York: Charles Hansen, 1971.

208 Brown, R. *Ray Brown Bass Method.* Los Angeles: First Place Music.

209 Cacibauda, J. *No Nonsense Electric Bass* (Vol. I). Lebanon, IN: Studio P/R, 1975.

210 Cacibauda, J. *No Nonsense Electric Bass* (Vol. II). Lebanon, IN: Studio P/R, 1979.

211 Cacibauda, J. *No Nonsense Electric Bass* (Vol. III). Lebanon, IN: Studio P/R, 1979.

212 Clayton, J. *Big Band Bass.* Lebanon, IN: Studio P/R, 1978.

213 Davis, A. *The Arthur Davis System for Double Bass.* Crugers, NY: K.M.V. Enterprises, 1976.

214 DeWitt, J. *Rhythmic Figures for Bassists* (Vols. I & II). New York: Charles Hansen, 1976.

215 Filiberto, R. *Play Electric Bass from Chord Symbols.* Pacific, MO: Mel Bay, 1978.

216 Gately, E. *Bass Improvising.* Pacific, MO: Mel Bay, 1979.

217 Hammick, V. *Electric Bass Technique* (Vols. I & II). Sherman Oaks, CA: GWYN Publishing Co., 1975.

218 Hilliker, T., & J. Goldsby. *Ron Carter Bass Lines.* New Albany, IN: Jamey Aebersold, 1979.

219 Jackson, C. P. *How to Play Jazz Bass Lines.* Boston: Hornpipe Music, 1980.

220 Kaye, C. *Electric Bass Lines* (No. 1). Sherman Oaks, CA: GWYN, 1969.

221 Kaye, C. *Electric Bass Lines* (No. 2). Sherman Oaks, CA: GWYN, 1970.

222 Kaye, C. *Electric Bass Lines* (No. 3). Sherman Oaks, CA: GWYN, 1971.

223 Kaye, C. *Electric Bass Lines* (No. 4). Sherman Oaks, CA: GWYN, 1971.

224 Kaye, C. *Electric Bass Lines* (No. 5). Sherman Oaks, CA: GWYN, 1975.

225 Kaye, C. *How to Play the Electric Bass.* Sherman Oaks, CA: GWYN, 1969.

226 Kaye, C. *Personally Yours.* Camarillo, CA: GWYN, 1970.

227 Leonhart, D., & K. Slone. *Rufus Reid Bass Lines.* New Albany, IN: Jamey Aebersold, 1980.

228 Menke, T. *Bass Blues Bag.* Pacific, MO: Mel Bay, 1973.

229 Montgomery, M. *The Monk Montgomery Electric Bass Method.* Lebanon, IN: Studio P/R, 1978.

230 Pliskow, D. *Jazz Bass Lines.* Atlanta, GA: Dan Pliskow, 1975.

231 Reid, R. *The Evolving Bassist.* Chicago: Myriad Limited, 1974.

232 Reid, R. *Evolving Upward Bass Book.* Teaneck, NJ: Myriad Limited, 1977.

233 Sher, C. *The Improviser's Bass Method.* San Francisco: Sher Music Co., 1979.

234 Spera, D. *Blues and the Basics (bass).* Winona, MN: Hal Leonard Publications, 1977.

Publications

235 Hinton, M. "The Bass: A Way of Life." *NAJE Educator,* December/January 1978, 14–15.

236 Kaye, C. "The Electric Bassist in School." *NAJE Educator,* April/May 1976, 40–41.

237 Kaye, C. "Teaching Electric Bass." *The Instrumentalist,* October 1972, 27.

238 Tusa, F. "Pizzicato Power for Jazz Bassists." *The Instrumentalist,* August 1979, 34.

PIANO

Books

239 Aebersold, J. *Transcribed Piano Voicings.* New Albany, IN: Jamey Aebersold, 1980.

240 Burswold, L. *Topics in Jazz Piano Improvisation.* Lebanon, IN: Studio P/R, 1980.

241 Danko, H. *The Illustrated Keyboard Series for Improvising* (Books I & II). Lebanon, IN: Studio P/R, 1980.

242 Dobbins, B. *The Contemporary Jazz Pianist* (Vols. I, II, III, & IV). Jamestown, RI: GAMT Music Press, 1978.

243 Edison, R. *Learn to Play Jazz Piano.* Sherman Oaks, CA: Alfred Publishing Co., 1978.

244 Evans, L. *Jazz Keyboard Harmony.* Melville, NY: Belwin/Mills, 1981.

245 Gray, J. *Bluesblues.* Seattle, WA: Mitchell Madison, 1973.

246 Haerle, D. *Jazz Improvisation for Keyboard Players* (Books I, II, & III).

247 Haerle, D. *Jazz/Rock Voicings for the Contemporary Keyboard Player.*

248 Hyman, D., & C. DeRosa. *It's Time for Some Piano Changes*. Delevan, NY: Kendor Music, 1980.

249 Marohnic, C. *How to Create Jazz Chord Progressions*. Lebanon, IN: Studio P/R, 1979.

250 Matteson, R., & J. Peterson. *Improvisation Clinic Notes*. Elkhorn, WI: Getzen Co., 1973.

251 Mehegan, J. *Contemporary Piano Styles*. New York: Amsco Music Publishers, 1965.

252 Mehegan, J. *Jazz Rhythm and the Improvised Line*. New York: Amsco Music Publishers, 1962.

253 Mehegan, J. *Swing and Early Progressive Piano Styles*. New York: Amsco Music Publishers, 1964.

254 Mehegan, J. *Tonal and Rhythmic Principles*. New York: Amsco Music Publishers, 1959.

255 Southern, J. *Interpreting Popular Music at the Keyboard*. Lebanon, IN: Studio P/R, 1978.

256 Spera, D. *Blues and the Basics (piano)*. Winona, MN: Hal Leonard Publications, 1976.

257 Sumares, F. *Contemporary Jazz Piano from Voicings to Improvisation*. Castro Valley, CA: Lantana Music Publishers, 1978.

258 Swain, A. *Advanced Chord Construction*. Glenview, IL: Creative Music, 1969.

259 Swain, A. *Basic Chord Construction*. Glenview, IL: Creative Music, 1969.

260 Swain, A. *How to Play by Ear*. Glenview, IL: Creative Music, 1970.

261 Wheaton, J. *Basic Modal Improvisation Techniques for Keyboard Instruments*. Studio City, CA: 1972.

Periodicals

262 Ferguson, T. "Attention Directors: Some Do's and Don'ts for Stage Band Pianists." *NAJE Educator*, October/November 1975, 24, 34.

201 Henry, D.

263 Sumares, F. "The Delicate Art of Comping." *NAJE Educator*, February/March, 1980, 56–59.

GUITAR

Books

264 Baker, M. *Jazz Guitar* (Vols. I & II). Carlstadt, NJ: Lewis Music Publishing Co., 1978.

265 Bay, M. *Guitar Melody Chord Playing System*. Pacific, MO: Mel Bay, 1978.

266 Bay, M. *Rhythm Guitar Chord System*. Pacific, MO: Mel Bay, 1973.

267 Berle, A. *Jazz Improvisation Book for Guitar*. New York: Music-pring Corp., 1980.

268 Bruner, T. *The Arranger/Composer's Complete Guide to the Guitar*. Studio City, CA: Gresco Publishing Co., 1972.

269 Bruner, T. *How to Play Guitar in a Big Band*. Pacific, MO: Mel Bay, 1980.

270 Byrd, C. *Melodic Method for Guitar*. New York: Hollis Music, 1973.

271 Capuano, E. *Improvising Jazz Guitar*. Fairfield, NJ: Aquarius Publishing Co., 1978.

272 Carter, J. *Tonal Colors for Guitar*. Lebanon, IN: Studio P/R, 1979.

273 Diorio, J. *Fusion*. Canoga Park, CA: Dale Zdenek Publishing, 1979.

274 Edison, R. *Jazz Guitar*. Sherman Oaks, CA: Alfred Publishing, 1978.

275 Ellis, H. *Herb Ellis Jazz Guitar Style*. New York: Mills Music, 1963.

276 Fava, J. *Method for Guitar* (Vols. I, II, & III). Detroit: CRS Publishing, 1974.

277 Fowler, W. L. *Guitar Patterns for Improvisation*. Chicago: Maher Publications, 1972.

278 Green, T. *Chord Chemistry*. Canoga Park, CA: Dale Zdenek, 1971.

279 Greene, T. *Modern Chord Progressions*. Canoga Park, CA: Dale Zdenek, 1976.

280 Hanlon, A. *Basic Guitar* (Vols, I, II, & III). New York: Chappell Publishing, 1976.

281 Khan, S. *Wes Montgomery Guitar Folio*. New York: Gopam Enterprises, 1978.

282 Leavitt, W. G. *A Modern Method for Guitar* (Vol. I). Boston: Berklee Press, 1966.

283 Leavitt, W. G. *A Modern Method for Guitar* (Vol. II). Boston: Berklee Press, 1968.

284 Leavitt, W. G. *A Modern Method for Guitar* (Vol. III). Boston: Berklee Press, 1971.

285 Lee, R. *Jazz Guitar*. Pacific, MO: Mel Bay, 1963.

286 Lucas, P. *Jazz Improvising for the Rock/Blues Guitarist*. Lebanon, IN: Studio P/R, 1978.

287 McGuire, E. F. Guitar Fingerboard Harmony. Pacific, MO: Mel Bay, 1976.

288 Pass, J. *The Joe Pass Guitar Method*. New York: Chappell, 1977.

289 Pass, J., & B. Thrasher. *Joe Pass Guitar Style*. Sherman Oaks, CA: GWYN Publishing Co., 1970.

290   Petersen, J. *Jazz Styles & Analysis: Guitar.* Chicago: Maher Publications, 1979.

291   Rector, J. *Guitar Chord Progressions.* Pacific, MO: Mel Bay, 1977.

292   Silver, M. *Contemporary Guitar Improvisation.* New York: Dick Grove Publications, 1978.

293   Spera, D. *Blues and the Basics (guitar).* Winona, MN: Hal Leonard, 1976.

294   Summerfield, M. J. *The Jazz Guitar.* Gateshead, Tyne and Wear, England: Ashley Mark Publishing Co., 1978.

295   Van Eps, G. *Guitar Method.* New York: Plymouth Music, 1961.

Periodicals

296   Fowler, W. L. Contributing jazz education editor for *downbeat* magazine for various issues through many years.

297   Geissman, G. "Improvising on Major Family Chords." *NAJE Educator,* October/November 1975, 50–52.

298   *Guitar Player Magazine.*

RHYTHM SECTION

Periodicals

299   Bridge, N. W. "Care and Keeping of a Jazz Combo." *NAJE Educator,* April/May 1980, 9–10, 64.

300   Ferguson, T. "Tips on the Rhythm Section (Part I)." *The Instrumentalist,* November 1971, 44.

301   Ferguson, T. "Tips of the Rhythm Section (Part II)." *The Instrumentalist,* December 1971, 25.

201   Henry, D.

302   von Bergen, E. F. "Rufus Reid Speaks Out on Rhythm Section Playing." *The Instrumentalist,* June 1978, 63–67.

AUXILIARY PERCUSSION

Books

303   Almeida, L. *Latin Percussion Instruments and Rhythms.* Sherman Oaks, CA: Alfred Publishing Co., 1972.

304   Cohen, M. *Down to Basics.* Palisades Park, NJ: Latin Percussion Ventures, 1977.

305   Cohen, M. *Understanding Latin Rhythms.* Palisades Park, NJ: Latin Percussion Ventures, 1974.

306 Evans, B. *Authentic Bongo Rhythms.* Melville, NY: Belwin/Mills, 1966.

307 Evans, B. *Authentic Conga Rhythms.* Melville, NY: Belwin/Mills, 1960.

308 Joe, M. *Montego Joe Plays Conga/Bongos.* New York: Envolve Music, 1978.

309 Marrero, I. E. *Drumming the Latin-American Way.* New York: Edward B. Marks Music Corp., 1949.

310 Morales, H., & H. Adler. *Latin American Rhythm Instruments. Rockville Centre, NY: Belwin/Mills, 1954.*

Periodicals

311 Barr, W. L. "The Salsa Rhythm Section." *NAJE Educator,* December/January 1980, 15–18, 58–59.

312 Delp, R. "The Conga Drum." *The Instrumentalist,* February 1975, 29.

313 Soebling, H. W. "Latin American Instruments and Rhythms." *The Instrumentalist,* December 1977, 32.

VIBRAPHONE

Books

314 Brown, T. *Mallets in Mind.* Delevan, NY: Kendor Music, 1972.

315 Davis, T. L. *Improvise, Vibe-Wise and Otherwise.* New York: Phantom Music, 1974.

316 Delp, R. *Vibraphone Technique.* Boston: Berklee Press, 1973.

317 Feldman, V. *All Alone by the Vibraphone.* Sherman Oaks, CA: GWYN Publishing Co., 1971.

318 Friedman, D. *Vibraphone Technique.* Boston: Berklee Press, 1973.

319 Lecuona, E. *Mallet Go Latin.* New York: Edward B. Marks Music, 1967.

320 Rae, J. *Jazz Phrasing for Mallets.* New York: Henry Adler, 1961.

321 Viola, J., & R. Delp. *Chord Studies for Mallet Instruments.* Boston: Berklee Press, 1973.

322 Wechter, J. *Play Vibes.* New York: Henry Adler, 1962.

Periodicals

323 Lawson, R. "Mallets for Jazz Vibes." *Jazz Educators Journal,* October/November 1981, 58, 67.

52 Prebys, S. J.

Index